I0220307

After receiving feedback on my book, 1920 Population Census of Guam: Transcribed (ISBN 978-0-9851257-0-7), I have compiled this alphabetical Index as the book's companion to assist researchers.

This Index is the intellectual property of Bernard T. Punzalan (author, publisher and principal investigator) of the Chamorro Roots Genealogy Project™ (www.chamorroroots.com). No part of this Index may be reproduced or transmitted in any form or by any means, electronic or mechanical, including photocopying, recording, or by any information storage and retrieval system, without the written permission of the author. I would appreciate your support to this because all proceeds generated from the Chamorro Roots Genealogy Project are used to maintain and enhance the website, subscriptions and expenses for public presentations.

Si Yu'os Ma'åse,

Bernard Punzalan

Abrera, Rosa C -pg 368
Acfalle, Ana B -pg 481
Acfalle, Ana C -pg 435
Acfalle, Ana C -pg 497
Acfalle, Ana E -pg 493
Acfalle, Ana M -pg 493
Acfalle, Andrea N -pg 491
Acfalle, Antonia A -pg 479
Acfalle, Blas N -pg 491
Acfalle, Carmelo C -pg 491
Acfalle, Conception E -pg 493
Acfalle, Consolacion C -pg 434
Acfalle, Dimas A -pg 481
Acfalle, Dolores A -pg 479
Acfalle, Dominga B -pg 492
Acfalle, Emelirio C -pg 497
Acfalle, Estifania B -pg 492
Acfalle, Fausto C -pg 492
Acfalle, Felicidad A -pg 479
Acfalle, Felicidad A -pg 481
Acfalle, Felipe C -pg 479
Acfalle, Felix E -pg 493
Acfalle, Francisca M -pg 492
Acfalle, Genoveva C -pg 359
Acfalle, Geronimo SN -pg 434
Acfalle, Ignacio C -pg 372
Acfalle, Ingracia B -pg 481
Acfalle, Isabel C -pg 434
Acfalle, Isabel N -pg 491
Acfalle, Jesus A -pg 492
Acfalle, Jesus C -pg 372
Acfalle, Joaquin A -pg 385
Acfalle, Jose A -pg 27
Acfalle, Jose C -pg 359
Acfalle, Jose E -pg 493
Acfalle, Josefa B -pg 492
Acfalle, Juan B -pg 493
Acfalle, Juan E -pg 493
Acfalle, Juan N -pg 359
Acfalle, Margarita C -pg 435
Acfalle, Maria B -pg 492
Acfalle, Maria C -pg 434
Acfalle, Mariquita A -pg 493
Acfalle, Miguel M -pg 493
Acfalle, Natividad M -pg 493
Acfalle, Nicolas B -pg 481
Acfalle, Nieves C -pg 372
Acfalle, Rosa M -pg 493
Acfalle, Salamon C -pg 497
Acfalle, Santiago B -pg 481
Acfalle, Tedosia B -pg 481
Acfalle, Tomasa A -pg 479

Acfalle, Tomasa B -pg 492
Acfalle, Trinidad M -pg 493
Acfalle, Vicente E -pg 493
Achaigma, Esperanza S -pg 310
Achaigua, Ana S -pg 315
Achaigua, Angel C -pg 100
Achaigua, Concepcion S -pg 315
Achaigua, Dolores C -pg 99
Achaigua, Elisa S -pg 315
Achaigua, Enecasio C -pg 100
Achaigua, Felisa S -pg 315
Achaigua, Jose C -pg 100
Achaigua, Juan C -pg 100
Achaigua, Maria S -pg 315
Achaigua, Pedro S -pg 315
Achaigua, Regina C -pg 99
Acosta, Amalia B -pg 150
Acosta, Ana D -pg 137
Acosta, Antonia R -pg 129
Acosta, Antonia U -pg 133
Acosta, Antonio A -pg 147
Acosta, Carmen U -pg 133
Acosta, Concepcion R -pg 112
Acosta, Concepcion S -pg 134
Acosta, Dolores C -pg 147
Acosta, Dolores S -pg 134
Acosta, Felisa S -pg 134
Acosta, Felix S -pg 134
Acosta, Francisco B -pg 150
Acosta, Isabel A -pg 147
Acosta, Joaquin A -pg 137
Acosta, Joaquin C -pg 147
Acosta, Joaquin D -pg 137
Acosta, Joaquina S -pg 134
Acosta, Jose B -pg 150
Acosta, Jose C -pg 19
Acosta, Jose S -pg 134
Acosta, Jose V -pg 280
Acosta, Juan B -pg 150
Acosta, Juan B jr -pg 150
Acosta, Juan U -pg 134
Acosta, Justo U -pg 128
Acosta, Luis O -pg 59
Acosta, Manuel S -pg 134
Acosta, Maria A -pg 147
Acosta, Maria B -pg 150
Acosta, Maria D -pg 137
Acosta, Maria P -pg 280
Acosta, Mariano C -pg 15
Acosta, Miguel C -pg 134
Acosta, Pedro A -pg 112
Acosta, Ramon S -pg 134

Acosta, Rosa B -pg 150
Acosta, Rosa P -pg 280
Acosta, Rosa S -pg 134
Acosta, Rosario U -pg 133
Acosta, Vicenta S -pg 134
Ada, Ana C -pg 23
Ada, Antonio C -pg 23
Ada, Antonio F -pg 295
Ada, Antonio S -pg 295
Ada, Carmen F -pg 295
Ada, Cecilia T -pg 488
Ada, Felix B -pg 295
Ada, Herman T -pg 321
Ada, Ignacio F -pg 295
Ada, Jesus M -pg 34
Ada, Joaquin S -pg 293
Ada, Joaquin S -pg 295
Ada, Joaquina M -pg 34
Ada, Jose C -pg 23
Ada, Manuel S -pg 295
Ada, Maria A -pg 50
Ada, Maria F -pg 295
Ada, Maria M -pg 34
Ada, Maria M -pg 34
Ada, Maria S -pg 295
Ada, Nicolas B -pg 488
Ada, Nicolasa B -pg 45
Ada, Pedro T -pg 25
Ada, Ramon M -pg 34
Ada, Regino M -pg 23
Ada, Rita C -pg 23
Ada, Rosa A -pg 422
Ada, Rosa M -pg 34
Ada, Rosa S -pg 295
Ada, Vicente B -pg 34
Adriano, Joaquina G -pg 167
Adriano, Jose G -pg 167
Adriano, Juan O -pg 167
Adriano, Maria O -pg 174
Adriano, Maria G -pg 167
Afaisen, Ana SN -pg 529
Afaisen, Antonio N -pg 520
Afaisen, Cristina D -pg 519
Afaisen, Dolores -pg 505
Afaisen, Elisa SN -pg 529
Afaisen, Joaquin SN -pg 519
Afaisen, Josefa A -pg 328
Afaisen, Juan D -pg 519
Afaisen, Manuel M -pg 505
Afaisen, Manuel T -pg 529
Afaisen, Maria C -pg 520
Afaisen, Maria D -pg 519

Afaisen, Maria M -pg 505
Afaisen, Maria SN -pg 519
Afaisen, Miguel M -pg 505
Afaisen, Natividad SN -pg 529
Afaisen, Pas M -pg 505
Afaisen, Ramon SN -pg 328
Afaisen, Rita SN -pg 519
Afaisen, Romana A -pg 328
Afaisen, Santiago D -pg 519
Afaisen, Susana T -pg 102
Afaisen, Vicenta N -pg 520
Afaron, Francisca T -pg 244
Aflague, Alfonso C -pg 200
Aflague, Ana C -pg 24
Aflague, Ana C -pg 201
Aflague, Ana C -pg 321
Aflague, Ana R -pg 321
Aflague, Ana S -pg 314
Aflague, Ana S -pg 365
Aflague, Antonia -pg 328
Aflague, Antonio S -pg 365
Aflague, Concepcion L -pg 213
Aflague, Concepcion R -pg 321
Aflague, Concepcion S -pg 365
Aflague, Dolores SM -pg 315
Aflague, Fermin S -pg 213
Aflague, Francisca G -pg 70
Aflague, Francisco C -pg 201
Aflague, Francisco S -pg 314
Aflague, Francisco S -pg 365
Aflague, Frouctaso SN -pg 71
Aflague, Fructoso SM -pg 315
Aflague, Gregorio C -pg 201
Aflague, Inocencio S -pg 314
Aflague, Inocencio SM -pg 315
Aflague, Joaquin C -pg 201
Aflague, Jose C -pg 314
Aflague, Jose C -pg 364
Aflague, Jose S -pg 314
Aflague, Josefa P -pg 301
Aflague, Josefina SM -pg 315
Aflague, Justo R -pg 70
Aflague, Leola A -pg 383
Aflague, Lorenzo S -pg 365
Aflague, Magdalena -pg 360
Aflague, Manuel G -pg 70
Aflague, Maria C -pg 321
Aflague, Maria N -pg 364
Aflague, Miguel S -pg 321
Aflague, Pilar SM -pg 314
Aflague, Rigoberto R -pg 321
Aflague, Rita A -pg 323

Aflague, Rosa A -pg 323
Aflague, Rosa N -pg 364
Aflague, Rosa SM -pg 314
Aflague, Rosario R -pg 321
Aflague, Simeon R -pg 321
Aflague, Tomas SM -pg 315
Aflague, Vicenta C -pg 322
Aflague, Vicenta S -pg 314
Aflague, Vicente T -pg 24
Aflleje, Ana P -pg 418
Aflleje, Ana T -pg 366
Aflleje, Antonio T -pg 359
Aflleje, Catalina -pg 370
Aflleje, Cristina N -pg 381
Aflleje, Dolores G -pg 359
Aflleje, Dolores P -pg 367
Aflleje, Encarnacion P -pg 418
Aflleje, Ignacia P -pg 418
Aflleje, Isabel -pg 370
Aflleje, Joaquin P -pg 367
Aflleje, Joaquina T -pg 366
Aflleje, Jose G -pg 359
Aflleje, Jose T -pg 354
Aflleje, Jose T -pg 366
Aflleje, Josefa P -pg 367
Aflleje, Juan P -pg 366
Aflleje, Juan T -pg 381
Aflleje, Juana -pg 370
Aflleje, Magdalena -pg 370
Aflleje, Manuel P -pg 418
Aflleje, Marcela T -pg 359
Aflleje, Maria G -pg 359
Aflleje, Maria N -pg 381
Aflleje, Maria T -pg 370
Aflleje, Mariano -pg 370
Aflleje, Natividad G -pg 359
Aflleje, Nicolasa P -pg 360
Aflleje, Perpetua T -pg 370
Aflleje, Regina T -pg 366
Aflleje, Rita T -pg 366
Aflleje, Rosa C -pg 355
Aflleje, Rosa -pg 370
Aflleje, Rosario C -pg 354
Aflleje, Teresa G -pg 359
Aflleje, Vicenta P -pg 418
Aflleje, Vicente C -pg 370
Aflleje, Vicente T -pg 366
Aguahlo, Aleandro C -pg 373
Aguahlo, Ignacio T -pg 365
Aguahlo, Jose C -pg 373
Aguahlo, Maria C -pg 373
Aguahlo, Miguel C -pg 373

Aguahlo, Santiago T -pg 365
Aguajlo, Ana M -pg 101
Aguajlo, Ana S -pg 116
Aguajlo, Angelina O -pg 101
Aguajlo, Antonia S -pg 116
Aguajlo, Carmen O -pg 101
Aguajlo, Dominga T -pg 110
Aguajlo, Jesus C -pg 104
Aguajlo, Joaquina C -pg 104
Aguajlo, Jose C -pg 104
Aguajlo, Juan A -pg 110
Aguajlo, Juan S -pg 116
Aguajlo, Luis S -pg 116
Aguajlo, Miguel M -pg 101
Aguajlo, Pedro C -pg 103
Aguajlo, Rita M -pg 101
Aguajlo, Serefina C -pg 104
Aguajlo, Vicente O -pg 101
Aguajlo, Vicente A -pg 116
Agualo, Juana Q -pg 544
Agualo, Ramon T -pg 549
Aguero, Ana O -pg 161
Aguero, Concepcion Q -pg 308
Aguero, Emeliana Q -pg 308
Aguero, Felix Q -pg 308
Aguero, Jesus SN -pg 548
Aguero, Jose O -pg 161
Aguero, Jose SN -pg 548
Aguero, Juan O -pg 161
Aguero, Juan SN -pg 548
Aguero, Juana SN -pg 538
Aguero, Maria SN -pg 538
Aguero, Maria SN -pg 548
Aguero, Maria SN -pg 548
Aguero, Rita O -pg 161
Aguero, Vicente SN -pg 538
Aguigui, Amabble R -pg 437
Aguigui, Ana C -pg 434
Aguigui, Ana SN -pg 446
Aguigui, Antonia C -pg 67
Aguigui, Antonia C -pg 432
Aguigui, Antonio C -pg 434
Aguigui, Beneda M -pg 490
Aguigui, Benedicto SN -pg 434
Aguigui, Carmen M -pg 490
Aguigui, Carmen SN -pg 447
Aguigui, Concepcion C -pg 432
Aguigui, Consolacion SN -pg 447
Aguigui, Dolores SN -pg 444
Aguigui, Donicio C -pg 434
Aguigui, Enrique C -pg 432
Aguigui, Felix A -pg 458

Aguigui, Francisco SN -pg 447
Aguigui, Geronimo R -pg 437
Aguigui, Guadalupe SN -pg 447
Aguigui, Ignacio B -pg 490
Aguigui, Ignacio R -pg 437
Aguigui, Joaquin A -pg 443
Aguigui, Joaquin C -pg 67
Aguigui, Joaquina T -pg 443
Aguigui, Jose R -pg 437
Aguigui, Jose SN -pg 447
Aguigui, Josefa C -pg 432
Aguigui, Josefa R -pg 437
Aguigui, Josefina SN -pg 447
Aguigui, Juan A -pg 437
Aguigui, Juan C -pg 67
Aguigui, Juan SN -pg 444
Aguigui, Juan -pg 210
Aguigui, Juan -pg 317
Aguigui, Juan -pg 376
Aguigui, Juana C -pg 434
Aguigui, Leon A -pg 58
Aguigui, Luis P -pg 376
Aguigui, Luis SN -pg 432
Aguigui, Luisa C -pg 434
Aguigui, Manuel SN -pg 447
Aguigui, Margarita M -pg 490
Aguigui, Maria C -pg 434
Aguigui, Maria P -pg 376
Aguigui, Miguel SN -pg 67
Aguigui, Milagro C -pg 434
Aguigui, Pedro A -pg 458
Aguigui, Pedro SN -pg 444
Aguigui, Rosa M -pg 490
Aguigui, Santos A -pg 27
Aguigui, Tomasa SN -pg 444
Aguigui, Trinidad C -pg 432
Aguigui, Vicente SN -pg 444
Aguiningoc, Jesus C -pg 412
Agulto, Ana C -pg 408
Agulto, Antonio C -pg 408
Agulto, Emilia C -pg 408
Agulto, Juan M -pg 408
Agulto, Pedro C -pg 408
Aguon, Adriano A -pg 15
Aguon, Amadeo T -pg 470
Aguon, Amparo T -pg 470
Aguon, Ana A -pg 469
Aguon, Ana C -pg 462
Aguon, Ana F -pg 212
Aguon, Ana O -pg 556
Aguon, Ana Q -pg 471
Aguon, Ana S -pg 40

Aguon, Ana S -pg 155
Aguon, Ana T -pg 70
Aguon, Ana T -pg 471
Aguon, Ana U -pg 316
Aguon, Andrea S -pg 155
Aguon, Angela B -pg 460
Aguon, Antonia B -pg 224
Aguon, Antonia C -pg 198
Aguon, Antonia T -pg 472
Aguon, Antonio C -pg 473
Aguon, Antonio I -pg 277
Aguon, Antonio R -pg 467
Aguon, Asuncion C -pg 466
Aguon, Atanacio M -pg 461
Aguon, Bernadita M -pg 461
Aguon, Blandina S -pg 155
Aguon, Calistra T -pg 468
Aguon, Candaleria P -pg 343
Aguon, Carlos C -pg 47
Aguon, Carmen M -pg 354
Aguon, Catalina C -pg 343
Aguon, Catalina M -pg 65
Aguon, Concepcion C -pg 539
Aguon, Concepcion F -pg 530
Aguon, Concepcion M -pg 195
Aguon, Concepcion O -pg 38
Aguon, Conception M -pg 461
Aguon, Consuelo Q -pg 471
Aguon, Cristina C -pg 466
Aguon, Dolores B -pg 224
Aguon, Dolores B -pg 490
Aguon, Dolores C -pg 472
Aguon, Dolores F -pg 530
Aguon, Edevis Q -pg 466
Aguon, Emilia C -pg 400
Aguon, Engracia C -pg 342
Aguon, Faustina B -pg 490
Aguon, Felicita T -pg 290
Aguon, Felipe L -pg 462
Aguon, Felipe T -pg 471
Aguon, Felix D -pg 221
Aguon, Felix P -pg 543
Aguon, Filipe R -pg 467
Aguon, Francis S -pg 155
Aguon, Francisco L -pg 559
Aguon, Francisco M -pg 384
Aguon, Francisco S -pg 56
Aguon, Francisco S -pg 155
Aguon, Genoveva I -pg 221
Aguon, Gregorio T -pg 471
Aguon, Ignacia C -pg 71
Aguon, Ignacio I -pg 277

Aguon, Ignacio I -pg 466
Aguon, Ignacio M -pg 408
Aguon, Ignacio O -pg 38
Aguon, Ignacio O -pg 556
Aguon, Ignacio T -pg 558
Aguon, Ignacio U -pg 170
Aguon, Ingracia T -pg 357
Aguon, Isabel C -pg 342
Aguon, Isabel C -pg 468
Aguon, Isabel O -pg 38
Aguon, Jesus C -pg 46
Aguon, Jesus I -pg 277
Aguon, Jesus L -pg 559
Aguon, Jesus P -pg 545
Aguon, Jesus T -pg 461
Aguon, Jesus T -pg 470
Aguon, Joaquin C -pg 342
Aguon, Joaquin C -pg 539
Aguon, Joaquin C -pg 539
Aguon, Joaquin L -pg 559
Aguon, Joaquin LG -pg 38
Aguon, Joaquin M -pg 195
Aguon, Joaquin Q -pg 466
Aguon, Joaquin Q -pg 471
Aguon, Joaquin S -pg 155
Aguon, Joaquin T -pg 290
Aguon, Joaquina B -pg 461
Aguon, Joaquina B -pg 490
Aguon, Joaquina C -pg 539
Aguon, Joaquina T -pg 468
Aguon, Jose B -pg 460
Aguon, Jose C -pg 210
Aguon, Jose C -pg 539
Aguon, Jose I -pg 472
Aguon, Jose L -pg 559
Aguon, Jose M -pg 195
Aguon, Jose M -pg 408
Aguon, Jose O -pg 556
Aguon, Jose P -pg 292
Aguon, Jose P -pg 343
Aguon, Jose P -pg 545
Aguon, Jose Q -pg 466
Aguon, Jose Q -pg 466
Aguon, Jose S -pg 155
Aguon, Jose T -pg 290
Aguon, Jose T -pg 357
Aguon, Jose T -pg 468
Aguon, Jose T -pg 471
Aguon, Jose T -pg 544
Aguon, Jose T -pg 554
Aguon, Jose V -pg 224
Aguon, Josefa I -pg 221

INDEX
1920 Population Census of Guam: Transcribed

Aguon, Josefa L -pg 46
Aguon, Josefina C -pg 60
Aguon, Josefina M -pg 65
Aguon, Juan C -pg 342
Aguon, Juan C -pg 354
Aguon, Juan C -pg 468
Aguon, Juan G -pg 15
Aguon, Juan L -pg 46
Aguon, Juan L -pg 559
Aguon, Juan M -pg 65
Aguon, Juan M -pg 408
Aguon, Juan P -pg 343
Aguon, Juan S -pg 155
Aguon, Juan T -pg 40
Aguon, Juan T -pg 306
Aguon, Juan T -pg 316
Aguon, Juan T -pg 530
Aguon, Juan U -pg 316
Aguon, Juana C -pg 466
Aguon, Julian LG -pg 306
Aguon, Justo C -pg 471
Aguon, Librada C -pg 462
Aguon, Lorenzo Q -pg 408
Aguon, Lucas T -pg 461
Aguon, Luis I -pg 221
Aguon, Luis L -pg 559
Aguon, Luisa C -pg 343
Aguon, Luisa T -pg 60
Aguon, Magdalena C -pg 462
Aguon, Magdalena S -pg 155
Aguon, Magdalena T -pg 357
Aguon, Manuel B -pg 460
Aguon, Manuel L -pg 559
Aguon, Manuel S -pg 56
Aguon, Manuela LG -pg 306
Aguon, Manuela U -pg 316
Aguon, Maria B -pg 460
Aguon, Maria C -pg 462
Aguon, Maria C -pg 470
Aguon, Maria F -pg 212
Aguon, Maria L -pg 46
Aguon, Maria L -pg 46
Aguon, Maria L -pg 559
Aguon, Maria LG -pg 306
Aguon, Maria M -pg 65
Aguon, Maria M -pg 383
Aguon, Maria M -pg 461
Aguon, Maria O -pg 38
Aguon, Maria O -pg 556
Aguon, Maria P -pg 343
Aguon, Maria P -pg 545
Aguon, Maria S -pg 56

Aguon, Maria T -pg 70
Aguon, Maria T -pg 470
Aguon, Mariana M -pg 65
Aguon, Mariano T -pg 357
Aguon, Martina C -pg 342
Aguon, Maximo C -pg 466
Aguon, Milagros C -pg 466
Aguon, Milagros P -pg 545
Aguon, Milagros Q -pg 466
Aguon, Nicolas M -pg 65
Aguon, Nicolasa C -pg 47
Aguon, Nieves C -pg 47
Aguon, Pedro B -pg 490
Aguon, Pedro I -pg 221
Aguon, Pedro S -pg 40
Aguon, Pedro S -pg 155
Aguon, Pedro T -pg 470
Aguon, Pedro T -pg 559
Aguon, Pedro -pg 240
Aguon, Petra C -pg 468
Aguon, Ramon O -pg 38
Aguon, Ramon P -pg 545
Aguon, Ramon S -pg 40
Aguon, Ramon T -pg 40
Aguon, Remedios A -pg 15
Aguon, Remedios S -pg 56
Aguon, Remedios S -pg 240
Aguon, Rita U -pg 316
Aguon, Rosa B -pg 460
Aguon, Rosa F -pg 530
Aguon, Rosa I -pg 221
Aguon, Rosa M -pg 195
Aguon, Rosa S -pg 56
Aguon, Rosa S -pg 155
Aguon, Rosa S -pg 240
Aguon, Rosa T -pg 530
Aguon, Rosa V -pg 296
Aguon, Rosalia C -pg 466
Aguon, Rosario S -pg 240
Aguon, Rosauro U -pg 155
Aguon, Sabina I -pg 277
Aguon, Sabina R -pg 467
Aguon, Santiago Q -pg 490
Aguon, Santiago T -pg 357
Aguon, Segundo C -pg 342
Aguon, Simon C -pg 469
Aguon, Simon M -pg 65
Aguon, Soledad M -pg 408
Aguon, Soledad O -pg 38
Aguon, Soledad P -pg 46
Aguon, Soledad P -pg 343
Aguon, Teresa C -pg 539

Aguon, Tomasa A -pg 15
Aguon, Tomasa O -pg 556
Aguon, Tomasa P -pg 343
Aguon, Trinidad C -pg 462
Aguon, Trinidad L -pg 559
Aguon, Trinidad M -pg 384
Aguon, Venancio T -pg 556
Aguon, Vicenta M -pg 195
Aguon, Vicente A -pg 469
Aguon, Vicente B -pg 224
Aguon, Vicente C -pg 70
Aguon, Vicente C -pg 295
Aguon, Vicente C -pg 343
Aguon, Vicente C -pg 462
Aguon, Vicente C -pg 466
Aguon, Vicente F -pg 530
Aguon, Vicente L -pg 46
Aguon, Vicente L -pg 559
Aguon, Vicente M -pg 384
Aguon, Vicente P -pg 543
Aguon, Vicente R -pg 460
Aguon, Vicente S -pg 56
Aguon, Vicente T -pg 195
Aguon, Vicente T -pg 277
Aguon, Vicente T -pg 471
Akiyama, Jose S -pg 193
Alam, Carmen D -pg 199
Alam, Leon D -pg 199
Alam, Pilar D -pg 199
Albarez, Joaquin Q -pg 14
Alcantara, Antonia -pg 520
Alcantara, Francisco D -pg 520
Alcantara, Joaquin S -pg 409
Alcantara, Luis S -pg 409
Alcantara, Maria S -pg 409
Alecto, Agustin D -pg 163
Alecto, Felix C -pg 163
Alecto, Merchot C -pg 163
Alecto, Natividad C -pg 163
Alecto, Pedro C -pg 163
Alejandro, Martin -pg 211
Algarao, Francisca C -pg 227
Algarao, T -pg 227
Altero, Antonio C -pg 36
Altero, Asuncion C -pg 36
Altero, Consuelo C -pg 36
Altero, Isabel C -pg 36
Altero, Jesus C -pg 36
Altero, Jose C -pg 36
Altero, Maria C -pg 36
Altero, Pascual C -pg 36
Altero, Pascual S -pg 36

Alufaq, Candida 0 -pg 167
Alufaq, Rita 0 -pg 167
Alvarez, Ana SA -pg 160
Alvarez, Dolores M -pg 157
Alvarez, Dolores SA -pg 160
Alvarez, J SN -pg 160
Alvarez, Jose G -pg 160
Alvarez, Juan SA -pg 160
Alvarez, Rufina SA -pg 160
Anderson, Ana B -pg 345
Anderson, Antonia B -pg 346
Anderson, Antonia P -pg 233
Anderson, Antonia -pg 413
Anderson, Antonio LG -pg 214
Anderson, Antonio Q -pg 320
Anderson, Arthur G -pg 252
Anderson, Arthur -pg 252
Anderson, Concepcion D -pg 422
Anderson, Dolores B -pg 346
Anderson, Emelia M -pg 321
Anderson, Engracia P -pg 233
Anderson, Felix LG -pg 407
Anderson, Fidela A -pg 407
Anderson, Fidela LG -pg 214
Anderson, Francisco B -pg 345
Anderson, Francisco Q -pg 345
Anderson, Francisco -pg 407
Anderson, Henry C -pg 252
Anderson, Isabel A -pg 407
Anderson, Jesus A -pg 407
Anderson, Jesusa P -pg 233
Anderson, Joaquin M -pg 214
Anderson, Joaquina M -pg 320
Anderson, John C -pg 252
Anderson, Jose A -pg 407
Anderson, Jose B -pg 345
Anderson, Jose C -pg 422
Anderson, Josefa B -pg 345
Anderson, Josefina LG -pg 215
Anderson, Joseph C -pg 253
Anderson, Juan M -pg 321
Anderson, Juan -pg 422
Anderson, Leon -pg 233
Anderson, Lillian C -pg 252
Anderson, Maria B -pg 346
Anderson, Maria M -pg 321
Anderson, Mariano A -pg 407
Anderson, Pedro M -pg 320
Anderson, Ramon B -pg 345
Anderson, Ramona M -pg 321
Anderson, Rita M -pg 320
Anderson, Rosa C -pg 252

Anderson, Rosalina C -pg 422
Anderson, Rosario LG -pg 214
Anderson, Tomas B -pg 346
Anderson, Tomasa LG -pg 214
Anderson, Vicenta -pg 407
Anderson, Vicente P -pg 233
Angoco, Agustina C -pg 207
Angoco, Ana G -pg 203
Angoco, Dolores D -pg 202
Angoco, Francisco M -pg 197
Angoco, Jesus D -pg 202
Angoco, Joaquin T -pg 202
Angoco, Juan T -pg 202
Angoco, Manuel D -pg 202
Angoco, Manuela M -pg 197
Angoco, Mariano -pg 203
Angoco, Pedro A -pg 197
Angoco, Pedro T -pg 203
Angoco, Ramona D -pg 202
Angoco, Rosa T -pg 202
Angoco, Santiago D -pg 202
Angoco, Teodora C -pg 207
Angoco, Vicenta D -pg 202
Angoco, Vicente D -pg 202
Aparon, Alberta T -pg 218
Aparon, Francisca T -pg 218
Aparon, Manuel T -pg 218
Aparon, Ricardo S -pg 218
Aparon, Simeon T -pg 218
Aquinigoc, Ana B -pg 453
Aquinigoc, Antonia C -pg 453
Aquinigoc, Carmelo C -pg 453
Aquinigoc, Carmen C -pg 453
Aquinigoc, Enrique C -pg 59
Aquinigoc, Enrique C -pg 453
Aquinigoc, Felipe C -pg 453
Aquinigoc, Jose B -pg 453
Aquinigoc, Juan C -pg 453
Aquiningoc, Amparo P -pg 410
Aquiningoc, Ana A -pg 50
Aquiningoc, Ana D -pg 417
Aquiningoc, Ana Q -pg 467
Aquiningoc, Ana T -pg 423
Aquiningoc, Ana W -pg 421
Aquiningoc, Antonio B -pg 410
Aquiningoc, Antonio D -pg 417
Aquiningoc, Antonio T -pg 423
Aquiningoc, Antonio W -pg 421
Aquiningoc, Carmen Q -pg 467
Aquiningoc, Dolores A -pg 420
Aquiningoc, Dolores P -pg 410
Aquiningoc, Dolores Q -pg 467

Aquiningoc, Felicidad Q -pg 467
Aquiningoc, Francisco -pg 411
Aquiningoc, Francisco -pg 420
Aquiningoc, Grabiel P -pg 410
Aquiningoc, Joaquin T -pg 423
Aquiningoc, Joaquin W -pg 421
Aquiningoc, Jose C -pg 420
Aquiningoc, Jose Q -pg 467
Aquiningoc, Josefa F -pg 41
Aquiningoc, Juan B -pg 423
Aquiningoc, Juan Q -pg 467
Aquiningoc, Macrina A -pg 50
Aquiningoc, Magdalena W -pg 421
Aquiningoc, Manuel A -pg 467
Aquiningoc, Manuel C -pg 417
Aquiningoc, Maria C -pg 411
Aquiningoc, Maria F -pg 41
Aquiningoc, Maria Q -pg 467
Aquiningoc, Maria T -pg 423
Aquiningoc, Mariano C -pg 421
Aquiningoc, Rosalia C -pg 411
Aquiningoc, Rosario Q -pg 420
Aquiningoc, Santiago P -pg 410
Aquiningoc, Susana P -pg 410
Aquiningoc, Trinidad P -pg 410
Aquiningoc, Vicente B -pg 421
Aquiningoc, Vicente D -pg 417
Aquininog, Joaquina -pg 301
Aquino, Barsalisa C -pg 277
Aquino, Carmen C -pg 277
Aquino, Concepcion M -pg 293
Aquino, Ignacia C -pg 277
Aquino, Jose C -pg 277
Aquino, Juan C -pg 277
Aquino, Matias C -pg 293
Aquino, Nicolasa C -pg 277
Aquino, Pedro C -pg 277
Aquino, Ramon M -pg 293
Aquino, Rosa M -pg 293
Aquino, Rufina M -pg 293
Aquino, Vicenta M -pg 293
Arceo, Ana G -pg 430
Arceo, Ana S -pg 304
Arceo, Antonia S -pg 305
Arceo, Antonia S -pg 432
Arceo, Carmen S -pg 432
Arceo, Felicita S -pg 305
Arceo, Francisco C -pg 175
Arceo, Francisco G -pg 430
Arceo, Francisco S -pg 432
Arceo, Gregoria C -pg 175
Arceo, Gregorio C -pg 303

Arceo, Guadalupe N -pg 423
Arceo, Ignacio C -pg 302
Arceo, Joaquina T -pg 303
Arceo, Jose B -pg 430
Arceo, Jose C -pg 175
Arceo, Jose C -pg 302
Arceo, Jose M -pg 423
Arceo, Josefa S -pg 304
Arceo, Lucia S -pg 305
Arceo, Lydia C -pg 175
Arceo, Maria C -pg 302
Arceo, Maria C -pg 302
Arceo, Maria G -pg 430
Arceo, Maria M -pg 407
Arceo, Maria S -pg 305
Arceo, Natividad N -pg 423
Arceo, Nicolasa C -pg 302
Arceo, Rosa S -pg 304
Arceo, Rosalia C -pg 302
Arceo, Rosario -pg 302
Arceo, Trinidad T -pg 303
Arceo, Vicente A -pg 175
Arceo, Vicente C -pg 175
Arceo, Vicente C -pg 304
Arceo, Vicente G -pg 430
Arima, T 0 -pg 166
Arriola, Ana A -pg 352
Arriola, Ana C -pg 113
Arriola, Ana C -pg 149
Arriola, Antonio F -pg 167
Arriola, Concepcion A -pg 157
Arriola, Consolacion C -pg 149
Arriola, Dolores C -pg 149
Arriola, Felomena M -pg 521
Arriola, Filomena C -pg 149
Arriola, Francisco D -pg 25
Arriola, Francisco R -pg 149
Arriola, Jose 0 -pg 157
Arriola, Jose 0 -pg 157
Arriola, Jose -pg 290
Arriola, Josefa C -pg 149
Arriola, Juan C -pg 149
Arriola, Juana A -pg 157
Arriola, Juana F -pg 167
Arriola, Luis M -pg 170
Arriola, Margarita -pg 291
Arriola, Maria C -pg 149
Arriola, Rufina A -pg 157
Arriola, Vicente A -pg 157
Arriola, Vicente F -pg 54
Arriola, Vicente F -pg 167
Arse, Ki -pg 541

Asa, Ono -pg 251
Asano, Isabel F -pg 281
Asano, Maria F -pg 281
Asano, Toshiro -pg 281
Asanoma, Francisco C -pg 525
Asanoma, Jesus C -pg 525
Asanoma, Jose C -pg 525
Asanoma, Maria C -pg 525
Asanoma, Sabina C -pg 525
Asanoma, Tito R -pg 525
Ascension, Juana B -pg 111
Asuncion, Andres SL -pg 57
Asuncion, Manuel B -pg 138
Asuncion, Vicente B -pg 130
Atao, Ana M -pg 372
Atao, Dolores M -pg 372
Atao, Juan M -pg 372
Atoigue, Alejandrina M -pg 159
Atoigue, Ana A -pg 102
Atoigue, Ana C -pg 558
Atoigue, Ana L -pg 99
Atoigue, Ana Q -pg 101
Atoigue, Antonia C -pg 103
Atoigue, Antonia T -pg 27
Atoigue, Antonio A -pg 552
Atoigue, Antonio C -pg 291
Atoigue, Antonio T -pg 27
Atoigue, Asuncion T -pg 27
Atoigue, Bernadino A -pg 102
Atoigue, Carlos Q -pg 101
Atoigue, Carmen B -pg 347
Atoigue, Carmen T -pg 103
Atoigue, Dolores A -pg 102
Atoigue, Dolores B -pg 347
Atoigue, Eufracia C -pg 146
Atoigue, Felipe M -pg 103
Atoigue, Francisco M -pg 552
Atoigue, Francisco Q -pg 101
Atoigue, Francisco T -pg 27
Atoigue, Jesus 0 -pg 101
Atoigue, Jesus C -pg 332
Atoigue, Jesus L -pg 152
Atoigue, Jesus Q -pg 101
Atoigue, Joaquin 0 -pg 103
Atoigue, Joaquin C -pg 332
Atoigue, Joaquin C -pg 347
Atoigue, Joaquin M -pg 552
Atoigue, Joaquina C -pg 103
Atoigue, Joaquina C -pg 146
Atoigue, Joaquina C -pg 332
Atoigue, Joaquina L -pg 152
Atoigue, Joaquina P -pg 269

Atoigue, Joaquina T -pg 27
Atoigue, Jose A -pg 523
Atoigue, Jose B -pg 347
Atoigue, Jose C -pg 146
Atoigue, Jose R -pg 26
Atoigue, Jose T -pg 102
Atoigue, Jose T -pg 103
Atoigue, Jose U -pg 159
Atoigue, Josefa U -pg 291
Atoigue, Juan B -pg 347
Atoigue, Juan M -pg 103
Atoigue, Juan M -pg 552
Atoigue, Juan SN -pg 103
Atoigue, Juliana SN -pg 102
Atoigue, Leonardo C -pg 558
Atoigue, Magdalena T -pg 103
Atoigue, Manuel A -pg 102
Atoigue, Manuel T -pg 552
Atoigue, Maria A -pg 102
Atoigue, Maria L -pg 99
Atoigue, Maria M -pg 159
Atoigue, Maria U -pg 291
Atoigue, Natividad C -pg 103
Atoigue, Pablo 0 -pg 101
Atoigue, Remedio A -pg 69
Atoigue, Rita T -pg 26
Atoigue, Rosa M -pg 552
Atoigue, Rosario C -pg 103
Atoigue, Teresa T -pg 27
Atoigue, Tomas M -pg 552
Atoigue, Trinidad A -pg 99
Atoigue, Ursula T -pg 348
Atoigue, Vicente 0 -pg 102
Atoigue, Vicente C -pg 269
Atoigue, Vicente Q -pg 101
Atoigue, Vicente T -pg 552
Atoigue, Vicente U -pg 291
Austria, Emeterio 0 -pg 18
Babauta, Ana A -pg 396
Babauta, Ana A -pg 461
Babauta, Ana C -pg 498
Babauta, Ana D -pg 379
Babauta, Ana S -pg 81
Babauta, Ana SN -pg 439
Babauta, Andrea B -pg 380
Babauta, Angel B -pg 476
Babauta, Angelina C -pg 87
Babauta, Antonia R -pg 437
Babauta, Antonia R -pg 438
Babauta, Antonio A -pg 436
Babauta, Antonio B -pg 391
Babauta, Antonio B -pg 492

Babauta, Antonio C -pg 440
Babauta, Antonio C -pg 451
Babauta, Antonio D -pg 392
Babauta, Antonio R -pg 438
Babauta, Barcelio T -pg 456
Babauta, Benjamin T -pg 430
Babauta, Candelario C -pg 87
Babauta, Carmen C -pg 411
Babauta, Carmen C -pg 441
Babauta, Carmen T -pg 430
Babauta, Catalina R -pg 438
Babauta, Concepcion Q -pg 539
Babauta, Consolacion T -pg 430
Babauta, Dolores Q -pg 533
Babauta, Dolores Q -pg 539
Babauta, Dolores S -pg 449
Babauta, Dolores T -pg 430
Babauta, Domingo D -pg 542
Babauta, Donicio C -pg 443
Babauta, Engracia Q -pg 532
Babauta, Faustino B -pg 450
Babauta, Felistina Q -pg 461
Babauta, Felix C -pg 411
Babauta, Felix SN -pg 439
Babauta, Florencia A -pg 462
Babauta, Francisco B -pg 492
Babauta, Francisco L -pg 451
Babauta, Francisco M -pg 456
Babauta, Francisco Q -pg 540
Babauta, Francisco R -pg 438
Babauta, Francisco SN -pg 137
Babauta, Francisco SN -pg 439
Babauta, Ignacia T -pg 430
Babauta, Ignacio G -pg 461
Babauta, Ignacio G -pg 532
Babauta, Jesus A -pg 437
Babauta, Jesus A -pg 462
Babauta, Jesus B -pg 493
Babauta, Jesus C -pg 479
Babauta, Jesus L -pg 451
Babauta, Joaquin C -pg 441
Babauta, Joaquin Q -pg 539
Babauta, Joaquin SN -pg 439
Babauta, Joaquina A -pg 462
Babauta, Joaquina B -pg 492
Babauta, Jose A -pg 449
Babauta, Jose A -pg 462
Babauta, Jose B -pg 436
Babauta, Jose B -pg 489
Babauta, Jose B -pg 492
Babauta, Jose D -pg 539
Babauta, Jose G -pg 440

Babauta, Jose G -pg 472
Babauta, Jose L -pg 451
Babauta, Jose P -pg 438
Babauta, Jose Q -pg 540
Babauta, Jose R -pg 438
Babauta, Josefa R -pg 438
Babauta, Juan B -pg 438
Babauta, Juan C -pg 411
Babauta, Juan C -pg 451
Babauta, Juan G -pg 461
Babauta, Juan SN -pg 438
Babauta, Juana A -pg 436
Babauta, Juana T -pg 430
Babauta, Julian D -pg 377
Babauta, Largrimas A -pg 462
Babauta, Luisa C -pg 87
Babauta, Manuel M -pg 462
Babauta, Manuel R -pg 209
Babauta, Maria A -pg 436
Babauta, Maria A -pg 449
Babauta, Maria A -pg 461
Babauta, Maria C -pg 443
Babauta, Maria C -pg 451
Babauta, Maria M -pg 456
Babauta, Maria Q -pg 539
Babauta, Maria R -pg 438
Babauta, Maria S -pg 449
Babauta, Pedro C -pg 443
Babauta, Pedro C -pg 449
Babauta, Pedro M -pg 454
Babauta, Portunato J -pg 81
Babauta, Ramona P -pg 454
Babauta, Remedio A -pg 449
Babauta, Rita B -pg 438
Babauta, Rita C -pg 411
Babauta, Rita M -pg 456
Babauta, Rita Q -pg 532
Babauta, Robinio G -pg 462
Babauta, Rosa B -pg 438
Babauta, Rosa C -pg 451
Babauta, Rosa G -pg 440
Babauta, Rosa L -pg 451
Babauta, Rosa Q -pg 532
Babauta, Rosalia Q -pg 540
Babauta, Rosalia S -pg 449
Babauta, Rosario T -pg 430
Babauta, Santiago C -pg 441
Babauta, Tedora SN -pg 438
Babauta, Venancio R -pg 442
Babauta, Vicenta C -pg 476
Babauta, Vicente B -pg 437
Babauta, Vicente B -pg 437

Babauta, Vicente B -pg 492
Babauta, Vicente C -pg 443
Babauta, Vicente L -pg 449
Babauta, Vicente Q -pg 533
Babauta, Vicente R -pg 209
Babauta, Vicente T -pg 430
Babauta, Virginia M -pg 456
Bae, Aguida O -pg 124
Bae, Angela LG -pg 159
Balajadia, Ana S -pg 548
Balajadia, Antonio I -pg 546
Balajadia, Catalina I -pg 545
Balajadia, Cornelia I -pg 545
Balajadia, Enrique S -pg 549
Balajadia, Felix S -pg 548
Balajadia, Francisca I -pg 545
Balajadia, Francisco C -pg 337
Balajadia, Ines LG -pg 337
Balajadia, Jesus S -pg 549
Balajadia, Joaquin J -pg 547
Balajadia, Joaquina B -pg 548
Balajadia, Joaquina S -pg 549
Balajadia, Jose I -pg 545
Balajadia, Jose J -pg 545
Balajadia, Jose P -pg 547
Balajadia, Josefa LG -pg 337
Balajadia, Juan I -pg 545
Balajadia, Manuel I -pg 545
Balajadia, Pedro I -pg 545
Balajadia, Remedios P -pg 547
Balajadia, Rita T -pg 356
Balajadia, Rosa I -pg 548
Balajadia, Susana P -pg 547
Balajadia, Vicenta R -pg 549
Balajadia, Vicente L -pg 337
Balajadia, Vicente M -pg 548
Balajadia, Vicente P -pg 547
Baleto, Andrea J -pg 426
Baleto, Antonio S -pg 398
Baleto, Francisco S -pg 398
Baleto, Jesus S -pg 398
Baleto, Jose S -pg 398
Baleto, Maria S -pg 398
Baleto, Maria S -pg 398
Baleto, Remedios S -pg 398
Baleto, Sebastian V -pg 426
Baleto, Sixto J -pg 426
Baleto, Vicente D -pg 398
Baleto, Vicente S -pg 398
Baliesta, Francisco B -pg 397
Bamba, Amalia C -pg 171
Bamba, Carmen B -pg 119

Bamba, Concepcion C -pg 171
Bamba, Dolores SA -pg 171
Bamba, Felisa -pg 316
Bamba, Jesus -pg 316
Bamba, Jose -pg 316
Bamba, Josefa -pg 316
Bamba, Juan SA -pg 171
Bamba, Manuel -pg 316
Bamba, Maria B -pg 309
Bamba, Maria C -pg 171
Bamba, Maria S -pg 119
Bamba, Maria S -pg 316
Bamba, Rita M -pg 316
Bamba, Vicente SA -pg 171
Bamba, Vicente -pg 316
Barbour, James -pg 357
Barbour, Maria C -pg 357
Barcinas, Ana C -pg 475
Barcinas, Ana C -pg 491
Barcinas, Antonia C -pg 491
Barcinas, Antonio B -pg 491
Barcinas, Benita C -pg 490
Barcinas, Gravier C -pg 476
Barcinas, Ignacio B -pg 491
Barcinas, Isaac LG -pg 532
Barcinas, Jesus C -pg 475
Barcinas, Joaquin C -pg 476
Barcinas, Jose A -pg 532
Barcinas, Jose C -pg 476
Barcinas, Jose D -pg 532
Barcinas, Jose S -pg 475
Barcinas, Josefa D -pg 532
Barcinas, Juan D -pg 532
Barcinas, Juan S -pg 491
Barcinas, Magdalena D -pg 532
Barcinas, Maria A -pg 532
Barcinas, Martin C -pg 475
Barcinas, Mercedes D -pg 532
Barcinas, Pedro B -pg 491
Barcinas, Pedro C -pg 490
Barcinas, Rita A -pg 532
Barcinas, Tomas C -pg 475
Barcinas, Tomas LG -pg 491
Barcinas, Tomasa B -pg 491
Barcinas, Ynigo C -pg 476
Bargas, Maria U -pg 22
Barnabas, de Caseda -pg 473
Bautista, Aguilino O -pg 18
Bautista, Andres S -pg 113
Bautista, Antonio C -pg 106
Bautista, Antonio L -pg 106
Bautista, Concepcion C -pg 116

Bautista, Dolores S -pg 113
Bautista, Encarnacion L -pg 106
Bautista, Enrique C -pg 116
Bautista, Francisca C -pg 116
Bautista, Francisco B -pg 127
Bautista, Ignacio C -pg 116
Bautista, Isabel C -pg 116
Bautista, Jesus L -pg 106
Bautista, Jose C -pg 116
Bautista, Jose S -pg 113
Bautista, Juan C -pg 113
Bautista, Juan D -pg 113
Bautista, Juan S -pg 113
Bautista, Luis P -pg 199
Bautista, Manuel S -pg 113
Bautista, Manuela A -pg 199
Bautista, Maria C -pg 116
Bautista, Maria P -pg 199
Bautista, Maria S -pg 113
Bautista, Matias L -pg 106
Bautista, Pablo C -pg 116
Bautista, Pedro L -pg 106
Bautista, Rosa C -pg 116
Bautista, Rosa L -pg 106
Bautista, Vicente C -pg 199
Bautista, Vicente P -pg 200
Bautista, Vicente S -pg 113
Bayona, Antonio I -pg 191
Bayona, Catalina I -pg 192
Bayona, Jose G -pg 192
Bayona, Juan I -pg 191
Bayona, Maria I -pg 191
Bayona, Rosa G -pg 191
Baza, Adela C -pg 548
Baza, Agustin U -pg 228
Baza, Ana C -pg 294
Baza, Ana I -pg 144
Baza, Ana P -pg 557
Baza, Ana S -pg 547
Baza, Ana T -pg 495
Baza, Ana M P -pg 30
Baza, Antonio C -pg 152
Baza, Biatris C -pg 550
Baza, Concepcion LG -pg 559
Baza, Dolores C -pg 480
Baza, Dolores M -pg 496
Baza, Faustina T -pg 495
Baza, Feliza C -pg 152
Baza, Francisca C -pg 558
Baza, Ignacia B -pg 30
Baza, Ignacio C -pg 294
Baza, Isabel A -pg 160

Baza, Jesus C -pg 294
Baza, Jesus C -pg 559
Baza, Joaquin C -pg 96
Baza, Jose B -pg 44
Baza, Jose C -pg 152
Baza, Jose C -pg 548
Baza, Jose C -pg 558
Baza, Jose LG -pg 294
Baza, Jose T -pg 496
Baza, Jose H D -pg 30
Baza, Josefa D -pg 96
Baza, Josefina C -pg 480
Baza, Juan B -pg 30
Baza, Juan C -pg 294
Baza, Luis C -pg 152
Baza, Luis M -pg 152
Baza, Manuel B -pg 30
Baza, Manuel C -pg 294
Baza, Manuela C -pg 548
Baza, Margarita C -pg 549
Baza, Maria A -pg 30
Baza, Maria B -pg 30
Baza, Maria B -pg 30
Baza, Maria C -pg 30
Baza, Maria C -pg 152
Baza, Maria C -pg 294
Baza, Maria C -pg 480
Baza, Maria C -pg 548
Baza, Maria C -pg 550
Baza, Maria LG -pg 294
Baza, Maria LG -pg 559
Baza, Maria T -pg 228
Baza, Pedro T -pg 228
Baza, Pedro T -pg 495
Baza, Pedro T -pg 557
Baza, Pilar C -pg 550
Baza, Prebiterio A -pg 160
Baza, Ramon C -pg 495
Baza, Ramon C -pg 558
Baza, Ramon S -pg 547
Baza, Ramona C -pg 44
Baza, Rita T -pg 228
Baza, Rosa C -pg 152
Baza, Rosa C -pg 480
Baza, Rosa C -pg 550
Baza, Rosa M -pg 496
Baza, Rosa T -pg 495
Baza, Rosa T -pg 557
Baza, Telesforo Q -pg 549
Baza, Teresa C -pg 550
Baza, Tito C -pg 550
Baza, Venancio T -pg 480

Baza, Vicente C -pg 294
Baza, Vicente C -pg 548
Baza, Vicente C -pg 549
Baza, Vicente S -pg 550
Baza, Vicente U -pg 160
Baza, Vicitacion M -pg 496
Benavente, Agripina S -pg 82
Benavente, Ana 0 -pg 74
Benavente, Ana 0 -pg 171
Benavente, Ana B -pg 346
Benavente, Ana C -pg 81
Benavente, Ana G -pg 86
Benavente, Ana L -pg 87
Benavente, Ana L -pg 120
Benavente, Ana R -pg 129
Benavente, Antonia Q -pg 75
Benavente, Antonio M -pg 74
Benavente, Candelaria 0 -pg 171
Benavente, Candelaria C -pg 81
Benavente, Carmen G -pg 120
Benavente, Carmen L -pg 120
Benavente, Cecilia Q -pg 74
Benavente, Concepcion C -pg 81
Benavente, Dolores D -pg 120
Benavente, Dolores P -pg 546
Benavente, Dolores Q -pg 543
Benavente, Eloi Q -pg 75
Benavente, Enrique R -pg 129
Benavente, Eufrasia SA -pg 83
Benavente, Felix R -pg 83
Benavente, Filipe C -pg 59
Benavente, Francisca SA -pg 83
Benavente, Francisco C -pg 81
Benavente, Gabriela M -pg 129
Benavente, Ignacia G -pg 78
Benavente, Ignacio G -pg 120
Benavente, Ignacio T -pg 144
Benavente, Ines G -pg 78
Benavente, Isabel G -pg 78
Benavente, Jesus G -pg 86
Benavente, Jesus R -pg 543
Benavente, Jesus SA -pg 83
Benavente, Joaquin A -pg 87
Benavente, Joaquin G -pg 78
Benavente, Joaquin G -pg 86
Benavente, Joaquin M -pg 82
Benavente, Joaquin S -pg 82
Benavente, Jose G -pg 78
Benavente, Jose G -pg 86
Benavente, Jose L -pg 120
Benavente, Jose L jr -pg 120
Benavente, Jose Q -pg 75

Benavente, Jose R -pg 81
Benavente, Josefa C -pg 297
Benavente, Josefa D -pg 120
Benavente, Josefa L -pg 120
Benavente, Juan L -pg 120
Benavente, Juan R -pg 129
Benavente, Justo B -pg 120
Benavente, Manuel Q -pg 75
Benavente, Manuel T -pg 75
Benavente, Manuela D -pg 144
Benavente, Manuela G -pg 78
Benavente, Maria C -pg 81
Benavente, Maria G -pg 78
Benavente, Maria G -pg 86
Benavente, Maria I -pg 168
Benavente, Maria L -pg 120
Benavente, Maria M -pg 129
Benavente, Maria Q -pg 74
Benavente, Maria SA -pg 83
Benavente, Maria SN -pg 114
Benavente, Mariano G -pg 78
Benavente, Nicolasa Q -pg 543
Benavente, Nieves L -pg 87
Benavente, Pedro M -pg 77
Benavente, Pedro SA -pg 83
Benavente, Ramon Q -pg 543
Benavente, Rita Q -pg 75
Benavente, Rita S -pg 82
Benavente, Teresa Q -pg 75
Benavente, Tomas Q -pg 75
Benavente, Vicenta G -pg 86
Benavente, Vicente A -pg 144
Benavente, Vicente B -pg 78
Benavente, Vicente M -pg 86
Benavente, Vicente R -pg 546
Benavente, Vicente SA -pg 83
Benavente, Victoria 0 -pg 171
Benito, Pedro R -pg 278
Bernardo, Ana T -pg 289
Bernardo, Andres C -pg 289
Bernardo, Artemio C -pg 289
Bernardo, Dominga C -pg 289
Bernardo, Guillermo C -pg 289
Bernardo, Joaquin C -pg 289
Bernardo, Pedro C -pg 289
Bitanga, Anatalio A -pg 266
Bitanga, Firmin G -pg 267
Bitanga, Francisca G -pg 267
Bitanga, Inocencio G -pg 267
Bitanga, Jose G -pg 266
Bitanga, Maria G -pg 266
Bitanga, Maria G -pg 267

Bitanga, Vicente G -pg 267
Blanco, Consolacion F -pg 21
Blanco, Delfina F -pg 21
Blanco, Felipe P -pg 21
Blanco, Joaquina F -pg 21
Blas, Alice A -pg 45
Blas, Ana A -pg 139
Blas, Ana A -pg 370
Blas, Ana C -pg 53
Blas, Ana C -pg 53
Blas, Ana C -pg 114
Blas, Ana G -pg 53
Blas, Ana M -pg 158
Blas, Angelina E -pg 30
Blas, Antonia F -pg 92
Blas, Antonia G -pg 53
Blas, Antonia L -pg 365
Blas, Antonio B -pg 91
Blas, Antonio C -pg 30
Blas, Antonio C -pg 115
Blas, Antonio L -pg 84
Blas, Antonio LG -pg 266
Blas, Apolonia T -pg 179
Blas, Asuncion M -pg 173
Blas, Asuncion R -pg 158
Blas, Atanasio 0 -pg 31
Blas, Biatris E -pg 31
Blas, Brigida B -pg 185
Blas, Carlos -pg 185
Blas, Concepcion C -pg 115
Blas, Consolacion A -pg 370
Blas, Consuelo M -pg 173
Blas, Consuelo M -pg 386
Blas, Dolores C -pg 32
Blas, Dolores C -pg 114
Blas, Dolores C -pg 137
Blas, Encarnacion C -pg 53
Blas, Esperanza C -pg 32
Blas, Francisca C -pg 32
Blas, Francisco A -pg 185
Blas, Francisco A -pg 370
Blas, Francisco C -pg 114
Blas, Francisco F -pg 91
Blas, Francisco G -pg 53
Blas, Francisco R -pg 137
Blas, Gregorio B -pg 44
Blas, Gregorio F -pg 137
Blas, Guido F -pg 91
Blas, Ignacio A -pg 370
Blas, Ignacio B -pg 370
Blas, Isabel G -pg 53
Blas, Jesus 0 -pg 167

Blas, Jesus A -pg 139
Blas, Jesus B -pg 185
Blas, Jesus C -pg 53
Blas, Jesus C -pg 115
Blas, Jesus E -pg 30
Blas, Joaquin A -pg 139
Blas, Joaquin C -pg 53
Blas, Joaquin F -pg 158
Blas, Joaquin G -pg 53
Blas, Joaquin L -pg 364
Blas, Joaquin T -pg 53
Blas, Joaquina R -pg 31
Blas, Jose A -pg 44
Blas, Jose A -pg 137
Blas, Jose A -pg 139
Blas, Jose B -pg 185
Blas, Jose C -pg 53
Blas, Jose C -pg 115
Blas, Jose E -pg 30
Blas, Jose F -pg 91
Blas, Jose F -pg 92
Blas, Jose T -pg 91
Blas, Josefa A -pg 139
Blas, Josefa A -pg 370
Blas, Josefa F -pg 158
Blas, Josefa R -pg 137
Blas, Juan A -pg 44
Blas, Juan A -pg 185
Blas, Juan C -pg 31
Blas, Juan L -pg 365
Blas, Juan S -pg 92
Blas, Juan S -pg 184
Blas, Juana A -pg 370
Blas, Juana C -pg 91
Blas, Julia F -pg 91
Blas, Juliana A -pg 44
Blas, Lagrimas R -pg 137
Blas, Leonardo A -pg 91
Blas, Lorenso L -pg 173
Blas, Lorenzo L -pg 364
Blas, Luis C -pg 108
Blas, Manuel A -pg 50
Blas, Manuel A -pg 139
Blas, Manuel A -pg 184
Blas, Manuel C -pg 53
Blas, Maria 0 -pg 114
Blas, Maria A -pg 44
Blas, Maria A -pg 50
Blas, Maria A -pg 139
Blas, Maria A -pg 139
Blas, Maria B -pg 185
Blas, Maria C -pg 53

Blas, Maria C -pg 53
Blas, Maria F -pg 91
Blas, Maria F -pg 91
Blas, Maria M -pg 173
Blas, Maria M -pg 173
Blas, Mariano R -pg 137
Blas, Matias P -pg 211
Blas, Nicolasa B -pg 185
Blas, Nicolasa S -pg 184
Blas, Pedro C -pg 53
Blas, Pedro G -pg 53
Blas, Ramon F -pg 158
Blas, Ramon T -pg 185
Blas, Ramon -pg 185
Blas, Rebeca C -pg 32
Blas, Regina R -pg 137
Blas, Rita C -pg 115
Blas, Rosa 0 -pg 139
Blas, Rosa B -pg 185
Blas, Rosa R -pg 137
Blas, Rosa S -pg 184
Blas, Rosa -pg 185
Blas, Rosalia E -pg 31
Blas, Rosario R -pg 137
Blas, Soledad A -pg 370
Blas, Teresa C -pg 32
Blas, Teresa C -pg 91
Blas, Thomas E A -pg 31
Blas, Trinidad B -pg 185
Blas, Vicente A -pg 45
Blas, Vicente A -pg 50
Blas, Vicente C -pg 53
Blas, Vicente D -pg 125
Blas, Vicente F -pg 139
Blaz, Ana I -pg 268
Blaz, Ana M -pg 351
Blaz, Angustia B -pg 328
Blaz, Antonia B -pg 328
Blaz, Antonia U -pg 312
Blaz, Antonio I -pg 268
Blaz, Carmen B -pg 328
Blaz, Concepcion U -pg 312
Blaz, Demetro U -pg 312
Blaz, Dolores U -pg 312
Blaz, Domingo C -pg 301
Blaz, Felisa I -pg 268
Blaz, Flora U -pg 312
Blaz, Francisca S -pg 287
Blaz, Francisco B -pg 301
Blaz, Francisco I -pg 268
Blaz, Henry B -pg 328
Blaz, Jesusa B -pg 328

Blaz, Jose B -pg 312
Blaz, Jose B -pg 328
Blaz, Jose C -pg 301
Blaz, Jose I -pg 268
Blaz, Jose P -pg 276
Blaz, Jose U -pg 312
Blaz, Jose -pg 268
Blaz, Josefa C -pg 301
Blaz, Josefa I -pg 268
Blaz, Josefa P -pg 276
Blaz, Lourdes C -pg 301
Blaz, Luis A -pg 287
Blaz, Magdalena I -pg 268
Blaz, Maria C -pg 220
Blaz, Maria I -pg 268
Blaz, Maria P -pg 268
Blaz, Maria P -pg 276
Blaz, Maria U -pg 312
Blaz, Maria -pg 224
Blaz, Natividad P -pg 276
Blaz, Nicolasa L -pg 329
Blaz, Rita L -pg 329
Blaz, Rosa C -pg 301
Blaz, Rosa I -pg 268
Blaz, Rosa U -pg 312
Blaz, Rosa U -pg 312
Blaz, Tomasa I -pg 268
Blaz, Vicenta P -pg 276
Blaz, Vicente C -pg 32
Blaz, Vicente S -pg 220
Bondshu, Frank R -pg 225
Bondshu, Gregoria R -pg 225
Bondshu, Theodore R -pg 225
Bontugan, Antonio C -pg 348
Bontugan, Francisca F -pg 348
Bordallo, Alfredo P -pg 457
Bordallo, Baltazar B -pg 457
Bordallo, Baltazar P -pg 457
Bordallo, Carlos P -pg 457
Bordallo, Delfina P -pg 457
Bordallo, Rita P -pg 457
Borja, Agustina S -pg 143
Borja, Amelia S -pg 404
Borja, Ana C -pg 262
Borja, Ana M -pg 294
Borja, Ana M -pg 404
Borja, Ana Q -pg 21
Borja, Ana S -pg 143
Borja, Ana S -pg 261
Borja, Ana S -pg 404
Borja, Ana S -pg 404
Borja, Ana T -pg 136

Borja, Antonio A -pg 443
Borja, Antonio B -pg 20
Borja, Antonio C -pg 405
Borja, Antonio G -pg 136
Borja, Antonio M -pg 442
Borja, Antonio P -pg 294
Borja, Antonio Q -pg 21
Borja, Antonio R -pg 485
Borja, Antonio T -pg 136
Borja, Asemcion A -pg 443
Borja, Beatrice G -pg 276
Borja, Bernadita S -pg 136
Borja, Carmen M -pg 404
Borja, Carmen N -pg 396
Borja, Catalina C -pg 341
Borja, Concepcion G -pg 276
Borja, Concepcion M -pg 404
Borja, Concepcion S -pg 287
Borja, Consuelo M -pg 309
Borja, Crecensia Q -pg 21
Borja, Daniel M -pg 405
Borja, Delfina C -pg 299
Borja, Delfina O -pg 284
Borja, Dolores A -pg 468
Borja, Dolores B -pg 477
Borja, Dolores C -pg 299
Borja, Dolores F -pg 92
Borja, Dolores M -pg 404
Borja, Dolores O -pg 283
Borja, Dolores S -pg 287
Borja, Eduvegis O -pg 284
Borja, Ejinio Q -pg 21
Borja, Emeliana L -pg 136
Borja, Engracia C -pg 262
Borja, Felicidad Q -pg 21
Borja, Filomena Q -pg 163
Borja, Francisca C -pg 217
Borja, Francisca C -pg 217
Borja, Francisco B -pg 20
Borja, Francisco C -pg 262
Borja, Francisco C -pg 299
Borja, Francisco C -pg 341
Borja, Francisco N -pg 396
Borja, Francisco S -pg 143
Borja, Francisco S -pg 181
Borja, Francisco S -pg 396
Borja, Francisco S -pg 450
Borja, Gabriela L -pg 136
Borja, Gabriela T -pg 136
Borja, Gregorio A -pg 468
Borja, Gregorio C -pg 52
Borja, Gregorio C -pg 262

Borja, Gregorio M -pg 404
Borja, Gregorio N -pg 396
Borja, Gregorio S -pg 404
Borja, Guadalupe M -pg 405
Borja, Ignacia R -pg 19
Borja, Ignacia R -pg 95
Borja, Ignacia -pg 217
Borja, Ignacio M -pg 405
Borja, Ignacio Q -pg 21
Borja, Ignacio R -pg 485
Borja, Ignacio T -pg 287
Borja, Isabel L -pg 169
Borja, Isabel M -pg 396
Borja, Isabel S -pg 242
Borja, Jesus B -pg 20
Borja, Jesus C -pg 341
Borja, Jesus Q -pg 136
Borja, Jesus S -pg 143
Borja, Joaquin C -pg 217
Borja, Joaquin M -pg 262
Borja, Joaquin M -pg 294
Borja, Joaquin S -pg 143
Borja, Joaquin T -pg 136
Borja, Joaquin T -pg 468
Borja, Joaquina C -pg 127
Borja, Joaquina S -pg 242
Borja, Jose A -pg 442
Borja, Jose B -pg 20
Borja, Jose B -pg 20
Borja, Jose C -pg 262
Borja, Jose D -pg 163
Borja, Jose F -pg 92
Borja, Jose L -pg 136
Borja, Jose L -pg 162
Borja, Jose M -pg 404
Borja, Jose O -pg 283
Borja, Jose R -pg 95
Borja, Jose S -pg 143
Borja, Jose S -pg 450
Borja, Jose S -pg 450
Borja, Jose T -pg 85
Borja, Jose T -pg 119
Borja, Jose -pg 283
Borja, Jose -pg 309
Borja, Josefa LG -pg 274
Borja, Josefa S -pg 143
Borja, Josefa T -pg 136
Borja, Josefina G -pg 276
Borja, Juan B -pg 20
Borja, Juan C -pg 127
Borja, Juan C -pg 299
Borja, Juan M -pg 95

Borja, Juan M -pg 404
Borja, Juan O -pg 284
Borja, Juan Q -pg 163
Borja, Juan R -pg 485
Borja, Juan S -pg 137
Borja, Juan S -pg 242
Borja, Juan S -pg 287
Borja, Juan S -pg 299
Borja, Juan T -pg 516
Borja, Juan W -pg 477
Borja, Juan -pg 427
Borja, Juan V S -pg 450
Borja, Julian A -pg 468
Borja, Lorenso R -pg 153
Borja, Lorenzo L -pg 217
Borja, Lucas C -pg 405
Borja, Lucas T -pg 404
Borja, Luis A -pg 442
Borja, Luis G -pg 317
Borja, Luis Q -pg 163
Borja, Luisa C -pg 341
Borja, Magdalena L -pg 338
Borja, Manuel A -pg 468
Borja, Manuel B -pg 20
Borja, Manuel B -pg 276
Borja, Manuel G -pg 276
Borja, Manuel L -pg 338
Borja, Manuel S -pg 92
Borja, Maraquita R -pg 485
Borja, Maria A -pg 442
Borja, Maria B -pg 20
Borja, Maria B -pg 20
Borja, Maria B -pg 20
Borja, Maria C -pg 127
Borja, Maria C -pg 341
Borja, Maria F -pg 22
Borja, Maria G -pg 177
Borja, Maria L -pg 169
Borja, Maria L -pg 338
Borja, Maria M -pg 294
Borja, Maria M -pg 338
Borja, Maria M -pg 338
Borja, Maria M -pg 404
Borja, Maria O -pg 283
Borja, Maria R -pg 95
Borja, Maria R -pg 162
Borja, Maria S -pg 242
Borja, Maria S -pg 262
Borja, Maria S -pg 404
Borja, Maria SN -pg 85
Borja, Maria T -pg 136
Borja, Maria T -pg 516

Borja, Mariano R -pg 162
Borja, Martina A -pg 442
Borja, Merigilda S -pg 262
Borja, Nicolasa C -pg 262
Borja, Nicolasa S -pg 181
Borja, Paulina C -pg 127
Borja, Paulino B -pg 341
Borja, Paz C -pg 317
Borja, Pedro B -pg 20
Borja, Pedro C -pg 127
Borja, Pedro M -pg 294
Borja, Pedro N -pg 396
Borja, Pedro Q -pg 163
Borja, Pedro Q -pg 351
Borja, Pilar O -pg 284
Borja, Rafael N -pg 396
Borja, Rafael T -pg 396
Borja, Ramon S -pg 169
Borja, Rita B -pg 477
Borja, Rita R -pg 162
Borja, Rita S -pg 404
Borja, Rita U -pg 406
Borja, Rosa A -pg 442
Borja, Rosa M -pg 294
Borja, Rosa M -pg 404
Borja, Rosa SN -pg 85
Borja, Santiago M -pg 261
Borja, Soledad S -pg 450
Borja, Soledad -pg 217
Borja, Susana Q -pg 20
Borja, Vicenta C -pg 405
Borja, Vicenta S -pg 42
Borja, Vicenta S -pg 287
Borja, Vicente C -pg 299
Borja, Vicente C -pg 341
Borja, Vicente D -pg 143
Borja, Vicente I -pg 127
Borja, Vicente M -pg 241
Borja, Vicente R -pg 485
Borja, Vicente S -pg 143
Borja, Vicente S -pg 143
Borja, Vicente S -pg 404
Borja, Vicente T -pg 404
Brown, Frank -pg 399
Brown, Maria -pg 399
Brown, Teodora -pg 399
Butler, Beatrice R -pg 240
Butler, Carl C -pg 240
Butler, Clara M -pg 240
Butler, Ignacia B -pg 240
Butler, James B -pg 240
Cabo, Angel D -pg 305

Cabo, Antonio D -pg 193
Cabo, Dolores C -pg 293
Cabo, Jose D -pg 293
Cabo, Manuela D -pg 305
Cabo, Maria D -pg 305
Cabo, Nicolasa D -pg 193
Cabrera, Ana D -pg 537
Cabrera, Ana D -pg 537
Cabrera, Ana SN -pg 29
Cabrera, Benita D -pg 538
Cabrera, Concepcion C -pg 28
Cabrera, Concepcion M -pg 156
Cabrera, Consolacion D -pg 537
Cabrera, Dolores SN -pg 29
Cabrera, Enrique V -pg 28
Cabrera, Francisco C -pg 28
Cabrera, Ignacia O -pg 156
Cabrera, Ignacio M -pg 156
Cabrera, Isabel D -pg 538
Cabrera, Joaquin V -pg 537
Cabrera, Jose D -pg 537
Cabrera, Juan D -pg 537
Cabrera, Juan M -pg 156
Cabrera, Maria C -pg 351
Cabrera, Maria D -pg 537
Cabrera, Maria M -pg 156
Cabrera, Maria T -pg 156
Cabrera, Pedro D -pg 537
Cabrera, Rosa M -pg 156
Cabrera, Rosalia SN -pg 29
Cabrera, Rosario M pg 156
Cabrera, Soledad D -pg 537
Cabrera, Vicente C -pg 28
Calvo, Adela T -pg 222
Calvo, Ana A -pg 222
Calvo, Angusto A -pg 222
Calvo, Antonia B -pg 53
Calvo, Antonio B -pg 189
Calvo, Carlos T -pg 222
Calvo, Clotilde T -pg 222
Calvo, Eduardo T -pg 222
Calvo, Fedela B -pg 53
Calvo, Felix P -pg 53
Calvo, Felix V -pg 189
Calvo, Flora T -pg 222
Calvo, Gregorio LG -pg 41
Calvo, Gregorio P -pg 244
Calvo, Guadalupe M -pg 189
Calvo, Hermina T -pg 222
Calvo, Isabel L -pg 248
Calvo, Ismael T -pg 222
Calvo, Jacinto A -pg 222

Calvo, Jose LG -pg 236
Calvo, Juana P -pg 244
Calvo, Leon P -pg 236
Calvo, Magdalena A -pg 320
Calvo, Manuel A -pg 41
Calvo, Maria A -pg 41
Calvo, Maria A -pg 41
Calvo, Maria LG -pg 236
Calvo, Oscar L -pg 248
Calvo, Pedro A -pg 41
Calvo, Pilar L -pg 248
Calvo, Pilar M -pg 189
Calvo, Ramon P -pg 248
Calvo, Regina T -pg 222
Calvo, Ricardo T -pg 222
Calvo, Rita A -pg 41
Calvo, Rufina T -pg 189
Calvo, Tomas A -pg 222
Calvo, Tomas L -pg 248
Calvo, Trinidad T -pg 222
Calvo, Vicente P -pg 244
Camacho, Alejandra T -pg 276
Camacho, Alfonso M -pg 39
Camacho, Amable D -pg 67
Camacho, Ana O -pg 173
Camacho, Ana B -pg 547
Camacho, Ana C -pg 67
Camacho, Ana D -pg 67
Camacho, Ana M -pg 39
Camacho, Ana M -pg 40
Camacho, Ana M -pg 44
Camacho, Ana M -pg 96
Camacho, Ana M -pg 295
Camacho, Ana M -pg 296
Camacho, Ana O -pg 16
Camacho, Ana R -pg 123
Camacho, Ana S -pg 29
Camacho, Ana S -pg 159
Camacho, Ana S -pg 406
Camacho, Ana SN -pg 48
Camacho, Antonia A -pg 64
Camacho, Antonia B -pg 131
Camacho, Antonia LG -pg 153
Camacho, Antonia O -pg 16
Camacho, Antonia S -pg 406
Camacho, Antonio C -pg 140
Camacho, Antonio M -pg 417
Camacho, Antonio P -pg 242
Camacho, Atanasio R -pg 243
Camacho, Barbara C -pg 199
Camacho, Beatris C -pg 38
Camacho, Candelaria M -pg 39

Camacho, Candelaria R -pg 123
Camacho, Carlos M -pg 292
Camacho, Carmen B -pg 108
Camacho, Carmen C -pg 29
Camacho, Carmen C -pg 38
Camacho, Carmen C -pg 215
Camacho, Carmen C -pg 253
Camacho, Carmen O -pg 16
Camacho, Carmen P -pg 32
Camacho, Carmen R -pg 243
Camacho, Catalina E -pg 286
Camacho, Cecilio G -pg 279
Camacho, Cecilio M -pg 295
Camacho, Concepcion C -pg 130
Camacho, Concepcion C -pg 140
Camacho, Concepcion C -pg 327
Camacho, Concepcion G -pg 278
Camacho, Concepcion O -pg 16
Camacho, Concepcion R -pg 242
Camacho, Concepcion S -pg 29
Camacho, Cristina B -pg 131
Camacho, Cristina C -pg 199
Camacho, Dolores A -pg 64
Camacho, Dolores M -pg 416
Camacho, Emeteria O -pg 153
Camacho, Emilia R -pg 81
Camacho, Encarnacion R -pg 81
Camacho, Engracia O -pg 173
Camacho, Enrique M -pg 152
Camacho, Enrique O -pg 16
Camacho, Feliciana O -pg 173
Camacho, Felicita G -pg 279
Camacho, Felicitas G -pg 45
Camacho, Felisidad P -pg 322
Camacho, Felix A -pg 64
Camacho, Filomena C -pg 253
Camacho, Florentina C -pg 470
Camacho, Francisco B -pg 554
Camacho, Francisco C -pg 67
Camacho, Francisco C -pg 253
Camacho, Francisco F -pg 40
Camacho, Francisco L -pg 43
Camacho, Francisco M -pg 39
Camacho, Francisco M -pg 292
Camacho, Francisco S -pg 29
Camacho, Francisco S -pg 262
Camacho, Francisco S -pg 406
Camacho, Geronimo O -pg 131
Camacho, Gregoria C -pg 469
Camacho, Gregorio C -pg 29
Camacho, Gregorio D -pg 67
Camacho, Gregorio R -pg 243

Camacho, Gregorio S -pg 29
Camacho, Gregorio SN -pg 48
Camacho, Guilermo S -pg 420
Camacho, Hazel P -pg 402
Camacho, Ignacia A -pg 64
Camacho, Ignacia P -pg 293
Camacho, Ignacio A -pg 81
Camacho, Ignacio C -pg 80
Camacho, Ignacio D -pg 67
Camacho, Ignacio G -pg 279
Camacho, Ignacio L -pg 292
Camacho, Ignacio N -pg 67
Camacho, Ines C -pg 416
Camacho, Isabel D -pg 40
Camacho, Isabel G -pg 45
Camacho, Jesus O -pg 131
Camacho, Jesus O -pg 173
Camacho, Jesus C -pg 38
Camacho, Jesus C -pg 199
Camacho, Jesus C -pg 470
Camacho, Jesus G -pg 45
Camacho, Jesus M -pg 292
Camacho, Jesus O -pg 16
Camacho, Jesus P -pg 33
Camacho, Jesus P -pg 322
Camacho, Jesus S -pg 29
Camacho, Jesus SN -pg 48
Camacho, Jesus -pg 225
Camacho, Joaquin F -pg 278
Camacho, Joaquin M -pg 295
Camacho, Joaquin O -pg 16
Camacho, Joaquin P -pg 322
Camacho, Joaquina C -pg 29
Camacho, Joaquina S -pg 262
Camacho, Jose O -pg 160
Camacho, Jose O -pg 173
Camacho, Jose A -pg 64
Camacho, Jose A -pg 109
Camacho, Jose C -pg 139
Camacho, Jose C -pg 406
Camacho, Jose C -pg 416
Camacho, Jose D -pg 40
Camacho, Jose D -pg 48
Camacho, Jose G -pg 96
Camacho, Jose G -pg 279
Camacho, Jose G -pg 296
Camacho, Jose J -pg 286
Camacho, Jose M -pg 40
Camacho, Jose M -pg 199
Camacho, Jose M -pg 286
Camacho, Jose M -pg 292
Camacho, Jose O -pg 554

Camacho, Jose R -pg 122
Camacho, Jose R -pg 242
Camacho, Jose S -pg 29
Camacho, Jose S -pg 60
Camacho, Jose S -pg 67
Camacho, Jose SN -pg 38
Camacho, Jose SN -pg 48
Camacho, Josefa O -pg 160
Camacho, Josefa A -pg 64
Camacho, Josefa A -pg 64
Camacho, Josefa O -pg 554
Camacho, Josefa R -pg 242
Camacho, Josefa S -pg 406
Camacho, Josefa -pg 253
Camacho, Josefina G -pg 60
Camacho, Josefina M -pg 96
Camacho, Josefina M -pg 296
Camacho, Josefina O -pg 554
Camacho, Josephine O -pg 16
Camacho, Juan B -pg 131
Camacho, Juan B -pg 160
Camacho, Juan C -pg 427
Camacho, Juan D -pg 31
Camacho, Juan F -pg 294
Camacho, Juan G -pg 45
Camacho, Juan G -pg 279
Camacho, Juan R -pg 123
Camacho, Juan S -pg 29
Camacho, Juan T -pg 83
Camacho, Juan -pg 220
Camacho, Juana P -pg 33
Camacho, Juana Q -pg 83
Camacho, Julita S -pg 406
Camacho, Lucia R -pg 43
Camacho, Luis C -pg 22
Camacho, Luis M -pg 292
Camacho, Luis P -pg 232
Camacho, Manuel C -pg 406
Camacho, Manuel C -pg 469
Camacho, Manuel F -pg 45
Camacho, Manuel M -pg 39
Camacho, Manuel SN -pg 39
Camacho, Manuela C -pg 29
Camacho, Manuela S -pg 29
Camacho, Maria O -pg 161
Camacho, Maria O -pg 173
Camacho, Maria A -pg 64
Camacho, Maria B -pg 547
Camacho, Maria C -pg 38
Camacho, Maria C -pg 38
Camacho, Maria C -pg 67
Camacho, Maria C -pg 189

Camacho, Maria C -pg 199
Camacho, Maria C -pg 253
Camacho, Maria C -pg 327
Camacho, Maria C -pg 470
Camacho, Maria D -pg 31
Camacho, Maria D -pg 40
Camacho, Maria D -pg 67
Camacho, Maria D -pg 68
Camacho, Maria G -pg 45
Camacho, Maria G -pg 279
Camacho, Maria LG -pg 153
Camacho, Maria M -pg 40
Camacho, Maria M -pg 40
Camacho, Maria M -pg 66
Camacho, Maria M -pg 292
Camacho, Maria M -pg 295
Camacho, Maria O -pg 16
Camacho, Maria O -pg 554
Camacho, Maria P -pg 322
Camacho, Maria R -pg 43
Camacho, Maria R -pg 122
Camacho, Maria S -pg 29
Camacho, Maria S -pg 406
Camacho, Maria SN -pg 64
Camacho, Maria T -pg 420
Camacho, Maria S S -pg 29
Camacho, Mariana P -pg 322
Camacho, Mariano R -pg 43
Camacho, Mercedes G -pg 45
Camacho, Miguel B -pg 108
Camacho, Natividad B -pg 137
Camacho, Natividad G -pg 45
Camacho, Nicolasa M -pg 317
Camacho, Nicolasa R -pg 243
Camacho, Pedro C -pg 67
Camacho, Pedro C -pg 327
Camacho, Pedro G -pg 286
Camacho, Pedro M -pg 40
Camacho, Pedro M -pg 292
Camacho, Pedro O -pg 554
Camacho, Pedro R -pg 123
Camacho, Pedro SN -pg 48
Camacho, Raimundo V -pg 286
Camacho, Ramon D -pg 64
Camacho, Ramon O -pg 554
Camacho, Rita C -pg 140
Camacho, Rita M -pg 253
Camacho, Rita M -pg 286
Camacho, Rita P -pg 293
Camacho, Rita T -pg 420
Camacho, Roque B -pg 548
Camacho, Rosa C -pg 22

Camacho, Rosa C -pg 253
Camacho, Rosa M -pg 66
Camacho, Rosa O -pg 554
Camacho, Rosa R -pg 243
Camacho, Rosa S -pg 29
Camacho, Rosa S -pg 60
Camacho, Rosalia C -pg 327
Camacho, Rosario B -pg 547
Camacho, Rosario C -pg 29
Camacho, Rosario S -pg 29
Camacho, Saturnina F -pg 32
Camacho, Serlala M -pg 66
Camacho, Sigena M -pg 286
Camacho, Silvestre O -pg 131
Camacho, Silvestre P -pg 293
Camacho, Simeon R -pg 243
Camacho, Teresa B -pg 131
Camacho, Tomas S -pg 416
Camacho, Tomas T -pg 420
Camacho, Tomasa P -pg 232
Camacho, Trinidad C -pg 33
Camacho, Trinidad C -pg 38
Camacho, Vicenta B -pg 108
Camacho, Vicenta C -pg 29
Camacho, Vicenta R -pg 43
Camacho, Vicente C -pg 38
Camacho, Vicente C -pg 83
Camacho, Vicente C -pg 177
Camacho, Vicente C -pg 528
Camacho, Vicente D -pg 40
Camacho, Vicente G -pg 45
Camacho, Vicente L -pg 88
Camacho, Vicente L -pg 286
Camacho, Vicente M -pg 41
Camacho, Vicente O -pg 554
Camacho, Vicente P -pg 33
Camacho, Vicente P -pg 293
Camacho, Vicente P -pg 317
Camacho, Vicente R -pg 81
Camacho, Vicente R -pg 243
Camacho, Vicente S -pg 547
Camacho, Vicente SN -pg 48
Camacho, Vicente T -pg 72
Camacho, Victoriano P -pg 327
Camacho, Vidal A -pg 293
Camacho, Zuilo LG -pg 153
Campos, Antonia R -pg 328
Campos, Antonio C -pg 327
Campos, Dominga G -pg 553
Campos, Joaquin R -pg 328
Campos, Jose R -pg 348
Campos, Jose SN -pg 553

Campos, Juan R -pg 328
Campos, Luisa R -pg 328
Campos, Maria G -pg 553
Campos, Ramon R -pg 328
Candaso, Antonia F -pg 479
Candaso, Antonio F -pg 479
Candaso, Brijeda T -pg 477
Candaso, Carmen T -pg 477
Candaso, Consolacion F -pg 479
Candaso, Jesus F -pg 479
Candaso, Jose F -pg 477
Candaso, Jose T -pg 477
Candaso, Maria F -pg 479
Candaso, Maria T -pg 477
Candaso, Vicente F -pg 479
Carbuillido, Concepcion M -pg 431
Carbuillido, Engracia M -pg 431
Carbuillido, Luisa M -pg 431
Carbuillido, Remedio M -pg 431
Carbuillido, Sebastian B -pg 431
Carbullido, Alberto T -pg 434
Carbullido, Amparo P -pg 430
Carbullido, Ana M -pg 430
Carbullido, Andres L -pg 436
Carbullido, Antonio P -pg 434
Carbullido, Baltazar -pg 414
Carbullido, Barbara C -pg 435
Carbullido, Carmen M -pg 430
Carbullido, Concepcion C -pg 436
Carbullido, Dolores C -pg 435
Carbullido, Enriqueta T -pg 434
Carbullido, Felicita C -pg 451
Carbullido, Felix T -pg 434
Carbullido, Francisco A -pg 458
Carbullido, Francisco M -pg 432
Carbullido, Ignacio M -pg 430
Carbullido, Jesus B -pg 429
Carbullido, Joaquin C -pg 451
Carbullido, Joaquin P -pg 430
Carbullido, Jose B -pg 430
Carbullido, Jose M -pg 432
Carbullido, Josefa B -pg 436
Carbullido, Josefa C -pg 435
Carbullido, Luis A -pg 458
Carbullido, Luis B -pg 435
Carbullido, Maria A -pg 458
Carbullido, Maria C -pg 435
Carbullido, Maria C -pg 451
Carbullido, Maria M -pg 432
Carbullido, Maria T -pg 434
Carbullido, Martina A -pg 458
Carbullido, Natividad C -pg 435

Carbullido, Regina P -pg 430
Carbullido, Rita M -pg 430
Carbullido, Rosa C -pg 435
Carbullido, Trinidad C -pg 451
Carbullido, Vicente C -pg 458
Cariaga, Carmen P -pg 181
Cariaga, Felix S -pg 181
Cariaga, Juan P -pg 181
Carlos, Maria P -pg 129
Carlos, Vicente M -pg 129
Carlson, Oscar -pg 426
Castro, Amalia C -pg 222
Castro, Amparo P -pg 540
Castro, Ana A -pg 121
Castro, Ana B -pg 152
Castro, Ana B -pg 169
Castro, Ana C -pg 259
Castro, Ana C -pg 453
Castro, Ana G -pg 497
Castro, Ana LG -pg 150
Castro, Ana LG -pg 518
Castro, Ana M -pg 238
Castro, Ana M -pg 247
Castro, Ana R -pg 133
Castro, Ana S -pg 30
Castro, Ana S -pg 248
Castro, Ana S -pg 262
Castro, Ana SN -pg 65
Castro, Ana SN -pg 509
Castro, Ana T -pg 274
Castro, Ana U -pg 238
Castro, Angela P -pg 253
Castro, Angelina T -pg 361
Castro, Antanasio P -pg 540
Castro, Antonia B -pg 147
Castro, Antonia LG -pg 320
Castro, Antonia LG -pg 518
Castro, Antonia P -pg 242
Castro, Antonia SN -pg 509
Castro, Antonia T -pg 274
Castro, Antonio I -pg 274
Castro, Antonio SN -pg 65
Castro, Anuncia T -pg 361
Castro, Ascemcion L -pg 67
Castro, Atanasio S -pg 409
Castro, Baronica SN -pg 65
Castro, Beatrice S -pg 248
Castro, Brigida C -pg 214
Castro, Carmen C -pg 148
Castro, Carmen P -pg 242
Castro, Carmen S -pg 379
Castro, Catalina LG -pg 35

Castro, Concepcion B -pg 152
Castro, Concepcion B -pg 168
Castro, Concepcion C -pg 142
Castro, Concepcion C -pg 156
Castro, Concepcion C -pg 542
Castro, Concepcion C -pg 542
Castro, Concepcion G -pg 541
Castro, Concepcion M -pg 247
Castro, Concepcion S -pg 409
Castro, Concepcion -pg 268
Castro, Consolacion C -pg 540
Castro, Consolacion R -pg 284
Castro, Cristina T -pg 361
Castro, Cristobal LG -pg 518
Castro, Delfina C -pg 542
Castro, Delfina LG -pg 320
Castro, Delfina S -pg 30
Castro, Dolores C -pg 52
Castro, Dolores C -pg 216
Castro, Dolores C -pg 453
Castro, Dolores C -pg 542
Castro, Dolores M -pg 115
Castro, Dolores S -pg 262
Castro, Dolores SN -pg 65
Castro, Elena G -pg 541
Castro, Emelia R -pg 284
Castro, Engracia LG -pg 150
Castro, Enrique M -pg 248
Castro, Enrique P -pg 540
Castro, Enrique R -pg 284
Castro, Enrique S -pg 279
Castro, Ernestina C -pg 216
Castro, Ester C -pg 542
Castro, Felecita M -pg 115
Castro, Feliciana G -pg 283
Castro, Feliciana R -pg 132
Castro, Feliciana -pg 253
Castro, Felicita C -pg 216
Castro, Felisa L -pg 67
Castro, Felix C -pg 238
Castro, Felix P -pg 242
Castro, Felix R -pg 158
Castro, Felix R -pg 284
Castro, Fernando A -pg 109
Castro, Florentina G -pg 497
Castro, Francisca R -pg 132
Castro, Francisco A -pg 217
Castro, Francisco B -pg 147
Castro, Francisco F -pg 131
Castro, Francisco N -pg 525
Castro, Francisco P -pg 242
Castro, Francisco R -pg 150

Castro, Francisco T -pg 361
Castro, Francisco W -pg 242
Castro, Geronimo R -pg 133
Castro, Gertrudes LG -pg 518
Castro, Ignacio J -pg 549
Castro, Ignacio P -pg 540
Castro, Ignacio T -pg 361
Castro, Isabel C -pg 238
Castro, Jesus B -pg 168
Castro, Jesus C -pg 29
Castro, Jesus C -pg 147
Castro, Jesus C -pg 453
Castro, Jesus LG -pg 35
Castro, Jesus LG -pg 518
Castro, Jesus M -pg 68
Castro, Jesus P -pg 540
Castro, Jesus R -pg 133
Castro, Jesus SN -pg 509
Castro, Jesus -pg 238
Castro, Joaquin C -pg 540
Castro, Joaquin LG -pg 518
Castro, Joaquin O -pg 149
Castro, Joaquin R -pg 132
Castro, Joaquina L -pg 67
Castro, Joaquina R -pg 149
Castro, Joaquina R -pg 156
Castro, Joaquina R -pg 284
Castro, Joaquina SN -pg 509
Castro, Jose A -pg 67
Castro, Jose B -pg 147
Castro, Jose B -pg 152
Castro, Jose B -pg 169
Castro, Jose C -pg 30
Castro, Jose C -pg 148
Castro, Jose C -pg 216
Castro, Jose C -pg 222
Castro, Jose C -pg 453
Castro, Jose C -pg 540
Castro, Jose C -pg 542
Castro, Jose D -pg 518
Castro, Jose G -pg 320
Castro, Jose G -pg 497
Castro, Jose I -pg 253
Castro, Jose L -pg 67
Castro, Jose L -pg 540
Castro, Jose LG -pg 518
Castro, Jose M -pg 63
Castro, Jose M -pg 115
Castro, Jose P -pg 279
Castro, Jose P -pg 540
Castro, Jose R -pg 132
Castro, Jose R -pg 284

Castro, Jose R -pg 296
Castro, Jose S -pg 220
Castro, Jose S -pg 279
Castro, Jose T -pg 361
Castro, Josefa B -pg 181
Castro, Josefa B -pg 217
Castro, Josefa G -pg 497
Castro, Josefa L -pg 67
Castro, Josefa S -pg 19
Castro, Josefa S -pg 63
Castro, Josefa S -pg 262
Castro, Josefa T -pg 274
Castro, Josefina R -pg 284
Castro, Juan B -pg 181
Castro, Juan C -pg 30
Castro, Juan C -pg 148
Castro, Juan C -pg 156
Castro, Juan C -pg 361
Castro, Juan I -pg 132
Castro, Juan LG -pg 518
Castro, Juan M -pg 115
Castro, Juan R -pg 88
Castro, Juan R -pg 149
Castro, Juan S -pg 19
Castro, Juan S -pg 379
Castro, Juan W -pg 247
Castro, Juan -pg 238
Castro, Juana L -pg 291
Castro, Juana R -pg 538
Castro, Juliana L -pg 506
Castro, Librada M pg 115
Castro, Librada P -pg 540
Castro, Lucas R -pg 132
Castro, Lucia C -pg 214
Castro, Lucia -pg 247
Castro, Luis P -pg 168
Castro, Luis R -pg 156
Castro, Luisa L -pg 291
Castro, Manuel C -pg 259
Castro, Manuel R -pg 149
Castro, Manuela C -pg 397
Castro, Manuela C -pg 453
Castro, Marcas A -pg 63
Castro, Margarita LG -pg 518
Castro, Margarita P -pg 242
Castro, Margarita R -pg 133
Castro, Maria B -pg 147
Castro, Maria B -pg 169
Castro, Maria B -pg 181
Castro, Maria C -pg 29
Castro, Maria C -pg 149
Castro, Maria C -pg 214

Castro, Maria C -pg 222
Castro, Maria F -pg 22
Castro, Maria F -pg 131
Castro, Maria L -pg 506
Castro, Maria LG -pg 35
Castro, Maria M -pg 66
Castro, Maria M -pg 248
Castro, Maria O -pg 115
Castro, Maria P -pg 242
Castro, Maria P -pg 242
Castro, Maria P -pg 540
Castro, Maria P -pg 540
Castro, Maria R -pg 133
Castro, Maria R -pg 149
Castro, Maria S -pg 19
Castro, Maria SN -pg 65
Castro, Maria SN -pg 509
Castro, Maria T -pg 274
Castro, Maria T -pg 361
Castro, Mariano C -pg 29
Castro, Mariano C -pg 152
Castro, Marta S -pg 409
Castro, Mercedes L -pg 291
Castro, Miguel C -pg 148
Castro, Miguel S -pg 66
Castro, Natividad LG -pg 320
Castro, Natividad M -pg 514
Castro, Nicolas M -pg 286
Castro, Nicolasa C -pg 259
Castro, Nicolasa M -pg 247
Castro, Nieves R -pg 149
Castro, Oliva LG -pg 321
Castro, Pedro C -pg 259
Castro, Pedro D -pg 509
Castro, Pilar S -pg 30
Castro, Rafael LG -pg 320
Castro, Ramon C -pg 29
Castro, Ramon D -pg 497
Castro, Ramon S -pg 19
Castro, Ramon S -pg 65
Castro, Regina B -pg 223
Castro, Regina M -pg 247
Castro, Ricardo LG -pg 320
Castro, Rita B -pg 152
Castro, Rita C -pg 259
Castro, Rita C -pg 540
Castro, Rita M -pg 66
Castro, Rita T -pg 238
Castro, Rosa B -pg 223
Castro, Rosa LG -pg 35
Castro, Rosa S -pg 63
Castro, Rosa S -pg 279

Castro, Rosario -pg 247
Castro, Rufina SN -pg 509
Castro, Santiago C -pg 115
Castro, Santiago L -pg 291
Castro, Santiago M -pg 248
Castro, Santiago O -pg 149
Castro, Sebastian B -pg 181
Castro, Soledad F -pg 131
Castro, Susana O -pg 150
Castro, Teresa C -pg 259
Castro, Tomas LG -pg 150
Castro, Trinidad B -pg 223
Castro, Trinidad C -pg 30
Castro, Trudes M -pg 68
Castro, Vicenta S -pg 19
Castro, Vicenta S -pg 286
Castro, Vicente C -pg 30
Castro, Vicente C -pg 223
Castro, Vicente C -pg 542
Castro, Vicente I -pg 131
Castro, Vicente L -pg 506
Castro, Vicente M -pg 68
Castro, Vicente P -pg 142
Castro, Vicente P -pg 242
Castro, Vicente P -pg 540
Castro, Vicente R -pg 156
Castro, Vicente T -pg 238
Cepeda, Alfredo M -pg 320
Cepeda, Amanda C -pg 218
Cepeda, Ana B -pg 555
Cepeda, Ana C -pg 26
Cepeda, Ana C -pg 276
Cepeda, Ana C -pg 510
Cepeda, Ana F -pg 276
Cepeda, Ana LG -pg 248
Cepeda, Ana M -pg 249
Cepeda, Ana Q -pg 256
Cepeda, Ana -pg 219
Cepeda, Andrea Q -pg 18
Cepeda, Antonia C -pg 510
Cepeda, Antonia C -pg 510
Cepeda, Antonia M -pg 94
Cepeda, Antonio M -pg 94
Cepeda, Antonio Q -pg 256
Cepeda, Concepcion A -pg 539
Cepeda, Concepcion M -pg 94
Cepeda, Concepcion M -pg 549
Cepeda, Dolores B -pg 555
Cepeda, Dolores C -pg 276
Cepeda, Dolores T -pg 525
Cepeda, Fraim T -pg 525
Cepeda, Francisca Q -pg 256

Cepeda, Francisco F -pg 276
Cepeda, Francisco S -pg 376
Cepeda, Francisco -pg 219
Cepeda, Ignacia M -pg 244
Cepeda, Ignacio C -pg 218
Cepeda, Jesus C -pg 219
Cepeda, Jesus M -pg 320
Cepeda, Jesus Q -pg 256
Cepeda, Jesus R -pg 555
Cepeda, Jesus S -pg 253
Cepeda, Joaquin C -pg 77
Cepeda, Joaquin C -pg 253
Cepeda, Joaquin C -pg 525
Cepeda, Joaquin Q -pg 256
Cepeda, Joaquina B -pg 81
Cepeda, Joaquina M -pg 320
Cepeda, Jose B -pg 555
Cepeda, Jose C -pg 218
Cepeda, Jose C -pg 253
Cepeda, Jose C -pg 555
Cepeda, Jose M -pg 320
Cepeda, Jose Q -pg 256
Cepeda, Jose S -pg 218
Cepeda, Jose S -pg 376
Cepeda, Jose T -pg 182
Cepeda, Jose -pg 219
Cepeda, Josefa B -pg 555
Cepeda, Juan C -pg 219
Cepeda, Juan C -pg 253
Cepeda, Juan C -pg 320
Cepeda, Juan C -pg 555
Cepeda, Juan M -pg 319
Cepeda, Juan Q -pg 256
Cepeda, Juan S -pg 75
Cepeda, Juan S -pg 376
Cepeda, Juan -pg 256
Cepeda, Leon M -pg 94
Cepeda, Lourdes C -pg 253
Cepeda, Manuel B -pg 555
Cepeda, Manuel -pg 376
Cepeda, Margarita S -pg 376
Cepeda, Maria C -pg 218
Cepeda, Maria C -pg 219
Cepeda, Maria C -pg 320
Cepeda, Maria C -pg 510
Cepeda, Maria LG -pg 248
Cepeda, Maria M -pg 319
Cepeda, Maria R -pg 555
Cepeda, Natividad M -pg 94
Cepeda, Nicolasa M -pg 219
Cepeda, Nicolasa Q -pg 256
Cepeda, Nicolasa -pg 219

Cepeda, Pancrasio M -pg 94
Cepeda, Paz R -pg 555
Cepeda, Pedro C -pg 320
Cepeda, Pedro F -pg 276
Cepeda, Pedro L -pg 319
Cepeda, Pedro M -pg 320
Cepeda, Rita C -pg 26
Cepeda, Rita Q -pg 256
Cepeda, Rita S -pg 376
Cepeda, Rosa B -pg 555
Cepeda, Rosa C -pg 510
Cepeda, Rosa Q -pg 256
Cepeda, Rosa T -pg 525
Cepeda, Rose Concepcion 0 -pg 84
Cepeda, Teresa L -pg 344
Cepeda, Tomas -pg 268
Cepeda, Trinidad C -pg 218
Cepeda, Trinidad Q -pg 256
Cepeda, Vicenta C -pg 253
Cepeda, Vicente A -pg 320
Cepeda, Vicente A -pg 539
Cepeda, Vicente C -pg 510
Cepeda, Vicente F -pg 94
Cepeda, Vicente M -pg 94
Cepeda, Vicente R -pg 555
Cepeda, Vicente S -pg 81
Certeza, Grabiel A -pg 374
Certeza, Maria Q -pg 374
Chaco, Ana C -pg 437
Chaco, Ana R -pg 438
Chaco, Antonio C -pg 437
Chaco, Antonio Q -pg 438
Chaco, Antonio R -pg 435
Chaco, Carmen R -pg 435
Chaco, Consolacion R -pg 435
Chaco, Felipe Q -pg 435
Chaco, Francisco C -pg 437
Chaco, Francisco R -pg 438
Chaco, Ignacio L -pg 455
Chaco, Jesus C -pg 437
Chaco, Jesus R -pg 438
Chaco, Joaquin R -pg 438
Chaco, Joaquina R -pg 435
Chaco, Jose Q -pg 435
Chaco, Jose R -pg 438
Chaco, Juan C -pg 437
Chaco, Juan R -pg 438
Chaco, Magdalena L -pg 455
Chaco, Manuel Q -pg 437
Chaco, Margarita L -pg 455
Chaco, Maria L -pg 455
Chaco, Maria R -pg 438

Chaco, Mariano Q -pg 455
Chaco, Milagro R -pg 438
Chaco, Nieves C -pg 437
Chaco, Regina R -pg 438
Chaco, Soledad R -pg 438
Chaco, Tomas R -pg 435
Chaco, Trinidad Q -pg 435
Chaco, Vicente R -pg 438
Chafauros, Juan S -pg 446
Chagulaf, Geronimo T -pg 477
Chagulaf, Magdalena T -pg 477
Chamora, Doroteo C -pg 330
Chamora, Juana C -pg 330
Chamora, Rosita C -pg 330
Chamora, Ursula C -pg 330
Champaco, Ana C -pg 481
Champaco, Ana E -pg 484
Champaco, Ana M -pg 478
Champaco, Ascemcion M -pg 478
Champaco, Dolores E -pg 484
Champaco, Felicita E -pg 484
Champaco, Joaquina E -pg 484
Champaco, Jose E -pg 484
Champaco, Jose M -pg 478
Champaco, Juan C -pg 477
Champaco, Juan E -pg 484
Champaco, Manuela E -pg 484
Champaco, Maria M -pg 478
Champaco, Mariano M -pg 478
Champaco, Pedro C -pg 478
Champaco, Rosalia E -pg 484
Champaco, Vicente M -pg 478
Charfauros, Ana B -pg 429
Charfauros, Ana L -pg 496
Charfauros, Ana T -pg 413
Charfauros, Andres C -pg 59
Charfauros, Andres C -pg 444
Charfauros, Aniceto B -pg 441
Charfauros, Antonia B -pg 429
Charfauros, Antonio B -pg 431
Charfauros, Augustin C -pg 443
Charfauros, Barbara L -pg 479
Charfauros, Bardovina D -pg 300
Charfauros, Calota G -pg 461
Charfauros, Carmela B -pg 456
Charfauros, Carmen A -pg 449
Charfauros, Carmen B -pg 429
Charfauros, Carmen C -pg 480
Charfauros, Consolacion B -pg 441
Charfauros, Consolacion C -pg 444
Charfauros, Dolores C -pg 444
Charfauros, Dolores L -pg 454

Charfauros, Elena L -pg 496
Charfauros, Encarnation Q -pg 445
Charfauros, Faustino C -pg 453
Charfauros, Felix C -pg 429
Charfauros, Felix L -pg 451
Charfauros, Francisca B -pg 429
Charfauros, Francisco A -pg 441
Charfauros, Francisco Cruz -pg 431
Charfauros, Francisco N -pg 429
Charfauros, Francisco SN -pg 448
Charfauros, Ignacia N -pg 429
Charfauros, Ignacio C -pg 444
Charfauros, Ignacio N -pg 429
Charfauros, Jesus A -pg 449
Charfauros, Jesus B -pg 429
Charfauros, Jesus G -pg 461
Charfauros, Joaquin C -pg 65
Charfauros, Joaquin L -pg 451
Charfauros, Joaquin N -pg 429
Charfauros, Joaquin -pg 413
Charfauros, Joaquina L -pg 479
Charfauros, Jose B -pg 431
Charfauros, Jose C -pg 456
Charfauros, Jose F -pg 411
Charfauros, Jose G -pg 461
Charfauros, Jose L -pg 451
Charfauros, Jose L -pg 455
Charfauros, Jose M -pg 458
Charfauros, Jose N -pg 429
Charfauros, Jose S -pg 443
Charfauros, Juan A -pg 449
Charfauros, Juan B -pg 411
Charfauros, Juan C -pg 444
Charfauros, Juan C -pg 458
Charfauros, Juan L -pg 445
Charfauros, Juan L -pg 451
Charfauros, Juan SN -pg 448
Charfauros, Juan T -pg 461
Charfauros, Juana SN -pg 448
Charfauros, Luis A -pg 444
Charfauros, Manuel S -pg 443
Charfauros, Manuel T -pg 479
Charfauros, Maria B -pg 429
Charfauros, Maria B -pg 456
Charfauros, Maria G -pg 300
Charfauros, Maria G -pg 461
Charfauros, Maria L -pg 454
Charfauros, Maria L -pg 496
Charfauros, Maria SN -pg 448
Charfauros, Maria SN -pg 448
Charfauros, Maria T -pg 413
Charfauros, Mariano A -pg 448

Charfauros, Mariano T -pg 429
Charfauros, Pedro C -pg 431
Charfauros, Pedro L -pg 451
Charfauros, Ramona L -pg 455
Charfauros, Rejina L -pg 455
Charfauros, Rita T -pg 441
Charfauros, Rosa B -pg 212
Charfauros, Rosa B -pg 431
Charfauros, Rosa C -pg 444
Charfauros, Rosa L -pg 451
Charfauros, Rosa T -pg 441
Charfauros, Teordora F -pg 411
Charfauros, Tomas B -pg 431
Charfauros, Tomas C -pg 431
Charfauros, Venancio B -pg 429
Charfauros, Vicente A -pg 451
Charfauros, Victoria M -pg 458
Chargiliya, Rita B -pg 549
Chargiliya, Rosa B -pg 549
Chargualaf, Agustin M -pg 264
Chargualaf, Agustin T -pg 533
Chargualaf, Ana A -pg 533
Chargualaf, Ana C -pg 372
Chargualaf, Ana R -pg 232
Chargualaf, Ana T -pg 360
Chargualaf, Angelina -pg 404
Chargualaf, Antonia C -pg 264
Chargualaf, Antonia M -pg 524
Chargualaf, Antonio F -pg 513
Chargualaf, Antonio S -pg 361
Chargualaf, Antonio T -pg 355
Chargualaf, Carmela S -pg 361
Chargualaf, Carmen M -pg 505
Chargualaf, Cecilio T -pg 504
Chargualaf, Consolacion C -pg 372
Chargualaf, Consolacion T -pg 531
Chargualaf, Cornelia T -pg 513
Chargualaf, Cristina T -pg 516
Chargualaf, Damiana M -pg 527
Chargualaf, Dolores M -pg 524
Chargualaf, Dolores M -pg 527
Chargualaf, Dolores S -pg 361
Chargualaf, Dolores SN -pg 20
Chargualaf, Dolores T -pg 355
Chargualaf, Dometila M -pg 527
Chargualaf, Elias C -pg 220
Chargualaf, Encarnacion T -pg 355
Chargualaf, Engracia SN -pg 202
Chargualaf, Enrique C -pg 372
Chargualaf, Esperanza C -pg 372
Chargualaf, Estefania SN -pg 515
Chargualaf, Eugenio Q -pg 360

Chargualaf, Eugenio R -pg 220
Chargualaf, Felix -pg 230
Chargualaf, Filiomena -pg 372
Chargualaf, Francisco M -pg 525
Chargualaf, Francisco Q -pg 361
Chargualaf, Francisco R -pg 220
Chargualaf, Froilan M -pg 505
Chargualaf, Getrudes R -pg 297
Chargualaf, Ignacia L -pg 230
Chargualaf, Ignacio C -pg 445
Chargualaf, Ignacio M -pg 227
Chargualaf, Isabel D -pg 531
Chargualaf, Jesus M -pg 520
Chargualaf, Joaquin SN -pg 515
Chargualaf, Joaquina A -pg 533
Chargualaf, Joaquina S -pg 361
Chargualaf, Jose A -pg 533
Chargualaf, Jose C -pg 202
Chargualaf, Jose M -pg 506
Chargualaf, Jose N -pg 506
Chargualaf, Jose R -pg 227
Chargualaf, Jose R -pg 298
Chargualaf, Jose S -pg 361
Chargualaf, Jose SN -pg 515
Chargualaf, Jose T -pg 527
Chargualaf, Jose T -pg 531
Chargualaf, Josefa M -pg 512
Chargualaf, Josefa S -pg 130
Chargualaf, Josefina C -pg 505
Chargualaf, Juan C -pg 372
Chargualaf, Juan N -pg 506
Chargualaf, Juan R -pg 232
Chargualaf, Juan R -pg 232
Chargualaf, Julia C -pg 220
Chargualaf, Justo C -pg 264
Chargualaf, Justo Q -pg 355
Chargualaf, Justo T -pg 529
Chargualaf, Lino M -pg 525
Chargualaf, Lucas M -pg 505
Chargualaf, Lucia M -pg 524
Chargualaf, Manuel SN -pg 20
Chargualaf, Margarita SN -pg 515
Chargualaf, Maria C -pg 220
Chargualaf, Maria C -pg 264
Chargualaf, Maria L -pg 230
Chargualaf, Maria M -pg 512
Chargualaf, Maria M -pg 527
Chargualaf, Maria R -pg 227
Chargualaf, Maria S -pg 361
Chargualaf, Maria T -pg 355
Chargualaf, Nicolas Q -pg 361
Chargualaf, Pedro SN -pg 515

INDEX
1920 Population Census of Guam: Transcribed

Chargualaf, Preciosa S -pg 361
Chargualaf, Ramon M -pg 512
Chargualaf, Ramon M -pg 515
Chargualaf, Rita C -pg 264
Chargualaf, Rita T -pg 531
Chargualaf, Rosa C -pg 220
Chargualaf, Rosa SN -pg 20
Chargualaf, Rosario L -pg 230
Chargualaf, Sebastian S -pg 531
Chargualaf, Vicente C -pg 264
Chargualaf, Vicente C -pg 505
Chargualaf, Vicente R -pg 298
Chargualaf, Vicente SN -pg 515
Charguane, Francisco T -pg 427
Charguane, Guadalupe T -pg 427
Charguane, Justo T -pg 427
Charguane, Trinidad T -pg 427
Chargulaf, Ana B -pg 461
Chargulaf, Ana T -pg 483
Chargulaf, Angelina T -pg 497
Chargulaf, Antonia U -pg 484
Chargulaf, Antonio T -pg 497
Chargulaf, Balentina B -pg 485
Chargulaf, Barbara N -pg 491
Chargulaf, Carmen B -pg 485
Chargulaf, Carmen T -pg 497
Chargulaf, Cricencio M -pg 483
Chargulaf, Dimas B -pg 485
Chargulaf, Dimas T -pg 497
Chargulaf, Fidel N -pg 491
Chargulaf, Grelerma B -pg 485
Chargulaf, Ignacio T -pg 497
Chargulaf, Jacobo B -pg 490
Chargulaf, Jose T -pg 497
Chargulaf, Juan B -pg 475
Chargulaf, Juliana T -pg 497
Chargulaf, Manuela A -pg 475
Chargulaf, Mariano B -pg 476
Chargulaf, Mariano T -pg 497
Chargulaf, Natividad C -pg 476
Chargulaf, Nicolas T -pg 483
Chargulaf, Remedio C -pg 476
Chargulaf, Rosalia T -pg 483
Chargulaf, Ynigo C -pg 476
Charsagua, Concepcion S -pg 225
Charsagua, Magdalena S -pg 225
Charsagua, Maria S -pg 225
Charsagua, Ramona A -pg 60
Cheguina, Antonia S -pg 467
Cheguina, Calalena S -pg 467
Cheguina, Emiliana S -pg 467
Cheguina, Jose S -pg 467

Cheguina, Maxima S -pg 467
Cheguina, Polocarpio T -pg 467
Chigina, Vicente T -pg 462
Chiguina, Antonia M -pg 531
Chiguina, Antonio M -pg 106
Chiguina, Candelaria M -pg 105
Chiguina, Carmen T -pg 83
Chiguina, Enrique M -pg 105
Chiguina, Ingracia C -pg 397
Chiguina, Jesus D -pg 531
Chiguina, Jesus M -pg 106
Chiguina, Joaquina N -pg 181
Chiguina, Jose T -pg 83
Chiguina, Juan M -pg 531
Chiguina, Juan T -pg 83
Chiguina, Magdalena C -pg 524
Chiguina, Manuela T -pg 83
Chiguina, Marcela M -pg 105
Chiguina, Marcelo C -pg 83
Chiguina, Maria M -pg 90
Chiguina, Maria N -pg 517
Chiguina, Maria T -pg 83
Chiguina, Monica C -pg 524
Chiguina, Soledad M -pg 531
Chiguina, Vicente C -pg 105
Chin, Aleandro C -pg 418
Chin, Delfina C -pg 418
Chin, Engracia C -pg 418
Chin, Gregorio C -pg 418
Chin, Juan Q -pg 418
Chin, Regina C -pg 418
Chin, Regino C -pg 418
Chin, Rosalia C -pg 418
Chupaco, Alfonso O -pg 174
Chupaco, Luisa A -pg 174
Cleofas, Ana C -pg 197
Cleofas, Felecita C -pg 197
Cleofas, Joaquin C -pg 197
Cleofas, Maria C -pg 197
Cleofas, Sixto C -pg 197
Combado, Concepcion SN -pg 502
Combado, Guadalupe SN -pg 502
Combado, Juan SN -pg 502
Combado, Juan P -pg 502
Combado, Maria SN -pg 502
Combado, Remedios SN -pg 502
Concepcion, Albert -pg 424
Concepcion, Ana C -pg 208
Concepcion, Ana C -pg 258
Concepcion, Ana C -pg 394
Concepcion, Ana L -pg 411
Concepcion, Ana Q -pg 377

Concepcion, Ana SN -pg 331
Concepcion, Antonia C -pg 266
Concepcion, Antonia M -pg 229
Concepcion, Antonio T -pg 390
Concepcion, Antonio T -pg 399
Concepcion, Asuncion C -pg 208
Concepcion, Balbino T -pg 399
Concepcion, Beatris C -pg 391
Concepcion, Candelaria C -pg 208
Concepcion, Caridad C -pg 391
Concepcion, Catalina P -pg 341
Concepcion, Clara -pg 419
Concepcion, Concepcion M -pg 216
Concepcion, Cristina C -pg 391
Concepcion, Delfina D -pg 422
Concepcion, Dolores A -pg 203
Concepcion, Dolores B -pg 198
Concepcion, Dolores C -pg 209
Concepcion, Dolores C -pg 419
Concepcion, Dolores C -pg 508
Concepcion, Dolores M -pg 284
Concepcion, Dominga A -pg 203
Concepcion, Eduviges D -pg 422
Concepcion, Elizabeth D -pg 422
Concepcion, Engracia C -pg 391
Concepcion, Enrique P -pg 341
Concepcion, Enrique S -pg 341
Concepcion, Enrique T -pg 399
Concepcion, Enriqueta C -pg 552
Concepcion, Estefania SN -pg 331
Concepcion, Felecidad C -pg 208
Concepcion, Felisidad P -pg 341
Concepcion, Felix C -pg 266
Concepcion, Francisco A -pg 198
Concepcion, Francisco C -pg 552
Concepcion, Ignacia O -pg 116
Concepcion, Ignacio C -pg 552
Concepcion, Inocencio P -pg 341
Concepcion, Jesus C -pg 391
Concepcion, Jesus C -pg 394
Concepcion, Jesus G -pg 203
Concepcion, Jesus Q -pg 377
Concepcion, Joaquin A -pg 331
Concepcion, Joaquin C -pg 258
Concepcion, Joaquin P -pg 377
Concepcion, Jose B -pg 411
Concepcion, Jose C -pg 331
Concepcion, Jose C -pg 383
Concepcion, Jose C jr -pg 391
Concepcion, Jose E -pg 229
Concepcion, Jose M -pg 229
Concepcion, Jose M -pg 508

Concepcion, Jose Q -pg 377
Concepcion, Jose T -pg 399
Concepcion, Jose -pg 391
Concepcion, Josefa D -pg 399
Concepcion, Juan A -pg 331
Concepcion, Juan C -pg 258
Concepcion, Juan C -pg 258
Concepcion, Juan C -pg 390
Concepcion, Juan C -pg 411
Concepcion, Juan S -pg 399
Concepcion, Juan T -pg 399
Concepcion, Juan -pg 198
Concepcion, Juan -pg 202
Concepcion, Juana P -pg 341
Concepcion, Magdalena C -pg 258
Concepcion, Manuel C -pg 391
Concepcion, Manuel C -pg 394
Concepcion, Manuela R -pg 216
Concepcion, Maria C -pg 131
Concepcion, Maria C -pg 258
Concepcion, Maria C -pg 391
Concepcion, Maria M -pg 229
Concepcion, Maria Q -pg 377
Concepcion, Maria SN -pg 331
Concepcion, Maria T -pg 424
Concepcion, Prudencio D -pg 422
Concepcion, Ramon G -pg 266
Concepcion, Rosa G -pg 266
Concepcion, Rosa M -pg 383
Concepcion, Rosa T -pg 391
Concepcion, Rosalia T -pg 399
Concepcion, Rosario C -pg 258
Concepcion, Saturnina T -pg 390
Concepcion, Soledad T -pg 399
Concepcion, Susana A -pg 203
Concepcion, Teodoro L -pg 422
Concepcion, Teresa A -pg 331
Concepcion, Tomasa -pg 405
Concepcion, Vicenta C -pg 419
Concepcion, Vicente P -pg 377
Conception, Carmen C -pg 485
Conception, Jose R -pg 485
Contrares, Miguel -pg 277
Corella, Aniceto P -pg 246
Crisostomo, Ana A -pg 110
Crisostomo, Ana C -pg 180
Crisostomo, Ana G -pg 69
Crisostomo, Ana LG -pg 521
Crisostomo, Ana P -pg 342
Crisostomo, Ana SN -pg 100
Crisostomo, Ana T -pg 339
Crisostomo, Angel M -pg 511

Crisostomo, Angel P -pg 338
Crisostomo, Antonia M -pg 511
Crisostomo, Antonio D -pg 137
Crisostomo, Antonio P -pg 338
Crisostomo, Antonio P -pg 342
Crisostomo, Basilio -pg 334
Crisostomo, Caila C -pg 180
Crisostomo, Catalina A -pg 110
Crisostomo, Concepcion C -pg 305
Crisostomo, Concepcion M -pg 418
Crisostomo, Concepcion M -pg 419
Crisostomo, Concepcion T -pg 339
Crisostomo, Concepcion T -pg 340
Crisostomo, Delfina SN -pg 100
Crisostomo, Dolores A -pg 110
Crisostomo, Dolores C -pg 192
Crisostomo, Dolores C -pg 339
Crisostomo, Dolores P -pg 342
Crisostomo, Elena M -pg 511
Crisostomo, Faustino C -pg 342
Crisostomo, Felicita P -pg 342
Crisostomo, Felisitas C -pg 180
Crisostomo, Felix C -pg 100
Crisostomo, Francisco C -pg 305
Crisostomo, Francisco M -pg 418
Crisostomo, Francisco P -pg 342
Crisostomo, Francisco V -pg 334
Crisostomo, Hinaro M -pg 418
Crisostomo, Ignacia M -pg 418
Crisostomo, Ignacio S -pg 95
Crisostomo, Jesus A -pg 110
Crisostomo, Jesus C -pg 342
Crisostomo, Jesus D -pg 137
Crisostomo, Jesus M -pg 511
Crisostomo, Jesus P -pg 342
Crisostomo, Joaquin A -pg 110
Crisostomo, Joaquin M -pg 110
Crisostomo, Joaquin M -pg 511
Crisostomo, Joaquin M -pg 521
Crisostomo, Joaquin T -pg 339
Crisostomo, Jose A -pg 211
Crisostomo, Jose C -pg 511
Crisostomo, Jose D -pg 137
Crisostomo, Jose LG -pg 522
Crisostomo, Jose M -pg 511
Crisostomo, Jose P -pg 342
Crisostomo, Jose T -pg 339
Crisostomo, Josefa A -pg 211
Crisostomo, Josefa D -pg 137
Crisostomo, Josefa P -pg 342
Crisostomo, Josefina V -pg 334
Crisostomo, Juan B -pg 179

Crisostomo, Juan P -pg 305
Crisostomo, Juan P -pg 338
Crisostomo, Juan T -pg 339
Crisostomo, Juan T -pg 361
Crisostomo, Juana S -pg 95
Crisostomo, Juana S -pg 95
Crisostomo, Lorenzo B -pg 341
Crisostomo, Lourdes S -pg 95
Crisostomo, Lucia G -pg 69
Crisostomo, Manuel M -pg 511
Crisostomo, Marcelo C -pg 342
Crisostomo, Margarita M -pg 419
Crisostomo, Maria 0 -pg 180
Crisostomo, Maria A -pg 211
Crisostomo, Maria C -pg 179
Crisostomo, Maria C -pg 179
Crisostomo, Maria LG -pg 521
Crisostomo, Maria M -pg 418
Crisostomo, Maria M -pg 511
Crisostomo, Maria M -pg 513
Crisostomo, Maria P -pg 342
Crisostomo, Maria P -pg 342
Crisostomo, Mariano B -pg 95
Crisostomo, Mariano C -pg 342
Crisostomo, Miguel C -pg 305
Crisostomo, Paula C -pg 341
Crisostomo, Pedro C -pg 180
Crisostomo, Pedro C -pg 211
Crisostomo, Pedro C -pg 351
Crisostomo, Pedro LG -pg 521
Crisostomo, Pedro M -pg 511
Crisostomo, Pedro -pg 192
Crisostomo, Purification V -pg 334
Crisostomo, Ramon J -pg 418
Crisostomo, Ramon M -pg 511
Crisostomo, Remedios C -pg 342
Crisostomo, Rita V -pg 334
Crisostomo, Rosa C -pg 342
Crisostomo, Rosa M -pg 511
Crisostomo, Rosario M -pg 511
Crisostomo, Soledad M -pg 418
Crisostomo, Soledad V -pg 334
Crisostomo, Teodoro SN -pg 100
Crisostomo, Tomas D -pg 137
Crisostomo, Vicenta C -pg 180
Crisostomo, Vicenta P -pg 338
Crisostomo, Vicente C -pg 180
Crisostomo, Vicente C -pg 338
Crisostomo, Vicente LG -pg 522
Crisostomo, Vicente P -pg 342
Crisostomo, Vicente C -pg 511
Cristobal, Adriano M -pg 251

Cristobal, Canali -pg 500
Cristobal, Carmen U -pg 251
Cristobal, Fe G -pg 251
Cristobal, Jorge E -pg 251
Crusar, Antonia 0 -pg 163
Cruz, Adela C -pg 264
Cruz, Adela LG -pg 85
Cruz, Agosto P -pg 247
Cruz, Agustin R -pg 333
Cruz, Agustin S -pg 96
Cruz, Agustina C -pg 393
Cruz, Albert F -pg 523
Cruz, Amparo LG -pg 236
Cruz, Ana 0 -pg 152
Cruz, Ana A -pg 130
Cruz, Ana A -pg 175
Cruz, Ana A -pg 295
Cruz, Ana A -pg 382
Cruz, Ana A -pg 411
Cruz, Ana A -pg 413
Cruz, Ana A -pg 454
Cruz, Ana B -pg 127
Cruz, Ana B -pg 223
Cruz, Ana B -pg 414
Cruz, Ana B -pg 445
Cruz, Ana B -pg 549
Cruz, Ana C -pg 197
Cruz, Ana C -pg 229
Cruz, Ana C -pg 272
Cruz, Ana C -pg 319
Cruz, Ana C -pg 331
Cruz, Ana C -pg 375
Cruz, Ana C -pg 414
Cruz, Ana C -pg 415
Cruz, Ana G -pg 17
Cruz, Ana G -pg 99
Cruz, Ana G -pg 124
Cruz, Ana G -pg 481
Cruz, Ana L -pg 130
Cruz, Ana LG -pg 281
Cruz, Ana LG -pg 307
Cruz, Ana M -pg 212
Cruz, Ana M -pg 494
Cruz, Ana P -pg 333
Cruz, Ana Q -pg 341
Cruz, Ana R -pg 39
Cruz, Ana R -pg 53
Cruz, Ana S -pg 71
Cruz, Ana S -pg 223
Cruz, Ana S -pg 226
Cruz, Ana S -pg 381
Cruz, Ana S -pg 456

Cruz, Ana T -pg 19
Cruz, Ana T -pg 269
Cruz, Ana T -pg 307
Cruz, Ana T -pg 551
Cruz, Ana -pg 273
Cruz, Anacleto M -pg 175
Cruz, Andrea G -pg 124
Cruz, Andrea M -pg 255
Cruz, Andres LG -pg 203
Cruz, Antonia B -pg 82
Cruz, Antonia B -pg 223
Cruz, Antonia C -pg 375
Cruz, Antonia L -pg 130
Cruz, Antonia LG -pg 85
Cruz, Antonia LG -pg 307
Cruz, Antonia M -pg 196
Cruz, Antonia P -pg 247
Cruz, Antonia S -pg 206
Cruz, Antonia W -pg 178
Cruz, Antonio B -pg 127
Cruz, Antonio B -pg 415
Cruz, Antonio C -pg 205
Cruz, Antonio C -pg 241
Cruz, Antonio C -pg 264
Cruz, Antonio C -pg 349
Cruz, Antonio C -pg 475
Cruz, Antonio D -pg 440
Cruz, Antonio G -pg 124
Cruz, Antonio G -pg 127
Cruz, Antonio I -pg 210
Cruz, Antonio L -pg 480
Cruz, Antonio LG -pg 236
Cruz, Antonio LG -pg 250
Cruz, Antonio LG -pg 483
Cruz, Antonio M -pg 175
Cruz, Antonio M -pg 386
Cruz, Antonio P -pg 263
Cruz, Antonio Q -pg 99
Cruz, Antonio R -pg 210
Cruz, Antonio S -pg 175
Cruz, Antonio S -pg 370
Cruz, Antonio S -pg 381
Cruz, Antonio -pg 246
Cruz, Antonio -pg 302
Cruz, Antonio -pg 319
Cruz, Antonio -pg 387
Cruz, Ascencion C -pg 304
Cruz, Ascencion T -pg 269
Cruz, Ascencion T -pg 328
Cruz, Asencion C -pg 217
Cruz, Asencion P -pg 247
Cruz, Asencion R -pg 244

Cruz, Asuncion Ana 0 -pg 80
Cruz, Atanasio T -pg 19
Cruz, Balbina C -pg 389
Cruz, Baltasara M -pg 543
Cruz, Beatrice T -pg 269
Cruz, Beatris C -pg 382
Cruz, Benita C -pg 425
Cruz, Bruno F -pg 189
Cruz, Candaleria A -pg 295
Cruz, Candaleria T -pg 269
Cruz, Candalerio M -pg 244
Cruz, Caridad B -pg 414
Cruz, Caridad S -pg 296
Cruz, Caridad S -pg 381
Cruz, Carla P -pg 134
Cruz, Carlos J -pg 168
Cruz, Carmen A -pg 241
Cruz, Carmen A -pg 302
Cruz, Carmen A -pg 413
Cruz, Carmen B -pg 315
Cruz, Carmen C -pg 262
Cruz, Carmen C -pg 312
Cruz, Carmen C -pg 349
Cruz, Carmen C -pg 375
Cruz, Carmen C -pg 397
Cruz, Carmen C -pg 443
Cruz, Carmen N -pg 208
Cruz, Carmen P -pg 509
Cruz, Carmen SN -pg 452
Cruz, Carmen SN -pg 452
Cruz, Catalina T -pg 559
Cruz, Cerafina P -pg 247
Cruz, Clarita J -pg 202
Cruz, Concepcion A -pg 207
Cruz, Concepcion B -pg 318
Cruz, Concepcion C -pg 116
Cruz, Concepcion C -pg 229
Cruz, Concepcion C -pg 387
Cruz, Concepcion F -pg 39
Cruz, Concepcion L -pg 45
Cruz, Concepcion P -pg 120
Cruz, Concepcion R -pg 551
Cruz, Concepcion T -pg 307
Cruz, Consolacion B -pg 224
Cruz, Consolacion J -pg 358
Cruz, Consolacion L -pg 333
Cruz, Consolacion LG -pg 307
Cruz, Consolacion M -pg 402
Cruz, Consolacion -pg 393
Cruz, Cristina T -pg 356
Cruz, Cristobal L -pg 480
Cruz, Cristobal F P -pg 317

Cruz, Demetrio G -pg 17
Cruz, Derfina S -pg 456
Cruz, Dolores A -pg 382
Cruz, Dolores A -pg 411
Cruz, Dolores B -pg 223
Cruz, Dolores B -pg 315
Cruz, Dolores B -pg 453
Cruz, Dolores C -pg 116
Cruz, Dolores C -pg 176
Cruz, Dolores C -pg 209
Cruz, Dolores C -pg 272
Cruz, Dolores C -pg 311
Cruz, Dolores C -pg 425
Cruz, Dolores C -pg 475
Cruz, Dolores C -pg 480
Cruz, Dolores E -pg 86
Cruz, Dolores G -pg 461
Cruz, Dolores L -pg 333
Cruz, Dolores L -pg 480
Cruz, Dolores LG -pg 308
Cruz, Dolores M -pg 249
Cruz, Dolores M -pg 476
Cruz, Dolores O -pg 196
Cruz, Dolores O -pg 450
Cruz, Dolores P -pg 224
Cruz, Dolores P -pg 262
Cruz, Dolores P -pg 333
Cruz, Dolores R -pg 280
Cruz, Dolores W -pg 178
Cruz, Dometila F -pg 550
Cruz, Domingo A -pg 208
Cruz, Domingo J -pg 74
Cruz, Domingo S -pg 175
Cruz, Edward T -pg 530
Cruz, Elena G -pg 140
Cruz, Elena H -pg 130
Cruz, Eliza G -pg 17
Cruz, Encarnasion -pg 313
Cruz, Encarnation G -pg 483
Cruz, Engracia C -pg 176
Cruz, Engracia C -pg 425
Cruz, Engracia G -pg 17
Cruz, Engracia M -pg 543
Cruz, Engracia T -pg 354
Cruz, Engracio L -pg 480
Cruz, Enrique A -pg 80
Cruz, Enrique A -pg 454
Cruz, Enrique C -pg 196
Cruz, Enrique C -pg 349
Cruz, Enrique LG -pg 307
Cruz, Enrique M -pg 249
Cruz, Enrique -pg 389

Cruz, Estella R -pg 244
Cruz, Eugenio F -pg 283
Cruz, Eugenio V -pg 271
Cruz, Faustino LG -pg 272
Cruz, Fecundo C -pg 381
Cruz, Felecita S -pg 96
Cruz, Feliciana B -pg 127
Cruz, Feliciano D -pg 133
Cruz, Felicidad B -pg 445
Cruz, Felipe A -pg 85
Cruz, Felipe LG -pg 307
Cruz, Felisita O -pg 134
Cruz, Felix C -pg 112
Cruz, Felix C -pg 349
Cruz, Felix R -pg 280
Cruz, Felix S -pg 226
Cruz, Felix S -pg 512
Cruz, Felix -pg 217
Cruz, Felix -pg 304
Cruz, Felix -pg 509
Cruz, Feliza P -pg 140
Cruz, Fermina C -pg 126
Cruz, Filomena C -pg 376
Cruz, Filomena G -pg 121
Cruz, Flora C -pg 387
Cruz, Florentina C -pg 474
Cruz, Francisca B -pg 82
Cruz, Francisca B -pg 445
Cruz, Francisca C -pg 112
Cruz, Francisca E -pg 489
Cruz, Francisca M -pg 121
Cruz, Francisca P -pg 317
Cruz, Francisco A -pg 130
Cruz, Francisco A -pg 383
Cruz, Francisco B -pg 319
Cruz, Francisco C -pg 17
Cruz, Francisco C -pg 127
Cruz, Francisco C -pg 176
Cruz, Francisco C -pg 229
Cruz, Francisco C -pg 480
Cruz, Francisco C -pg 552
Cruz, Francisco D -pg 530
Cruz, Francisco J -pg 173
Cruz, Francisco LG -pg 191
Cruz, Francisco LG -pg 250
Cruz, Francisco M -pg 247
Cruz, Francisco P -pg 225
Cruz, Francisco P -pg 263
Cruz, Francisco P -pg 509
Cruz, Francisco Q -pg 454
Cruz, Francisco R -pg 332
Cruz, Francisco S -pg 86

Cruz, Francisco S -pg 381
Cruz, Francisco T -pg 307
Cruz, Francisco T -pg 452
Cruz, Froilan D -pg 402
Cruz, Genera Q -pg 454
Cruz, George M -pg 543
Cruz, Gertrudes C -pg 119
Cruz, Gertrudes P -pg 119
Cruz, Gertrudes T -pg 19
Cruz, Grabiel S -pg 379
Cruz, Graviel Q -pg 454
Cruz, Gregorio A -pg 383
Cruz, Gregorio B -pg 203
Cruz, Gregorio Q -pg 344
Cruz, Gregorio S -pg 407
Cruz, Guadalupe C -pg 415
Cruz, Guadalupe M -pg 412
Cruz, Guadalupe S -pg 407
Cruz, Herminihildo G -pg 295
Cruz, Ignacia C -pg 443
Cruz, Ignacia D -pg 412
Cruz, Ignacia H -pg 131
Cruz, Ignacia L -pg 199
Cruz, Ignacio A -pg 411
Cruz, Ignacio A -pg 413
Cruz, Ignacio B -pg 413
Cruz, Ignacio G -pg 124
Cruz, Ignacio M -pg 186
Cruz, Ignacio M -pg 283
Cruz, Ignacio M -pg 333
Cruz, Ignacio M -pg 338
Cruz, Ignacio M -pg 340
Cruz, Ignacio M -pg 411
Cruz, Ignacio P -pg 480
Cruz, Ignacio T -pg 19
Cruz, Ignacio T -pg 58
Cruz, Ignacio T -pg 201
Cruz, Ines C -pg 375
Cruz, Ingracia C -pg 443
Cruz, Iolala P -pg 319
Cruz, Isabel B -pg 550
Cruz, Isabel C -pg 229
Cruz, Isabel G -pg 17
Cruz, Isabel G -pg 486
Cruz, Isabel LG -pg 85
Cruz, Isabel S -pg 296
Cruz, Isabel SN -pg 215
Cruz, Isabel T -pg 559
Cruz, Jesus O -pg 126
Cruz, Jesus O -pg 175
Cruz, Jesus B -pg 549
Cruz, Jesus C -pg 19

Cruz, Jesus C -pg 226

Cruz, Jesus C -pg 229

Cruz, Jesus C -pg 349

Cruz, Jesus C -pg 414

Cruz, Jesus C -pg 416

Cruz, Jesus C -pg 474

Cruz, Jesus C -pg 475

Cruz, Jesus C -pg 480

Cruz, Jesus D -pg 523

Cruz, Jesus E -pg 86

Cruz, Jesus F -pg 80

Cruz, Jesus G -pg 17

Cruz, Jesus G -pg 291

Cruz, Jesus G -pg 481

Cruz, Jesus G -pg 486

Cruz, Jesus I -pg 255

Cruz, Jesus LG -pg 236

Cruz, Jesus LG -pg 281

Cruz, Jesus M -pg 186

Cruz, Jesus M -pg 212

Cruz, Jesus O -pg 450

Cruz, Jesus P -pg 262

Cruz, Jesus Q -pg 416

Cruz, Jesus R -pg 71

Cruz, Jesus S -pg 487

Cruz, Jesus T -pg 19

Cruz, Jesus T -pg 559

Cruz, Jesus V -pg 271

Cruz, Joaquin A -pg 86

Cruz, Joaquin A -pg 383

Cruz, Joaquin B -pg 407

Cruz, Joaquin C -pg 17

Cruz, Joaquin C -pg 264

Cruz, Joaquin C -pg 358

Cruz, Joaquin C -pg 382

Cruz, Joaquin C -pg 398

Cruz, Joaquin C -pg 551

Cruz, Joaquin D -pg 200

Cruz, Joaquin G -pg 291

Cruz, Joaquin G -pg 483

Cruz, Joaquin LG -pg 281

Cruz, Joaquin M -pg 206

Cruz, Joaquin M -pg 412

Cruz, Joaquin M -pg 494

Cruz, Joaquin P -pg 361

Cruz, Joaquin R -pg 559

Cruz, Joaquin S -pg 95

Cruz, Joaquin S -pg 206

Cruz, Joaquin S -pg 293

Cruz, Joaquin S -pg 356

Cruz, Joaquin T -pg 361

Cruz, Joaquina B -pg 329

Cruz, Joaquina C -pg 112

Cruz, Joaquina C -pg 209

Cruz, Joaquina S -pg 153

Cruz, Jose 0 -pg 27

Cruz, Jose 0 -pg 106

Cruz, Jose 0 -pg 106

Cruz, Jose 0 -pg 180

Cruz, Jose A -pg 80

Cruz, Jose A -pg 130

Cruz, Jose A -pg 269

Cruz, Jose A -pg 295

Cruz, Jose A -pg 303

Cruz, Jose A -pg 445

Cruz, Jose A -pg 454

Cruz, Jose B -pg 82

Cruz, Jose B -pg 127

Cruz, Jose B -pg 414

Cruz, Jose C -pg 52

Cruz, Jose C -pg 95

Cruz, Jose C -pg 112

Cruz, Jose C -pg 126

Cruz, Jose C -pg 184

Cruz, Jose C -pg 202

Cruz, Jose C -pg 229

Cruz, Jose C -pg 262

Cruz, Jose C -pg 312

Cruz, Jose C -pg 341

Cruz, Jose C -pg 349

Cruz, Jose C -pg 393

Cruz, Jose C -pg 415

Cruz, Jose C -pg 425

Cruz, Jose C -pg 443

Cruz, Jose C -pg 453

Cruz, Jose C -pg 474

Cruz, Jose C -pg 475

Cruz, Jose C -pg 480

Cruz, Jose D -pg 200

Cruz, Jose D -pg 509

Cruz, Jose F -pg 39

Cruz, Jose F -pg 196

Cruz, Jose F -pg 283

Cruz, Jose G -pg 17

Cruz, Jose G -pg 122

Cruz, Jose G -pg 126

Cruz, Jose G -pg 262

Cruz, Jose G -pg 474

Cruz, Jose G -pg 481

Cruz, Jose I -pg 210

Cruz, Jose L -pg 333

Cruz, Jose L -pg 481

Cruz, Jose LG -pg 85

Cruz, Jose LG -pg 236

Cruz, Jose LG -pg 281

Cruz, Jose LG -pg 307

Cruz, Jose M -pg 121

Cruz, Jose M -pg 212

Cruz, Jose M -pg 249

Cruz, Jose M -pg 250

Cruz, Jose M -pg 312

Cruz, Jose M -pg 332

Cruz, Jose M -pg 356

Cruz, Jose M -pg 412

Cruz, Jose M -pg 494

Cruz, Jose M -pg 543

Cruz, Jose N -pg 208

Cruz, Jose P -pg 139

Cruz, Jose P -pg 207

Cruz, Jose P -pg 249

Cruz, Jose P -pg 262

Cruz, Jose P -pg 317

Cruz, Jose P -pg 317

Cruz, Jose P -pg 333

Cruz, Jose P -pg 351

Cruz, Jose P -pg 474

Cruz, Jose P -pg 486

Cruz, Jose Q -pg 341

Cruz, Jose Q -pg 416

Cruz, Jose Q -pg 437

Cruz, Jose Q -pg 454

Cruz, Jose Q -pg 487

Cruz, Jose S -pg 154

Cruz, Jose S -pg 175

Cruz, Jose S -pg 324

Cruz, Jose S -pg 380

Cruz, Jose S -pg 381

Cruz, Jose S -pg 382

Cruz, Jose SN -pg 279

Cruz, Jose T -pg 555

Cruz, Jose U -pg 406

Cruz, Jose V -pg 271

Cruz, Jose -pg 255

Cruz, Josefa A -pg 126

Cruz, Josefa A -pg 303

Cruz, Josefa B -pg 549

Cruz, Josefa C -pg 389

Cruz, Josefa C -pg 414

Cruz, Josefa G -pg 17

Cruz, Josefa G -pg 486

Cruz, Josefa I -pg 254

Cruz, Josefa J -pg 450

Cruz, Josefa LG -pg 236

Cruz, Josefa LG -pg 281

Cruz, Josefa M -pg 186

Cruz, Josefa M -pg 196

Cruz, Josefa M -pg 494
Cruz, Josefa P -pg 58
Cruz, Josefa P -pg 119
Cruz, Josefa P -pg 279
Cruz, Josefa Q -pg 27
Cruz, Josefa Q -pg 341
Cruz, Josefa S -pg 80
Cruz, Josefa S -pg 153
Cruz, Josefa S -pg 381
Cruz, Josefa U -pg 202
Cruz, Josefa -pg 340
Cruz, Josefina A -pg 411
Cruz, Josefina B -pg 168
Cruz, Josefina C -pg 443
Cruz, Josefina C -pg 475
Cruz, Josefina D -pg 440
Cruz, Josefina S -pg 380
Cruz, Juan 0 -pg 175
Cruz, Juan A -pg 79
Cruz, Juan A -pg 235
Cruz, Juan A -pg 302
Cruz, Juan B -pg 82
Cruz, Juan B -pg 414
Cruz, Juan B -pg 549
Cruz, Juan C -pg 209
Cruz, Juan C -pg 229
Cruz, Juan C -pg 264
Cruz, Juan C -pg 272
Cruz, Juan C -pg 328
Cruz, Juan C -pg 349
Cruz, Juan C -pg 356
Cruz, Juan C -pg 402
Cruz, Juan C -pg 414
Cruz, Juan G -pg 17
Cruz, Juan G -pg 124
Cruz, Juan G -pg 229
Cruz, Juan G -pg 479
Cruz, Juan I -pg 186
Cruz, Juan L -pg 130
Cruz, Juan L -pg 480
Cruz, Juan LG -pg 236
Cruz, Juan LG -pg 250
Cruz, Juan LG -pg 307
Cruz, Juan LG -pg 550
Cruz, Juan M -pg 121
Cruz, Juan M -pg 173
Cruz, Juan M -pg 173
Cruz, Juan M -pg 375
Cruz, Juan M -pg 412
Cruz, Juan M -pg 554
Cruz, Juan N -pg 208
Cruz, Juan O -pg 450

Cruz, Juan P -pg 333
Cruz, Juan P -pg 372
Cruz, Juan P -pg 480
Cruz, Juan P -pg 500
Cruz, Juan Q -pg 416
Cruz, Juan R -pg 244
Cruz, Juan S -pg 39
Cruz, Juan S -pg 175
Cruz, Juan S -pg 206
Cruz, Juan S -pg 324
Cruz, Juan S -pg 381
Cruz, Juan S -pg 456
Cruz, Juan S -pg 487
Cruz, Juan SA -pg 124
Cruz, Juan T -pg 79
Cruz, Juan T -pg 328
Cruz, Juan V -pg 130
Cruz, Juan V -pg 271
Cruz, Juana C -pg 217
Cruz, Juana C -pg 304
Cruz, Juana M -pg 356
Cruz, Juana Q -pg 437
Cruz, Julia A -pg 241
Cruz, Juliana F -pg 523
Cruz, Juliana LG -pg 85
Cruz, Justa S -pg 487
Cruz, Justo C -pg 312
Cruz, Leocadio C -pg 509
Cruz, Loncia T -pg 452
Cruz, Lorenzo B -pg 380
Cruz, Lorenzo G -pg 324
Cruz, Loria B -pg 550
Cruz, Lourdes C -pg 272
Cruz, Lourdes C -pg 389
Cruz, Lucia T -pg 79
Cruz, Luis A -pg 387
Cruz, Luis C -pg 414
Cruz, Luis D -pg 443
Cruz, Luis M -pg 476
Cruz, Luisa B -pg 550
Cruz, Luisa C -pg 241
Cruz, Luisa D -pg 509
Cruz, Luisa T -pg 201
Cruz, Magdalena A -pg 454
Cruz, Magdalena C -pg 229
Cruz, Magdalena C -pg 264
Cruz, Magdalena M -pg 402
Cruz, Magdalena M -pg 402
Cruz, Magdalena M -pg 543
Cruz, Manuel 0 -pg 135
Cruz, Manuel A -pg 212
Cruz, Manuel A -pg 382

Cruz, Manuel B -pg 550
Cruz, Manuel C -pg 176
Cruz, Manuel C -pg 224
Cruz, Manuel C -pg 279
Cruz, Manuel C -pg 454
Cruz, Manuel G -pg 124
Cruz, Manuel I -pg 210
Cruz, Manuel L -pg 480
Cruz, Manuel M -pg 61
Cruz, Manuel M -pg 495
Cruz, Manuel P -pg 176
Cruz, Manuel P -pg 200
Cruz, Manuel S -pg 215
Cruz, Manuel S -pg 296
Cruz, Manuel V -pg 130
Cruz, Manuel -pg 262
Cruz, Manuela C -pg 128
Cruz, Manuela C -pg 375
Cruz, Manuela U -pg 406
Cruz, Marcela A -pg 383
Cruz, Marcela T -pg 344
Cruz, Margarita C -pg 554
Cruz, Margarita G -pg 481
Cruz, Maria A -pg 27
Cruz, Maria A -pg 27
Cruz, Maria A -pg 209
Cruz, Maria A -pg 293
Cruz, Maria A -pg 295
Cruz, Maria A -pg 303
Cruz, Maria A -pg 332
Cruz, Maria A -pg 380
Cruz, Maria A -pg 382
Cruz, Maria A -pg 383
Cruz, Maria A -pg 411
Cruz, Maria A -pg 411
Cruz, Maria A -pg 413
Cruz, Maria B -pg 112
Cruz, Maria B -pg 127
Cruz, Maria B -pg 168
Cruz, Maria B -pg 168
Cruz, Maria B -pg 203
Cruz, Maria B -pg 231
Cruz, Maria B -pg 414
Cruz, Maria B -pg 549
Cruz, Maria C -pg 33
Cruz, Maria C -pg 95
Cruz, Maria C -pg 112
Cruz, Maria C -pg 116
Cruz, Maria C -pg 126
Cruz, Maria C -pg 127
Cruz, Maria C -pg 176
Cruz, Maria C -pg 217

Cruz, Maria C -pg 229

Cruz, Maria C -pg 272

Cruz, Maria C -pg 272

Cruz, Maria C -pg 283

Cruz, Maria C -pg 304

Cruz, Maria C -pg 348

Cruz, Maria C -pg 349

Cruz, Maria C -pg 393

Cruz, Maria C -pg 414

Cruz, Maria C -pg 479

Cruz, Maria C -pg 480

Cruz, Maria C -pg 480

Cruz, Maria C -pg 554

Cruz, Maria D -pg 190

Cruz, Maria D -pg 440

Cruz, Maria D -pg 440

Cruz, Maria D -pg 509

Cruz, Maria G -pg 17

Cruz, Maria G -pg 291

Cruz, Maria G -pg 481

Cruz, Maria G -pg 486

Cruz, Maria G -pg 486

Cruz, Maria H -pg 130

Cruz, Maria H -pg 130

Cruz, Maria I -pg 210

Cruz, Maria J -pg 358

Cruz, Maria J -pg 450

Cruz, Maria L -pg 333

Cruz, Maria LG -pg 236

Cruz, Maria LG -pg 236

Cruz, Maria LG -pg 281

Cruz, Maria M -pg 17

Cruz, Maria M -pg 186

Cruz, Maria M -pg 196

Cruz, Maria M -pg 212

Cruz, Maria M -pg 249

Cruz, Maria M -pg 249

Cruz, Maria M -pg 356

Cruz, Maria M -pg 494

Cruz, Maria M -pg 543

Cruz, Maria O -pg 196

Cruz, Maria O -pg 450

Cruz, Maria P -pg 134

Cruz, Maria P -pg 189

Cruz, Maria P -pg 225

Cruz, Maria P -pg 319

Cruz, Maria P -pg 319

Cruz, Maria Q -pg 159

Cruz, Maria Q -pg 415

Cruz, Maria Q -pg 437

Cruz, Maria R -pg 280

Cruz, Maria R -pg 338

Cruz, Maria R -pg 356

Cruz, Maria S -pg 80

Cruz, Maria S -pg 206

Cruz, Maria S -pg 226

Cruz, Maria S -pg 380

Cruz, Maria S -pg 381

Cruz, Maria S -pg 456

Cruz, Maria T -pg 19

Cruz, Maria T -pg 269

Cruz, Maria T -pg 361

Cruz, Maria T -pg 530

Cruz, Maria T -pg 551

Cruz, Maria T -pg 559

Cruz, Maria V -pg 271

Cruz, Maria V -pg 271

Cruz, Maria Ana O -pg 80

Cruz, Mariano O -pg 135

Cruz, Mariano A -pg 201

Cruz, Mariano C -pg 450

Cruz, Mariano G -pg 379

Cruz, Mariano L -pg 333

Cruz, Mariano LG -pg 236

Cruz, Mariano M -pg 240

Cruz, Mariano M -pg 402

Cruz, Mariano R -pg 80

Cruz, Maricio C -pg 222

Cruz, Martina G -pg 483

Cruz, Matilde S -pg 324

Cruz, Mercedes A -pg 454

Cruz, Miguel J -pg 451

Cruz, Miguel L -pg 333

Cruz, Miguel M -pg 349

Cruz, Miguel P -pg 475

Cruz, Miguel R -pg 332

Cruz, Milagro -pg 227

Cruz, Natividad C -pg 118

Cruz, Natividad S -pg 324

Cruz, Natividad -pg 319

Cruz, Nicolas A -pg 412

Cruz, Nicolas C -pg 412

Cruz, Nicolas G -pg 82

Cruz, Nicolas G -pg 356

Cruz, Nicolas M -pg 356

Cruz, Nicolasa B -pg 168

Cruz, Nicolasa F -pg 338

Cruz, Nicolasa F -pg 340

Cruz, Nicolasa M -pg 280

Cruz, Pablo C -pg 476

Cruz, Paterno M -pg 186

Cruz, Paterno P -pg 120

Cruz, Paula G -pg 162

Cruz, Paulino G -pg 162

Cruz, Paz C -pg 375

Cruz, Pedro B -pg 223

Cruz, Pedro B -pg 316

Cruz, Pedro C -pg 118

Cruz, Pedro C -pg 375

Cruz, Pedro C -pg 450

Cruz, Pedro G -pg 99

Cruz, Pedro G -pg 124

Cruz, Pedro G -pg 130

Cruz, Pedro G -pg 291

Cruz, Pedro G -pg 533

Cruz, Pedro H -pg 131

Cruz, Pedro I -pg 254

Cruz, Pedro J -pg 168

Cruz, Pedro L -pg 480

Cruz, Pedro LG -pg 85

Cruz, Pedro M -pg 96

Cruz, Pedro M -pg 96

Cruz, Pedro O -pg 450

Cruz, Pedro P -pg 225

Cruz, Pedro R -pg 551

Cruz, Pedro S -pg 80

Cruz, Pedro S -pg 296

Cruz, Pedro S -pg 324

Cruz, Pedro -pg 319

Cruz, Pilar B -pg 82

Cruz, Polonia T -pg 384

Cruz, Potenciana S -pg 296

Cruz, Priciosa S -pg 296

Cruz, Ramon C -pg 474

Cruz, Ramon C -pg 475

Cruz, Ramon M -pg 383

Cruz, Ramon P -pg 263

Cruz, Ramon P -pg 487

Cruz, Ramona D -pg 190

Cruz, Raphael O -pg 450

Cruz, Raymundo C -pg 551

Cruz, Raymundo R -pg 279

Cruz, Redosindo A -pg 130

Cruz, Regina A -pg 379

Cruz, Regina F -pg 283

Cruz, Regina S -pg 206

Cruz, Remedio LG -pg 281

Cruz, Rita B -pg 173

Cruz, Rita B -pg 414

Cruz, Rita C -pg 86

Cruz, Rita D -pg 200

Cruz, Rita G -pg 291

Cruz, Rita LG -pg 250

Cruz, Rita N -pg 208

Cruz, Rita P -pg 175

Cruz, Rita S -pg 153

Cruz, Rita T -pg 269
Cruz, Robert F -pg 523
Cruz, Romana S -pg 380
Cruz, Rosa 0 -pg 134
Cruz, Rosa A -pg 295
Cruz, Rosa A -pg 303
Cruz, Rosa B -pg 173
Cruz, Rosa B -pg 549
Cruz, Rosa C -pg 272
Cruz, Rosa C -pg 414
Cruz, Rosa C -pg 474
Cruz, Rosa G -pg 99
Cruz, Rosa G -pg 162
Cruz, Rosa G -pg 486
Cruz, Rosa I -pg 210
Cruz, Rosa J -pg 358
Cruz, Rosa LG -pg 85
Cruz, Rosa M -pg 494
Cruz, Rosa R -pg 332
Cruz, Rosa S -pg 296
Cruz, Rosa S -pg 381
Cruz, Rosa T -pg 386
Cruz, Rosa T -pg 559
Cruz, Rosalia R -pg 551
Cruz, Rosario A -pg 80
Cruz, Rosario B -pg 316
Cruz, Rosario C -pg 387
Cruz, Rosario F -pg 283
Cruz, Rosario H -pg 130
Cruz, Rosario L -pg 45
Cruz, Rosario L -pg 333
Cruz, Rosario LG -pg 191
Cruz, Rosario M -pg 95
Cruz, Rufina C -pg 331
Cruz, Santiago 0 -pg 135
Cruz, Santiago LG -pg 549
Cruz, Saturnina B -pg 223
Cruz, Segundo A -pg 302
Cruz, Serafin P -pg 189
Cruz, Silvestre C -pg 333
Cruz, Simon B -pg 112
Cruz, Simona C -pg 443
Cruz, Soledad A -pg 295
Cruz, Soledad A -pg 383
Cruz, Soledad C -pg 116
Cruz, Soledad C -pg 415
Cruz, Soledad Q -pg 370
Cruz, Soledad R -pg 280
Cruz, Soledad T -pg 307
Cruz, Susana L -pg 45
Cruz, Susana P -pg 58
Cruz, Susana P -pg 236

Cruz, Teodora T -pg 361
Cruz, Teodoro S -pg 487
Cruz, Teordoro B -pg 223
Cruz, Teresa 0 -pg 130
Cruz, Tomas A -pg 281
Cruz, Tomas B -pg 112
Cruz, Tomas C -pg 197
Cruz, Tomas C -pg 202
Cruz, Tomas E -pg 481
Cruz, Tomas G -pg 481
Cruz, Tomas L -pg 287
Cruz, Tomas LG -pg 236
Cruz, Tomas S -pg 407
Cruz, Tomas T -pg 201
Cruz, Tomas T -pg 361
Cruz, Tomas T -pg 559
Cruz, Tomasa C -pg 264
Cruz, Tomasa G -pg 291
Cruz, Tomasa P -pg 333
Cruz, Tomasa Q -pg 416
Cruz, Trinidad A -pg 241
Cruz, Trinidad A -pg 380
Cruz, Trinidad P -pg 263
Cruz, Trudes C -pg 475
Cruz, Venancio T -pg 494
Cruz, Veronica C -pg 389
Cruz, Vicenta C -pg 475
Cruz, Vicenta LG -pg 85
Cruz, Vicenta M -pg 186
Cruz, Vicenta M -pg 379
Cruz, Vicenta R -pg 279
Cruz, Vicenta T -pg 354
Cruz, Vicente A -pg 130
Cruz, Vicente A -pg 295
Cruz, Vicente B -pg 74
Cruz, Vicente B -pg 168
Cruz, Vicente B -pg 203
Cruz, Vicente B -pg 414
Cruz, Vicente B -pg 543
Cruz, Vicente C -pg 241
Cruz, Vicente C -pg 264
Cruz, Vicente C -pg 272
Cruz, Vicente C -pg 283
Cruz, Vicente C -pg 312
Cruz, Vicente C -pg 380
Cruz, Vicente C -pg 415
Cruz, Vicente C -pg 474
Cruz, Vicente F -pg 283
Cruz, Vicente G -pg 452
Cruz, Vicente G -pg 483
Cruz, Vicente L -pg 39
Cruz, Vicente LG -pg 58

Cruz, Vicente LG -pg 236
Cruz, Vicente LG -pg 307
Cruz, Vicente M -pg 121
Cruz, Vicente M -pg 190
Cruz, Vicente M -pg 279
Cruz, Vicente M -pg 311
Cruz, Vicente P -pg 58
Cruz, Vicente P -pg 333
Cruz, Vicente S -pg 153
Cruz, Vicente S -pg 175
Cruz, Vicente S -pg 188
Cruz, Vicente S -pg 202
Cruz, Vicente S -pg 356
Cruz, Vicente S -pg 381
Cruz, Vicente T -pg 456
Cruz, Vicente T -pg 551
Cruz, Vicente U -pg 406
Cruz, Vicente W -pg 178
Cruz, Vidal J -pg 331
Custino, Annie T -pg 234
Custino, Charles T -pg 234
Custino, Edward T -pg 234
Custino, Helen T -pg 234
Custino, Joe K -pg 234
Custino, John E T -pg 234
Custino, Joseph K T -pg 234
Custino, Rosa T -pg 234
Custino, Ruth T -pg 234
Damian, Andres B -pg 336
Damian, Candido B -pg 336
Damian, Damazo B -pg 336
Damian, Egracio B -pg 336
Damian, Florentino B -pg 336
Damian, Greogria B -pg 336
Damian, Jose B -pg 335
Damian, Justo -pg 335
Damian, Petronila B -pg 335
Damian, Priscila B -pg 336
Daprosa, Catalina L -pg 427
Daprosa, Hermogines -pg 426
Day, John E -pg 199
Day, Josefina U -pg 199
Day, Petronila U -pg 199
De Gracia, Antonia A -pg 425
De Gracia, Dolores T -pg 427
De Gracia, Lorenzo A -pg 425
De Gracia, Manuel B -pg 427
De Gracia, Ponciano A -pg 425
De Gracia, Rosa A -pg 425
de la Cruz, Alejandro P -pg 291
de la Cruz, Candaleria P -pg 291
de la Cruz, Carlos P -pg 291

de la Cruz, Encarnacion P -pg 291
de la Cruz, Regina P -pg 291
de la Rosa, Agueda T -pg 334
de la Rosa, Antonia T -pg 334
de la Rosa, Dolores T -pg 334
de la Rosa, Francisco T -pg 334
de la Rosa, Maria T -pg 334
de la Rosa, Mariano R -pg 334
de la Torre, Felisidad U -pg 289
de la Torre, Joaquin B -pg 289
de la Torre, Jose U -pg 289
de la Torre, Vicente U -pg 289
de Leon, Adela P -pg 323
de Leon, Antonia P -pg 323
de Leon, Antonio C -pg 346
de Leon, Antonio P -pg 323
de Leon, Dolores P -pg 323
de Leon, Enrique M -pg 346
de Leon, Francisco P -pg 323
de Leon, Joaquin I -pg 323
de Leon, Joaquin P -pg 323
de Leon, Juan M -pg 346
De Leon, Juana B -pg 60
de Leon, Julia P -pg 323
de Leon, Lourdes M -pg 346
de Leon, Luisa P -pg 323
de Leon, Manuel P -pg 323
de Leon, Maria I -pg 251
de Leon, Maria P -pg 323
de Leon, Raimundo M -pg 346
de Leon Guerrero, Ana P -pg 299
de Leon Guerrero, Dolores P -pg 299
de Leon Guerrero, Francisca P -pg 299
de Leon Guerrero, Getrudes P -pg 299
de Leon Guerrero, Jesus P -pg 299
de Leon Guerrero, Joaquin P -pg 299
de Leon Guerrero, Jose P -pg 299
de Leon Guerrero, Justo S -pg 299
de Leon Guerrero, Maria P -pg 299
de Leon Guerrero, Maria P -pg 299
de los Santos, Ana G -pg 304
de los Santos, Felicita G -pg 304
de los Santos, Felisidad G -pg 304
de los Santos, Felix -pg 304
de los Santos, Joaquin G -pg 304
de los Santos, Jose G -pg 304
de los Santos, Juana G -pg 304
de Torres, Caridad C -pg 310

de Torres, Concepcion C -pg 311
de Torres, Luis C -pg 310
de Torres, Rita C -pg 310
de Torres, Vicente C -pg 310
Dejima, T -pg 302
dela Cruz, Eulogio C -pg 286
dela Cruz, Francisco M -pg 286
dela Cruz, Jose M -pg 286
dela Cruz, Maria U -pg 286
dela Rosa, Manuel M -pg 263
dela Rosa, Rita M -pg 263
Delgado, Alfonso M -pg 66
Delgado, Ana C -pg 64
Delgado, Ana G -pg 482
Delgado, Ana M -pg 81
Delgado, Ana SN -pg 510
Delgado, Ana D SN -pg 510
Delgado, Concepcion G -pg 482
Delgado, Consolacion SN -pg 510
Delgado, Elvina M -pg 81
Delgado, Enrique SN -pg 59
Delgado, Francisco M -pg 129
Delgado, Inacensio M -pg 129
Delgado, Jesus C -pg 64
Delgado, Jesus M -pg 66
Delgado, Jesus M -pg 81
Delgado, Jose C -pg 64
Delgado, Jose M -pg 48
Delgado, Jose M -pg 64
Delgado, Jose M -pg 527
Delgado, Jose M -pg 531
Delgado, Jose SN -pg 510
Delgado, Jose Maria 0 -pg 81
Delgado, Josefa C -pg 527
Delgado, Juan F -pg 81
Delgado, Juan M -pg 482
Delgado, Juan P -pg 383
Delgado, Juana D -pg 322
Delgado, Luis G -pg 482
Delgado, Manuel G -pg 482
Delgado, Maria C -pg 64
Delgado, Maria C -pg 64
Delgado, Maria G -pg 482
Delgado, Maria M -pg 49
Delgado, Maria M -pg 66
Delgado, Maria SN -pg 510
Delgado, Nicolas M -pg 527
Delgado, Nicolasa D -pg 322
Delgado, Pedro M -pg 81
Delgado, Pedro SN -pg 510
Delgado, Rita M -pg 81
Delgado, Rosa M -pg 66

Delgado, Rosa Maria 0 -pg 81
Delgado, Rufina M -pg 66
Delgado, Silvano M -pg 510
Delgado, Tomasa M -pg 531
Delgado, Vicenta M -pg 48
delos Santos, Lucindo C -pg 284
delos Santos, Narcisa M -pg 284
Demapan, Agueda M -pg 200
Demapan, Ana M -pg 200
Demapan, Ignacio M -pg 200
Demapan, Manuel -pg 399
Demapan, Maria M -pg 200
Demapan, Maria -pg 398
Demapan, Mariano A -pg 200
Demapan, Mercedes M -pg 200
Demapan, Pedro -pg 399
Desa, Nieves -pg 191
Deza, Josefa B -pg 31
Deza, Moses B -pg 46
Dias, David -pg 425
Dias, Rita -pg 426
Dias, Walter E -pg 426
Diaz, Amparo G -pg 250
Diaz, Ana C -pg 489
Diaz, Ana F -pg 385
Diaz, Ana G -pg 205
Diaz, Ana P -pg 410
Diaz, Ana P jr -pg 410
Diaz, Antonia F -pg 385
Diaz, Antonia SN -pg 383
Diaz, Antonio SN -pg 205
Diaz, Concepcion G -pg 250
Diaz, Concepcion L -pg 413
Diaz, Consolacion F -pg 385
Diaz, Dolores G -pg 250
Diaz, Dolores P -pg 410
Diaz, Doroteo D -pg 202
Diaz, Emilia F -pg 385
Diaz, Francisca P -pg 31
Diaz, Francisco S -pg 271
Diaz, Francisco S -pg 271
Diaz, Francisco T -pg 250
Diaz, Guadalupe C -pg 399
Diaz, Ignacia F -pg 271
Diaz, Ignacio F -pg 272
Diaz, Jesus F -pg 272
Diaz, Joaquin F -pg 272
Diaz, Joaquin F -pg 385
Diaz, Joaquin M -pg 412
Diaz, Jose C -pg 399
Diaz, Jose D -pg 202
Diaz, Jose D -pg 489

Diaz, Jose F -pg 385
Diaz, Josefa B -pg 309
Diaz, Josefa T -pg 250
Diaz, Josefina G -pg 250
Diaz, Juan M -pg 410
Diaz, Juan S -pg 271
Diaz, Juana P -pg 410
Diaz, Julia G -pg 205
Diaz, Lourdes C -pg 399
Diaz, Magdalena M -pg 410
Diaz, Maria F -pg 385
Diaz, Maria G -pg 205
Diaz, Maria S -pg 271
Diaz, Maria T -pg 199
Diaz, Pedro C -pg 399
Diaz, Rita G -pg 250
Diaz, Rosa C -pg 399
Diaz, Rosa G -pg 250
Diaz, Vicente F -pg 249
Diaz, Vicente P -pg 410
Diego, Ana SN -pg 514
Diego, Catalina LG -pg 519
Diego, Dolores SN -pg 513
Diego, Enemesio SN -pg 513
Diego, Florentina D -pg 513
Diego, Ignacia LG -pg 519
Diego, Jesus SN -pg 514
Diego, Joaquin C -pg 513
Diego, Joaquina SN -pg 514
Diego, Jose SN -pg 534
Diego, Juan SN -pg 514
Diego, Regina D -pg 513
Diego, Romualdo C -pg 513
Diego, Rosa SN -pg 514
Diego, Vicente C -pg 514
Diego, Vicente SN -pg 514
Diego, Victorina M -pg 513
Dimapan, Antonia A -pg 550
Dimapan, Carmen C -pg 251
Dimapan, Francisco C -pg 251
Dimapan, Jesus C -pg 251
Dimapan, Jose A -pg 338
Dimapan, Jose C -pg 251
Dimapan, Rosa C -pg 251
Dimapan, Vicente A -pg 250
Dimapan, Vicente I -pg 550
Divera, Antonia A -pg 178
Divera, Carmen B -pg 169
Divera, Jacoba B -pg 169
Divera, Juan B -pg 169
Divera, Lutilde G -pg 101
Divera, Marcus A -pg 178

Divera, Mercedes G -pg 101
Divera, Nicolas A -pg 169
Divera, Pablo B -pg 169
Divera, Ramon G -pg 101
Divera, Rogelio B -pg 178
Divera, Vicenta G -pg 101
Duenas, Agueda S -pg 412
Duenas, Agustin SN -pg 313
Duenas, Alfredo C -pg 45
Duenas, Amalia C -pg 135
Duenas, Ana B -pg 25
Duenas, Ana B -pg 77
Duenas, Ana C -pg 158
Duenas, Ana M -pg 33
Duenas, Ana M -pg 503
Duenas, Ana Q -pg 128
Duenas, Ana S -pg 172
Duenas, Antonia C -pg 158
Duenas, Antonia L -pg 286
Duenas, Antonia T -pg 165
Duenas, Antonia T -pg 190
Duenas, Antonia T -pg 537
Duenas, Antonio B -pg 284
Duenas, Antonio C -pg 135
Duenas, Antonio F -pg 25
Duenas, Antonio S -pg 422
Duenas, Antonio SN -pg 313
Duenas, Antonio T -pg 190
Duenas, Anunsacion T -pg 541
Duenas, Augustia T -pg 165
Duenas, Benita T -pg 537
Duenas, Bernadino F -pg 165
Duenas, Carmen A -pg 412
Duenas, Carmen C -pg 46
Duenas, Carmen C -pg 422
Duenas, Catalina B -pg 25
Duenas, Catalina D -pg 525
Duenas, Catalina LG -pg 187
Duenas, Catalina Q -pg 398
Duenas, Clemente C -pg 158
Duenas, Concepcion B -pg 282
Duenas, Concepcion C -pg 45
Duenas, Concepcion E -pg 76
Duenas, Dolores C -pg 135
Duenas, Dolores LG -pg 187
Duenas, Dolores S -pg 172
Duenas, Dolores S -pg 550
Duenas, Dometila A -pg 25
Duenas, Eduardo C -pg 45
Duenas, Enrique F -pg 25
Duenas, Eugenia SN -pg 313
Duenas, Felisa Q -pg 398

Duenas, Felix D -pg 537
Duenas, Fernando T -pg 541
Duenas, Florencio Q -pg 128
Duenas, Francisca D -pg 504
Duenas, Francisco A -pg 317
Duenas, Francisco B -pg 284
Duenas, Francisco C -pg 135
Duenas, Francisco C -pg 158
Duenas, Francisco M -pg 504
Duenas, Francisco Q -pg 128
Duenas, Fredecinda M -pg 503
Duenas, Gonzalo D -pg 526
Duenas, Gracie A -pg 317
Duenas, Guadalupe LG -pg 187
Duenas, Ignacia LG -pg 186
Duenas, Ignacio B -pg 284
Duenas, Ignacio C -pg 135
Duenas, Ignacio T -pg 190
Duenas, Ignacio T -pg 541
Duenas, Irene M -pg 230
Duenas, Isabel B -pg 77
Duenas, Isabel LG -pg 187
Duenas, Isabel M -pg 537
Duenas, Jesus B -pg 77
Duenas, Jesus B -pg 152
Duenas, Jesus B -pg 162
Duenas, Jesus C -pg 45
Duenas, Jesus D -pg 412
Duenas, Jesus E -pg 76
Duenas, Jesus Q -pg 128
Duenas, Jesus T -pg 526
Duenas, Joaquin A -pg 317
Duenas, Joaquin B -pg 25
Duenas, Joaquin B -pg 162
Duenas, Joaquin D -pg 543
Duenas, Joaquin F -pg 25
Duenas, Joaquin Q -pg 128
Duenas, Joaquin T -pg 165
Duenas, Joaquina T -pg 526
Duenas, Jose A -pg 313
Duenas, Jose B -pg 77
Duenas, Jose B -pg 162
Duenas, Jose C -pg 45
Duenas, Jose C -pg 45
Duenas, Jose C -pg 158
Duenas, Jose C -pg 417
Duenas, Jose C -pg 422
Duenas, Jose F -pg 158
Duenas, Jose LG -pg 186
Duenas, Jose M -pg 76
Duenas, Jose M -pg 526

Duenas, Jose M -pg 536
Duenas, Jose Q -pg 128
Duenas, Jose S -pg 172
Duenas, Jose S -pg 172
Duenas, Jose SN -pg 313
Duenas, Jose T -pg 165
Duenas, Jose T -pg 230
Duenas, Josefa B -pg 77
Duenas, Josefa B -pg 152
Duenas, Josefa D -pg 504
Duenas, Josefa L -pg 409
Duenas, Juan B -pg 25
Duenas, Juan B -pg 77
Duenas, Juan B -pg 162
Duenas, Juan D -pg 504
Duenas, Juan L -pg 286
Duenas, Juan M -pg 284
Duenas, Juan M -pg 504
Duenas, Juan Q -pg 128
Duenas, Juan S -pg 412
Duenas, Juan T -pg 165
Duenas, Juan T -pg 186
Duenas, Juan T -pg 503
Duenas, Juan T -pg 536
Duenas, Juana E -pg 76
Duenas, Juana T -pg 190
Duenas, Julia -pg 230
Duenas, Julian M -pg 128
Duenas, Luis P -pg 152
Duenas, Luisa B -pg 163
Duenas, Luisa M -pg 230
Duenas, Magdalena Q -pg 128
Duenas, Magdalena S -pg 536
Duenas, Manuel B -pg 77
Duenas, Manuel D -pg 536
Duenas, Manuel L -pg 128
Duenas, Manuel M -pg 230
Duenas, Manuel M -pg 504
Duenas, Manuel Q -pg 128
Duenas, Manuela C -pg 158
Duenas, Manuela F -pg 25
Duenas, Maria A -pg 25
Duenas, Maria A -pg 25
Duenas, Maria B -pg 77
Duenas, Maria B -pg 77
Duenas, Maria C -pg 135
Duenas, Maria D -pg 424
Duenas, Maria D -pg 504
Duenas, Maria D -pg 526
Duenas, Maria F -pg 317
Duenas, Maria L -pg 286
Duenas, Maria LG -pg 186

Duenas, Maria M -pg 504
Duenas, Maria Q -pg 128
Duenas, Maria Q -pg 398
Duenas, Maria S -pg 76
Duenas, Maria S -pg 550
Duenas, Maria SN -pg 313
Duenas, Maria SN -pg 379
Duenas, Mariano -pg 379
Duenas, Paz D -pg 412
Duenas, Pedro B -pg 152
Duenas, Pedro B -pg 284
Duenas, Pedro LG -pg 186
Duenas, Pedro M -pg 537
Duenas, Pedro Q -pg 398
Duenas, Pedro S -pg 398
Duenas, Pedro T -pg 541
Duenas, Ramon C -pg 76
Duenas, Ramon C -pg 158
Duenas, Ramon D -pg 526
Duenas, Ramon Q -pg 128
Duenas, Ramon S -pg 172
Duenas, Ramon T -pg 525
Duenas, Remedios B -pg 77
Duenas, Remedios D -pg 504
Duenas, Rita B -pg 77
Duenas, Rita T -pg 165
Duenas, Rita T -pg 537
Duenas, Rosa B -pg 77
Duenas, Rosa B -pg 162
Duenas, Rosa C -pg 225
Duenas, Rosa F -pg 190
Duenas, Rosa LG -pg 186
Duenas, Rosa M -pg 230
Duenas, Rosalia C -pg 135
Duenas, Rosalina M -pg 503
Duenas, Rufina L -pg 286
Duenas, Santiago S -pg 398
Duenas, Segundo A -pg 412
Duenas, Silvestre D -pg 526
Duenas, Soledad C -pg 422
Duenas, Supriana -pg 305
Duenas, Teresa LG -pg 186
Duenas, Teresa T -pg 526
Duenas, Tomasa T -pg 537
Duenas, Vicente A -pg 25
Duenas, Vicente C -pg 162
Duenas, Vicente D -pg 504
Duenas, Vicente D -pg 526
Duenas, Vicente M -pg 225
Duenas, Vicente M -pg 550
Duenas, Vicente SN -pg 313
Duenas, Vicente T -pg 165

Duenas, Vicente T -pg 537
Duenas, Vicente T -pg 541
Dumanal, Candelaria G -pg 406
Dumanal, Jose G -pg 406
Dumanal, Margarita G -pg 406
Dumanal, Maria G -pg 406
Dumanal, Martin L -pg 406
Dumanal, Rosalia G -pg 406
Dumanal, Vicenta G -pg 406
Dungca, Adela T -pg 302
Dungca, Concepcion -pg 226
Dungca, Constancia -pg 226
Dungca, Dolores -pg 226
Dungca, Emelia Q -pg 246
Dungca, Esparanca T -pg 302
Dungca, Felicita C -pg 246
Dungca, Felicita T -pg 302
Dungca, Felix G -pg 302
Dungca, Felix T -pg 302
Dungca, Francisco C -pg 246
Dungca, Jose S -pg 226
Dungca, Jose -pg 246
Dungca, Josefina T -pg 302
Dungca, Juana -pg 226
Dungca, Justo B -pg 246
Dungca, Justo T -pg 302
Dungca, Marcela G -pg 246
Dungca, Maria T -pg 302
Dungca, Soledad G -pg 246
Dungca, Teodoro G -pg 246
Dwyer, Harold -pg 426
Dydasco, Joaquin A -pg 169
Dydasco, Vicenta 0 -pg 130
Dydasco, Vicente A -pg 169
Dy-dasco, Ana F -pg 13
Dy-dasco, Concepcion F -pg 13
Dy-dasco, Felix F -pg 13
Dy-dasco, Gregorio F -pg 13
Dy-dasco, Jesus F -pg 13
Dy-dasco, Joaquin F -pg 13
Dy-dasco, Jose F -pg 13
Dy-dasco, Juan F -pg 13
Dy-dasco, Rosa F -pg 13
Eclavea, Antonio R -pg 42
Eclavea, Enrique R -pg 42
Eclavea, Gonzalo R -pg 42
Eclavea, Jose R -pg 42
Eclavea, Lucio Q -pg 42
Eclavea, Tomasa R -pg 42
Eclavea, Virginia R -pg 42
Edwards, Charles W -pg 376
Edwards, Edwin E -pg 376

Edwards, Frances D -pg 376

Edwards, Richard H -pg 377

Englacias, Luis C -pg 62

Englacias, Manuel C -pg 62

Englacias, Maria C -pg 62

Englacias, Maria C -pg 62

English, Carlos A -pg 459

English, Conception A -pg 459

English, Juana A -pg 459

English, Maria A -pg 459

English, Maria A -pg 459

Equiguan, Fidel E -pg 494

Equiguan, Ignacio B -pg 494

Equiguan, Maria B -pg 494

Espinosa, Ana C -pg 495

Espinosa, Ana F -pg 66

Espinosa, Ana N -pg 494

Espinosa, Carmen B -pg 494

Espinosa, Carmen C -pg 491

Espinosa, Carmen E -pg 65

Espinosa, Consuelo F -pg 66

Espinosa, Dolores B -pg 265

Espinosa, Dolores B -pg 494

Espinosa, Dolores F -pg 66

Espinosa, Enomisa N -pg 494

Espinosa, Estefania C -pg 495

Espinosa, Felemona SN -pg 439

Espinosa, Francisco B -pg 266

Espinosa, Francisco C -pg 66

Espinosa, Francisco F -pg 494

Espinosa, Ignacia C pg 491

Espinosa, Ignacia F -pg 494

Espinosa, Ignacio B -pg 494

Espinosa, Ignacio N -pg 495

Espinosa, Jacoba B -pg 494

Espinosa, Jesus B -pg 494

Espinosa, Jesus C -pg 495

Espinosa, Jesusa C -pg 495

Espinosa, Joaquina B -pg 498

Espinosa, Joaquina C -pg 495

Espinosa, Joaquina F -pg 494

Espinosa, Jose C -pg 67

Espinosa, Jose C -pg 495

Espinosa, Maria B -pg 266

Espinosa, Maria C -pg 67

Espinosa, Pedro C -pg 491

Espinosa, Serafin N -pg 494

Espinosa, Tomasa C -pg 495

Espinosa, Vicenta E -pg 453

Espinosa, Vicente b -pg 494

Espinosa, Vicente C -pg 495

Espinosa, Vicente N -pg 494

Espinosa, Ysidro F -pg 494

Esteban, Carmen E -pg 42

Esteban, Felipe E -pg 42

Esteban, Jesus E -pg 42

Esteban, Lagrimas E -pg 42

Esteban, Maria E -pg 42

Esteban, Maria E -pg 42

Esteban, Natividad E -pg 43

Esteban, Pedro P -pg 42

Estebes, Maria C -pg 268

Estrellas, Maria P -pg 339

Eustaquio, Ana C -pg 324

Eustaquio, Angel B -pg 324

Eustaquio, Antonio B -pg 324

Eustaquio, Cornelio P -pg 30

Eustaquio, Elena B -pg 324

Eustaquio, Felix B -pg 324

Eustaquio, Florencia B -pg 324

Eustaquio, Gregorio B -pg 324

Eustaquio, Jose B -pg 324

Eustaquio, Jose G -pg 324

Eustaquio, Maria B -pg 324

Eustaquio, Reducinda G -pg 325

Evangelista, Ana M -pg 55

Evangelista, Apolonio E -pg 55

Evangelista, Jesus M -pg 55

Evangelista, Jose M -pg 55

Evangelista, Josefa M -pg 55

Evangelista, Maria M -pg 55

Evangelista, Vicente M -pg 55

Evaristo, Jose E -pg 86

Evaristo, Maria 0 -pg 152

Evaristo, Maria L -pg 86

Evaristo, Pedro L -pg 86

Fabian, Braulio -pg 248

Fabian, Felisa G -pg 248

Fabian, Jesus G -pg 248

Fantas, Antonina A -pg 18

Fantas, Antonio A -pg 19

Fantas, Isabel A -pg 19

Farfan, Francisca C -pg 31

Farfan, Jesus C -pg 30

Farfan, Joaquina C -pg 30

Farfan, Jose C -pg 30

Farfan, Rosa C -pg 31

Farfan, Vicente C -pg 30

Farrol, Filomena A -pg 328

Farrol, Maria A -pg 328

Fausto, Agualia Y -pg 92

Fausto, Antonia M -pg 92

Fausto, Carmen -pg 336

Fausto, Felix -pg 340

Fausto, Francisco SN -pg 92

Fausto, Ignacia -pg 340

Fausto, Jesus -pg 341

Fausto, Joaquina G -pg 336

Fausto, Jose -pg 340

Fausto, Jose -pg 340

Fausto, Juan -pg 340

Fausto, Maria -pg 337

Fausto, Vicenta -pg 340

Fegurgur, Alexandra S -pg 489

Fegurgur, Ana F -pg 207

Fegurgur, Ana S -pg 489

Fegurgur, Ana T -pg 470

Fegurgur, Carmen F -pg 489

Fegurgur, Concepcion SN -pg 52

Fegurgur, Dolores N -pg 475

Fegurgur, Domingo C -pg 421

Fegurgur, Encarnation T -pg 470

Fegurgur, Enrique 0 -pg 117

Fegurgur, Enrique F -pg 105

Fegurgur, Francisco F -pg 207

Fegurgur, Guadalupe C -pg 404

Fegurgur, Isabel F -pg 207

Fegurgur, Jesus S -pg 421

Fegurgur, Jesus S -pg 466

Fegurgur, Joaquin S -pg 421

Fegurgur, Joaquin S -pg 489

Fegurgur, Jose 0 -pg 117

Fegurgur, Jose S -pg 466

Fegurgur, Juan N -pg 489

Fegurgur, Maria 0 -pg 117

Fegurgur, Maria S -pg 466

Fegurgur, Maria SN -pg 105

Fegurgur, Maria T -pg 470

Fegurgur, Rosa A -pg 471

Fegurgur, Rosauro C -pg 466

Fegurgur, Teresa 0 -pg 117

Fegurgur, Victoriana F -pg 207

Feja, Candelaria S -pg 411

Fejarang, Ana C -pg 225

Fejarang, Antonia A -pg 512

Fejarang, Antonia LG -pg 511

Fejarang, Antonia LG -pg 511

Fejarang, Catalina G -pg 27

Fejarang, Dolores A -pg 512

Fejarang, Enrique -pg 305

Fejarang, Fedela M -pg 39

Fejarang, Francisca C -pg 257

Fejarang, Francisco C -pg 258

Fejarang, Gregorio C -pg 225

Fejarang, Jesus C -pg 257

Fejarang, Joaquin C -pg 257

Fejarang, Joaquin C -pg 258
Fejarang, Joaquin P -pg 258
Fejarang, Joaquin -pg 225
Fejarang, Jose C -pg 225
Fejarang, Jose C -pg 257
Fejarang, Jose C -pg 257
Fejarang, Jose C -pg 305
Fejarang, Jose LG -pg 512
Fejarang, Jose P -pg 347
Fejarang, Jose R -pg 265
Fejarang, Jose S -pg 258
Fejarang, Josefa C -pg 257
Fejarang, Josefa G -pg 27
Fejarang, Juan LG -pg 511
Fejarang, Juan P -pg 257
Fejarang, Juana C -pg 220
Fejarang, Luis C -pg 257
Fejarang, Magdalena C -pg 257
Fejarang, Manuel C -pg 257
Fejarang, Manuel -pg 332
Fejarang, Maria C -pg 258
Fejarang, Maria G -pg 27
Fejarang, Maria M -pg 39
Fejarang, Maria S -pg 347
Fejarang, Mercedes C -pg 225
Fejarang, Pedro G -pg 27
Fejarang, Ramon C -pg 47
Fejarang, Ramon C -pg 220
Fejarang, Ramon G -pg 511
Fejarang, Rosa C -pg 257
Fejarang, Rosalia C -pg 257
Fejarang, Rufina LG -pg 511
Fejarang, Tomas A -pg 512
Fejarang, Vicenta P -pg 258
Fejarang, Vicente C -pg 257
Fejeran, Amanda P -pg 366
Fejeran, Ana C -pg 381
Fejeran, Antonia C -pg 389
Fejeran, Antonia SN -pg 365
Fejeran, Antonio R -pg 393
Fejeran, Antonio S -pg 390
Fejeran, Caridad R -pg 393
Fejeran, Carmela C -pg 381
Fejeran, Cerilo A -pg 358
Fejeran, Consolacion -pg 365
Fejeran, Dolores S -pg 382
Fejeran, Domingo S -pg 390
Fejeran, Domingo SN -pg 382
Fejeran, Elena C -pg 389
Fejeran, Encarnacion S -pg 390
Fejeran, Enrique P -pg 366
Fejeran, Felix S -pg 390

Fejeran, Florencio P -pg 366
Fejeran, Francisca C -pg 189
Fejeran, Francisca -pg 389
Fejeran, Francisco C -pg 382
Fejeran, Hermenguido J -pg 362
Fejeran, Ignacio A -pg 358
Fejeran, Isidro S -pg 393
Fejeran, Jesus C -pg 381
Fejeran, Jesus S -pg 382
Fejeran, Joaquin C -pg 381
Fejeran, Joaquin P -pg 361
Fejeran, Joaquin R -pg 395
Fejeran, Joaquin S -pg 382
Fejeran, Joaquin T -pg 389
Fejeran, Joaquina R -pg 393
Fejeran, Jose A -pg 358
Fejeran, Jose C -pg 382
Fejeran, Jose C -pg 389
Fejeran, Jose P -pg 367
Fejeran, Jose R -pg 395
Fejeran, Jose S -pg 390
Fejeran, Jose SN -pg 366
Fejeran, Juan C -pg 382
Fejeran, Juan S -pg 357
Fejeran, Juan S -pg 382
Fejeran, Juan -pg 394
Fejeran, Juana S -pg 390
Fejeran, Justo S -pg 381
Fejeran, Lucas S -pg 390
Fejeran, Luis A -pg 358
Fejeran, Magdalena R -pg 395
Fejeran, Manuel S -pg 390
Fejeran, Maria S -pg 382
Fejeran, Maria S -pg 390
Fejeran, Maria S jr -pg 382
Fejeran, Pedro A -pg 358
Fejeran, Pedro R -pg 395
Fejeran, Pilar S -pg 390
Fejeran, Ramona S -pg 390
Fejeran, Regina C -pg 381
Fejeran, Remedios A -pg 358
Fejeran, Remedios S -pg 382
Fejeran, Rosa Q -pg 362
Fejeran, Rosa SN -pg 365
Fejeran, Rosa T -pg 356
Fejeran, Rosario S -pg 390
Fejeran, Sabina C -pg 389
Fejeran, Soledad P -pg 366
Fejeran, Tomas R -pg 393
Fejeran, Vicente C -pg 189
Fejeran, Vicente SN -pg 365
Fergurgur, Remedios Q -pg 88

Fernandez, Ana Q -pg 547
Fernandez, Antonio Q -pg 547
Fernandez, Carmen Q -pg 547
Fernandez, Cristina Q -pg 547
Fernandez, Francisco L -pg 136
Fernandez, Gabriela Q -pg 547
Fernandez, Gonzalo L -pg 76
Fernandez, Jesus L -pg 76
Fernandez, Jesus L jr -pg 76
Fernandez, Jesus Q -pg 547
Fernandez, Joaquin Q -pg 547
Fernandez, Joaquina L -pg 76
Fernandez, Jose L -pg 76
Fernandez, Jose L jr -pg 76
Fernandez, Jose Q -pg 76
Fernandez, Jose Q -pg 547
Fernandez, Juan L -pg 76
Fernandez, Juan L jr -pg 76
Fernandez, Maria L -pg 76
Fernandez, Maria L jr -pg 76
Fernandez, Maria Q -pg 547
Fernandez, Paz L -pg 76
Fernandez, Potenciana Q -pg 547
Fernandez, Roque Q -pg 547
Fernandez, Rosario L -pg 61
Fernandez, Vicente L -pg 76
Finona, Ana F -pg 16
Finona, Antonia R -pg 31
Finona, Antonia T -pg 16
Finona, Antonio C -pg 392
Finona, Eliza T -pg 16
Finona, Estela R -pg 31
Finona, Francisco C -pg 392
Finona, Francisco G -pg 16
Finona, Ignacia T -pg 16
Finona, Jesus G -pg 16
Finona, Joaquin C -pg 392
Finona, Joaquin F -pg 31
Finona, Jose G -pg 16
Finona, Jose Q -pg 16
Finona, Jose SN -pg 392
Finona, Manuel C -pg 392
Finona, Manuel G -pg 16
Finona, Manuela C -pg 392
Finona, Maria G -pg 16
Finona, Maria M -pg 317
Finona, Maria R -pg 31
Finona, Maria SN -pg 391
Finona, Regina C -pg 392
Finona, Rita C -pg 392
Finona, Rita G -pg 16
Finona, Rita SN -pg 391

Finona, Rosalia T -pg 16
Finona, Rosario T -pg 16
Finona, Vicente T -pg 16
Flores, Alejo C -pg 426
Flores, Alfred SN -pg 512
Flores, Alice SN -pg 512
Flores, Ana B -pg 112
Flores, Ana B -pg 140
Flores, Ana C -pg 22
Flores, Ana C -pg 22
Flores, Ana C -pg 46
Flores, Ana C -pg 49
Flores, Ana C -pg 87
Flores, Ana C -pg 185
Flores, Ana G -pg 143
Flores, Ana G -pg 249
Flores, Ana L -pg 205
Flores, Ana P -pg 151
Flores, Ana SN -pg 135
Flores, Ana T -pg 179
Flores, Andrea C -pg 273
Flores, Angel LG -pg 145
Flores, Antonia G -pg 129
Flores, Antonio C -pg 273
Flores, Antonio C -pg 273
Flores, Antonio F -pg 140
Flores, Antonio M -pg 304
Flores, Aurora LG -pg 145
Flores, Benigno LG -pg 118
Flores, Bergnes A -pg 61
Flores, Candelaria S -pg 523
Flores, Carmen C -pg 47
Flores, Carmen S -pg 21
Flores, Catalina D -pg 509
Flores, Concepcion L -pg 205
Flores, Dolores C -pg 150
Flores, Dolores C -pg 273
Flores, Dolores C -pg 340
Flores, Dolores D -pg 509
Flores, Dolores R -pg 15
Flores, Dolores R -pg 60
Flores, Dolores SN -pg 135
Flores, Emelia T -pg 235
Flores, Engracia C -pg 340
Flores, Enrique D -pg 386
Flores, Enrique T -pg 235
Flores, Felisa -pg 261
Flores, Felix C -pg 283
Flores, Filomena LG -pg 118
Flores, Francisca B -pg 112
Flores, Francisca G -pg 22
Flores, Francisca G -pg 129

Flores, Francisco D -pg 386
Flores, Francisco G -pg 145
Flores, Francisco G -pg 249
Flores, Francisco M -pg 23
Flores, Gregorio B -pg 112
Flores, Gregorio T -pg 204
Flores, Guadalupe C -pg 426
Flores, Helen D -pg 386
Flores, Ida SN -pg 512
Flores, Ignacio C -pg 49
Flores, Ignacio G -pg 87
Flores, Ignacio T -pg 118
Flores, Jesus A -pg 509
Flores, Jesus C -pg 22
Flores, Jesus C -pg 151
Flores, Jesus L -pg 205
Flores, Jesus LG -pg 145
Flores, Jesus M -pg 23
Flores, Jesus P -pg 151
Flores, Jesus T -pg 204
Flores, Joaquin 0 -pg 135
Flores, Joaquin B -pg 52
Flores, Joaquin C -pg 340
Flores, Joaquin D -pg 340
Flores, Joaquin D -pg 509
Flores, Joaquin F -pg 140
Flores, Joaquin G -pg 87
Flores, Joaquin G -pg 249
Flores, Joaquin L -pg 60
Flores, Joaquin P -pg 151
Flores, Joaquin T -pg 204
Flores, Joaquin T -pg 234
Flores, Joaquina C -pg 49
Flores, Joaquina G -pg 507
Flores, Joaquina LG -pg 145
Flores, Jose 0 -pg 151
Flores, Jose A -pg 22
Flores, Jose A -pg 523
Flores, Jose B -pg 52
Flores, Jose C -pg 22
Flores, Jose C -pg 46
Flores, Jose C -pg 46
Flores, Jose C -pg 150
Flores, Jose C -pg 273
Flores, Jose D -pg 135
Flores, Jose D -pg 512
Flores, Jose F -pg 140
Flores, Jose G -pg 143
Flores, Jose G -pg 234
Flores, Jose L -pg 205
Flores, Jose LG -pg 118
Flores, Jose M -pg 23

Flores, Jose P -pg 150
Flores, Jose R -pg 15
Flores, Jose S -pg 21
Flores, Jose S -pg 523
Flores, Jose SN -pg 135
Flores, Jose T -pg 204
Flores, Josefa B -pg 140
Flores, Josefa C -pg 46
Flores, Josefa C -pg 49
Flores, Josefa C -pg 49
Flores, Josefa P -pg 151
Flores, Josefina C -pg 150
Flores, Joseph T -pg 235
Flores, Juan A -pg 53
Flores, Juan C -pg 46
Flores, Juan C -pg 49
Flores, Juan C -pg 87
Flores, Juan C -pg 340
Flores, Juan D -pg 509
Flores, Juan G -pg 87
Flores, Juan M -pg 23
Flores, Juan -pg 273
Flores, Juana A -pg 108
Flores, Juana M -pg 304
Flores, Julian L -pg 204
Flores, Kelly LG -pg 143
Flores, Laurete C -pg 309
Flores, Leon D jr -pg 185
Flores, Leon -pg 185
Flores, Lorenzo A -pg 15
Flores, Lorenzo R -pg 15
Flores, Luis A -pg 109
Flores, Magdalena S -pg 186
Flores, Magdalena B C -pg 22
Flores, Manuel A -pg 108
Flores, Manuel B -pg 52
Flores, Manuel D -pg 507
Flores, Manuel F -pg 205
Flores, Manuel G -pg 386
Flores, Manuel M -pg 23
Flores, Manuel P -pg 61
Flores, Manuel T -pg 23
Flores, Manuel T -pg 108
Flores, Maria C -pg 46
Flores, Maria C -pg 150
Flores, Maria C -pg 273
Flores, Maria C -pg 273
Flores, Maria C -pg 273
Flores, Maria C -pg 283
Flores, Maria C -pg 340
Flores, Maria F -pg 140
Flores, Maria G -pg 143

Flores, Maria G -pg 249
Flores, Maria L -pg 205
Flores, Maria LG -pg 304
Flores, Maria M -pg 23
Flores, Maria R -pg 15
Flores, Maria T -pg 204
Flores, Mariano S -pg 21
Flores, Mercedes LG -pg 118
Flores, Mercedez P -pg 151
Flores, Natividad LG -pg 145
Flores, Nicolasa C -pg 49
Flores, Nicolasa C -pg 87
Flores, Nieves M -pg 426
Flores, Oliva C -pg 49
Flores, Pedro C -pg 186
Flores, Pedro G -pg 112
Flores, Pedro LG -pg 146
Flores, Prudencio D -pg 509
Flores, Rafaela SN -pg 512
Flores, Ramon G -pg 249
Flores, Ramona F -pg 384
Flores, Remedios D -pg 386
Flores, Rita A -pg 385
Flores, Rita B -pg 52
Flores, Rita C -pg 49
Flores, Rita C -pg 273
Flores, Rita LG -pg 118
Flores, Rita M -pg 23
Flores, Rita T -pg 204
Flores, Rita T -pg 234
Flores, Rosa A -pg 61
Flores, Rosa C -pg 46
Flores, Rosa C -pg 53
Flores, Rosa G -pg 22
Flores, Rosario C -pg 273
Flores, Rosima S -pg 186
Flores, Rufina C -pg 87
Flores, Sabino C -pg 426
Flores, Sergio D -pg 185
Flores, Susana G -pg 87
Flores, Tomas G -pg 249
Flores, Trinidad A -pg 61
Flores, Vicente A -pg 108
Flores, Vicente A -pg 296
Flores, Vicente C -pg 49
Flores, Vicente C -pg 273
Flores, Vicente C -pg 273
Flores, Vicente D -pg 509
Flores, Vicente F -pg 384
Flores, Vicente G -pg 249
Flores, Vicente LG -pg 118
Flores, Vicente S -pg 283

Flores, Virginia T -pg 235
Francisco, Antonio C -pg 156
Francisco, Antonio C -pg 176
Francisco, Carmen C -pg 156
Francisco, Carmen C -pg 176
Francisco, Consolacion C -pg 166
Francisco, Dolores C -pg 156
Francisco, Domingo P -pg 176
Francisco, Ignacia C -pg 155
Francisco, Ignacia C -pg 176
Francisco, Ignacia S -pg 82
Francisco, Ignacio F -pg 46
Francisco, Jesus C -pg 176
Francisco, Joaquin C -pg 41
Francisco, Joaquin C -pg 156
Francisco, Joaquin C -pg 176
Francisco, Joaquina C -pg 176
Francisco, Jose C -pg 155
Francisco, Jose C -pg 166
Francisco, Jose F -pg 46
Francisco, Jose P -pg 46
Francisco, Jose S -pg 176
Francisco, Josefa S -pg 82
Francisco, Juan C -pg 156
Francisco, Juan C -pg 166
Francisco, Maria C -pg 155
Francisco, Nicolas P -pg 155
Francisco, Pedro C -pg 156
Francisco, Rita F -pg 46
Francisco, Rosa C -pg 176
Francisco, Rosario S -pg 82
Francisco, Saturnina C -pg 176
Francisco, Vicente C -pg 155
Francisco, Vicente S -pg 82
Francisco, Vicente T -pg 82
Franquez, Ana C -pg 24
Franquez, Ana I -pg 25
Franquez, Ana T -pg 19
Franquez, Antonia C -pg 15
Franquez, Emiliana P -pg 15
Franquez, George J -pg 214
Franquez, Isabel C -pg 25
Franquez, Jesus I -pg 25
Franquez, Jesus P -pg 15
Franquez, Jesus T -pg 19
Franquez, Joaquin I -pg 25
Franquez, Jose I -pg 19
Franquez, Jose T -pg 19
Franquez, Josefa L -pg 24
Franquez, Lorenzo C -pg 15
Franquez, Manuel I -pg 214
Franquez, Manuel T -pg 19

Franquez, Maria C -pg 25
Franquez, Maria P -pg 15
Franquez, Maria T -pg 19
Franquez, Maria T -pg 19
Franquez, Pedro C -pg 24
Franquez, Pedro I -pg 24
Franquez, Pedro T -pg 19
Franquez, Remedios C -pg 15
Franquez, Remedios I -pg 25
Franquez, Rita C -pg 24
Franquez, Rita C -pg 319
Franquez, Rosa C -pg 14
Franquez, Rosalia P -pg 214
Franquez, Vicente I -pg 14
Freegord, Guadalupe -pg 397
Fuerties, Joaquina T -pg 482
Fujikawa, Masayoshi -pg 310
Fulgencio, Garcia T -pg 61
Gamboa, Antonio P -pg 362
Gamboa, Isabel P -pg 362
Gamboa, Julia P -pg 362
Gamboa, Lorenzo P -pg 362
Gamboa, Vicente C -pg 362
Gamboa, Vicente P -pg 362
Garcia, Ana F -pg 300
Garcia, Angela C -pg 236
Garcia, Antonio L -pg 302
Garcia, Antonio SN -pg 300
Garcia, Demetro LG -pg 300
Garcia, Esparanca C -pg 236
Garcia, Florencio A -pg 236
Garcia, Francisco A -pg 236
Garcia, Francisco F -pg 300
Garcia, Francisco M -pg 235
Garcia, Fulencio -pg 248
Garcia, Gertrudes C -pg 302
Garcia, Gertrudes J -pg 28
Garcia, Jaime M -pg 235
Garcia, Jesus A -pg 236
Garcia, Jesus C -pg 302
Garcia, Jesus M -pg 235
Garcia, Jose C -pg 236
Garcia, Josefina M -pg 235
Garcia, Juan C -pg 302
Garcia, Juan J -pg 28
Garcia, Juan M -pg 235
Garcia, Juan SN -pg 235
Garcia, Justo A -pg 236
Garcia, Magdalena A -pg 236
Garcia, Maria F -pg 300
Garcia, Rosa J -pg 28
Garcia, Rosa M -pg 235

Garcia, Tomasa A -pg 236
Garcia, Trinidad SN -pg 300
Garcia, Vicenta J -pg 28
Garrido, Agueda A -pg 21
Garrido, Ana B -pg 263
Garrido, Ana L -pg 270
Garrido, Ana M -pg 297
Garrido, Ana N -pg 475
Garrido, Ana S -pg 499
Garrido, Ana T -pg 111
Garrido, Antonia B -pg 298
Garrido, Antonia E -pg 496
Garrido, Antonia S -pg 534
Garrido, Antonio S -pg 499
Garrido, Ascemcion E -pg 496
Garrido, Asuncion C -pg 83
Garrido, Augustin S -pg 499
Garrido, Carmen E -pg 496
Garrido, Carmen L -pg 231
Garrido, Concepcion S -pg 534
Garrido, Conception S -pg 498
Garrido, Dolores M -pg 297
Garrido, Dolores R -pg 84
Garrido, Dorotea L -pg 231
Garrido, Elena P -pg 21
Garrido, Enrique B -pg 298
Garrido, Enrique S -pg 534
Garrido, Enselmo B -pg 263
Garrido, Facundo B -pg 263
Garrido, Felis S -pg 534
Garrido, Felisa B -pg 263
Garrido, Francisco L -pg 270
Garrido, Ignacio L -pg 21
Garrido, Ignacio S -pg 534
Garrido, Isabel G -pg 300
Garrido, Jesus B -pg 298
Garrido, Jesus C -pg 83
Garrido, Jesus E -pg 496
Garrido, Jesus L -pg 231
Garrido, Jesus M -pg 297
Garrido, Jesus S -pg 184
Garrido, Jesus T -pg 111
Garrido, Joaquin G -pg 84
Garrido, Joaquin M -pg 297
Garrido, Joaquin N -pg 498
Garrido, Jose B -pg 111
Garrido, Jose C -pg 270
Garrido, Jose G -pg 300
Garrido, Jose G -pg 499
Garrido, Jose M -pg 298
Garrido, Jose P -pg 21
Garrido, Jose R -pg 489

Garrido, Jose S -pg 534
Garrido, Jose T -pg 111
Garrido, Juan C -pg 263
Garrido, Juan M -pg 297
Garrido, Juan R -pg 489
Garrido, Juan S -pg 499
Garrido, Lotirde A -pg 21
Garrido, Magdalena A -pg 21
Garrido, Magdalena P -pg 21
Garrido, Manuel T -pg 111
Garrido, Maria B -pg 298
Garrido, Maria B -pg 325
Garrido, Maria C -pg 83
Garrido, Maria C jr -pg 83
Garrido, Maria G -pg 300
Garrido, Maria G -pg 300
Garrido, Maria L -pg 231
Garrido, Maria M -pg 297
Garrido, Maria R -pg 489
Garrido, Maria R -pg 489
Garrido, Maria S -pg 534
Garrido, Maria T -pg 111
Garrido, Mariana C -pg 263
Garrido, Miguel S -pg 499
Garrido, Nicolas N -pg 475
Garrido, Ramon G -pg 475
Garrido, Ramon M -pg 499
Garrido, Ramona S -pg 499
Garrido, Rita P -pg 21
Garrido, Rosa B -pg 325
Garrido, Rosa E -pg 496
Garrido, Rosalia S -pg 534
Garrido, Rufina L -pg 270
Garrido, Salomon B -pg 325
Garrido, Simona B -pg 263
Garrido, Tomas S -pg 499
Garrido, Vicenta L -pg 231
Garrido, Vicenta T -pg 111
Garrido, Vicente B -pg 83
Garrido, Vicente B -pg 231
Garrido, Vicente C -pg 318
Garrido, Vicente C -pg 496
Garrido, Vicente E -pg 496
Garrido, Vicente L -pg 231
Garrido, Vicente L -pg 270
Garrido, Vicente L -pg 534
Garrido, Vicente P -pg 21
Garrido, Victorano J B -pg 263
George, Felix P -pg 289
George, Jose M -pg 289
George, Josefa M -pg 289
George, Luisa L -pg 337

George, Maria L -pg 337
George, Pilar L -pg 337
George, Regina L -pg 337
George, Rosa L -pg 337
George, Rosario L -pg 337
George, Vicente -pg 337
George, Zara M -pg 289
Giles, Albert H -pg 311
Giles, Elizabeth V -pg 311
Giles, Frank C -pg 311
Giles, Maud C -pg 311
Giles, Nancy M -pg 311
Gillespic, Elma E -pg 42
Gillespic, Jack M -pg 42
Gofigan, Geronimo Q -pg 469
Gofigan, Graviel Q -pg 469
Gofigan, Ramon Q -pg 469
Gofigan, Vicenta Q -pg 469
Gofigan, Vicente Q -pg 469
Gogo, Adela 0 -pg 100
Gogo, Amparo A -pg 103
Gogo, Ana C -pg 99
Gogo, Ana M -pg 66
Gogo, Ana N -pg 68
Gogo, Bernadita 0 -pg 103
Gogo, Carmela Q -pg 100
Gogo, Consolacion N -pg 67
Gogo, Daniel G -pg 103
Gogo, Emilio G -pg 105
Gogo, Enrique N -pg 68
Gogo, Felecita 0 -pg 100
Gogo, Felicita C -pg 103
Gogo, Felix C -pg 330
Gogo, Filomena A -pg 102
Gogo, Francisco N -pg 68
Gogo, Ignacia C -pg 103
Gogo, Ignacio A -pg 103
Gogo, Isabel M -pg 66
Gogo, Jesus N -pg 68
Gogo, Joaquina N -pg 68
Gogo, Jose 0 -pg 100
Gogo, Jose C -pg 66
Gogo, Jose C -pg 99
Gogo, Jose G -pg 103
Gogo, Juan G -pg 99
Gogo, Juan G -pg 102
Gogo, Juan S -pg 67
Gogo, Marcela A -pg 103
Gogo, Margarita C -pg 65
Gogo, Maria 0 -pg 100
Gogo, Maria C -pg 65
Gogo, Maria C -pg 99

Gogo, Maria G -pg 103

Gogo, Pedro C -pg 99

Gogo, Ramon G -pg 103

Gogo, Rosa N -pg 68

Gogo, Rosalia C -pg 65

Gogo, Rosario C -pg 65

Gogo, Teofera Q -pg 100

Gogo, Venancio G -pg 65

Gogo, Vicenta C -pg 330

Gogo, Vicente G -pg 103

Gogue, Agustin SL -pg 57

Gogue, Amalia T -pg 105

Gogue, Ana LG -pg 154

Gogue, Ana Q -pg 99

Gogue, Antonia S -pg 57

Gogue, Carmen A -pg 101

Gogue, Carmen G -pg 498

Gogue, Dolores G -pg 498

Gogue, Dolores T -pg 105

Gogue, Enrique W -pg 178

Gogue, Geronimo A -pg 71

Gogue, Ignacio B -pg 18

Gogue, Isabel -pg 427

Gogue, Isabel R G -pg 498

Gogue, Jesus A -pg 101

Gogue, Jesus G -pg 106

Gogue, Jesus LG -pg 154

Gogue, Joaquin B -pg 18

Gogue, Joaquina G -pg 100

Gogue, Joaquina G -pg 498

Gogue, Jose 0 -pg 101

Gogue, Jose A -pg 100

Gogue, Jose LG -pg 154

Gogue, Jose M -pg 153

Gogue, Jose Q -pg 99

Gogue, Jose S -pg 57

Gogue, Josefina A -pg 71

Gogue, Juan A -pg 99

Gogue, Juan G -pg 100

Gogue, Juan Q -pg 99

Gogue, Juana T -pg 105

Gogue, Justo LG -pg 154

Gogue, Magdalena B -pg 18

Gogue, Manuel G -pg 69

Gogue, Maria A -pg 71

Gogue, Maria A -pg 101

Gogue, Maria C -pg 70

Gogue, Maria S -pg 57

Gogue, Maria W -pg 178

Gogue, Maria R G -pg 498

Gogue, Pedro S -pg 69

Gogue, Prodencio R -pg 498

Gogue, Ramona W -pg 178

Gogue, Rita A -pg 71

Gogue, Rita A -pg 101

Gogue, Saturnina B -pg 18

Gogue, Tomas S -pg 57

Gogue, Vicenta W -pg 178

Gogue, Vicente SL -pg 71

Gogue, Vicente T -pg 105

Gogue, Vicente -pg 427

Gomes, Maria S -pg 441

Gomez, Artemio C -pg 114

Gomez, Emeteria P -pg 114

Gomez, Jesus A -pg 114

Gomez, Jose S -pg 114

Gomez, Maria C -pg 114

Gomez, Silvestre 0 -pg 114

Gomez, Vicente S -pg 97

Gonzalo, Antonia T -pg 204

Gonzalo, Josefina T -pg 204

Gonzalo, Pedro G -pg 204

Grey, Gustav -pg 417

Grey, Paul -pg 417

Grey, Rosario C -pg 417

Grey, Wilhelmina -pg 417

Guerrero, Amparo C -pg 221

Guerrero, Ana B -pg 439

Guerrero, Ana C -pg 272

Guerrero, Ana G -pg 43

Guerrero, Ana LG -pg 48

Guerrero, Ana M -pg 127

Guerrero, Ana Q -pg 456

Guerrero, Ana R -pg 50

Guerrero, Ana R -pg 436

Guerrero, Ana T -pg 267

Guerrero, Antonia C -pg 221

Guerrero, Antonia LG -pg 48

Guerrero, Antonia R -pg 123

Guerrero, Antonia S -pg 117

Guerrero, Antonina Q -pg 456

Guerrero, Antonio P -pg 400

Guerrero, Baltazar B -pg 439

Guerrero, Beatrice -pg 268

Guerrero, Benancio T -pg 267

Guerrero, Caesario P -pg 272

Guerrero, Caridad A -pg 308

Guerrero, Caridad M -pg 196

Guerrero, Carmelo G -pg 400

Guerrero, Carmen P -pg 400

Guerrero, Concepcion R -pg 123

Guerrero, Consuelo P -pg 402

Guerrero, Delfina R -pg 279

Guerrero, Dolores C -pg 268

Guerrero, Dolores G -pg 68

Guerrero, Dolores M -pg 127

Guerrero, Dolores M -pg 196

Guerrero, Dolores P -pg 400

Guerrero, Dolores R -pg 123

Guerrero, Dolores T -pg 322

Guerrero, Domingo B -pg 124

Guerrero, Domingo B -pg 124

Guerrero, Emelia G -pg 306

Guerrero, Encarnation B -pg 439

Guerrero, Enrique C -pg 399

Guerrero, Enrique P -pg 272

Guerrero, Felecita P -pg 400

Guerrero, Felicidad G -pg 68

Guerrero, Felipe G -pg 268

Guerrero, Felipe G -pg 279

Guerrero, Felix B -pg 439

Guerrero, Francesca P -pg 272

Guerrero, Francisca LG -pg 48

Guerrero, Francisca P -pg 400

Guerrero, Francisco B -pg 124

Guerrero, Francisco C -pg 119

Guerrero, Francisco G -pg 50

Guerrero, Higinio T -pg 323

Guerrero, Ignacia B -pg 439

Guerrero, Ignacia P -pg 272

Guerrero, Ignacia -pg 272

Guerrero, Ignacio C -pg 115

Guerrero, Ignacio F -pg 336

Guerrero, Ignacio G -pg 322

Guerrero, Ignacio T -pg 322

Guerrero, Ignacio V -pg 399

Guerrero, Jesus M -pg 127

Guerrero, Jesus M -pg 196

Guerrero, Jesus P -pg 272

Guerrero, Jesus R -pg 436

Guerrero, Jesus T -pg 267

Guerrero, Jesus T -pg 322

Guerrero, Jesus -pg 268

Guerrero, Joaquin C -pg 119

Guerrero, Joaquin P -pg 400

Guerrero, Joaquin R -pg 50

Guerrero, Joaquin T -pg 322

Guerrero, Joaquin -pg 306

Guerrero, Joaquina R -pg 209

Guerrero, Joaquina T -pg 322

Guerrero, Jose B -pg 119

Guerrero, Jose C -pg 209

Guerrero, Jose C -pg 221

Guerrero, Jose C -pg 279

Guerrero, Jose G -pg 306

Guerrero, Jose M -pg 123

Guerrero, Jose M -pg 196
Guerrero, Jose M -pg 399
Guerrero, Jose P -pg 272
Guerrero, Jose P -pg 272
Guerrero, Jose P -pg 456
Guerrero, Jose R -pg 279
Guerrero, Jose T -pg 267
Guerrero, Jose DL 0 -pg 34
Guerrero, Josefa C -pg 273
Guerrero, Josefa G -pg 177
Guerrero, Josefa M -pg 127
Guerrero, Josephina P -pg 272
Guerrero, Juan B -pg 119
Guerrero, Juan C -pg 268
Guerrero, Juan C -pg 273
Guerrero, Juan F -pg 48
Guerrero, Juan G -pg 43
Guerrero, Juan LG -pg 48
Guerrero, Juan P -pg 272
Guerrero, Juan P -pg 400
Guerrero, Juan S -pg 117
Guerrero, Juan T -pg 267
Guerrero, Juan V -pg 400
Guerrero, Juana 0 -pg 177
Guerrero, Julian M -pg 196
Guerrero, Leon C -pg 439
Guerrero, Lucio G -pg 68
Guerrero, Luis G -pg 43
Guerrero, Luisa A -pg 308
Guerrero, Manuel C -pg 127
Guerrero, Manuel C -pg 221
Guerrero, Manuel M -pg 196
Guerrero, Manuel -pg 268
Guerrero, Maria 0 -pg 177
Guerrero, Maria B -pg 111
Guerrero, Maria B -pg 124
Guerrero, Maria C -pg 115
Guerrero, Maria C -pg 119
Guerrero, Maria C -pg 221
Guerrero, Maria C -pg 268
Guerrero, Maria C -pg 268
Guerrero, Maria C -pg 273
Guerrero, Maria E -pg 322
Guerrero, Maria M -pg 127
Guerrero, Maria M -pg 196
Guerrero, Maria M -pg 399
Guerrero, Maria P -pg 265
Guerrero, Maria P -pg 272
Guerrero, Maria P -pg 400
Guerrero, Maria R -pg 50
Guerrero, Maria R -pg 123
Guerrero, Maria R -pg 124

Guerrero, Maria R -pg 436
Guerrero, Maria T -pg 267
Guerrero, Maria R T -pg 322
Guerrero, Maxima M -pg 399
Guerrero, Nicolas B -pg 124
Guerrero, Nicolas G -pg 402
Guerrero, Nicolas M -pg 127
Guerrero, Nieves LG -pg 124
Guerrero, Pedro B -pg 119
Guerrero, Pedro C -pg 221
Guerrero, Pedro F -pg 221
Guerrero, Pedro LG -pg 48
Guerrero, Ramon P -pg 308
Guerrero, Regina T -pg 322
Guerrero, Rita F -pg 336
Guerrero, Rita T -pg 267
Guerrero, Rita T -pg 267
Guerrero, Rita J T -pg 322
Guerrero, Rosa B -pg 119
Guerrero, Rosa C -pg 268
Guerrero, Rosa C -pg 439
Guerrero, Rosa T -pg 322
Guerrero, Rosalia R -pg 50
Guerrero, Rosario R -pg 279
Guerrero, Rufina P -pg 400
Guerrero, Santiago T -pg 322
Guerrero, Silvestre R -pg 124
Guerrero, Soledad B -pg 124
Guerrero, Soledad C -pg 439
Guerrero, Soledad M -pg 127
Guerrero, Soledad R -pg 436
Guerrero, Tomas R -pg 279
Guerrero, Vicente C -pg 267
Guerrero, Vicente C -pg 268
Guerrero, Vicente LG -pg 119
Guerrero, Vicente S -pg 68
Guerrero, Vicente S -pg 195
Guerrero, Victoriana V -pg 399
Guerrero, Virginia T -pg 322
Guevara, Antonio C -pg 69
Guevara, Aularia D -pg 69
Guevara, Cecilio C -pg 69
Guevara, Edwardo A -pg 72
Guevara, Enriqueta C -pg 69
Guevara, Enriqueta C -pg 70
Guevara, Fernando C -pg 69
Guevara, Fralon D -pg 69
Guevara, Gregorio D -pg 69
Guevara, Isabel C -pg 69
Guevara, Jose A -pg 72
Guevara, Juan C -pg 69
Guevara, Juliana D -pg 69

Guevara, Macario D -pg 69
Guevara, Maria A -pg 72
Guevara, Maria C -pg 69
Guevara, Maria C -pg 69
Guevara, Maria D -pg 69
Guevara, Rosa C -pg 69
Guevara, Simion C -pg 70
Guevara, Teodora C -pg 70
Guevara, Vicente A -pg 72
Guevara, Vicente C -pg 72
Guevara, Vicente R -pg 169
Gumabon, Ariston G -pg 171
Gumabon, Carmen N -pg 171
Gumabon, Jose N -pg 171
Gumabon, Vicente N -pg 171
Gumataotao, Adela D -pg 403
Gumataotao, Agustin U -pg 261
Gumataotao, Ana L -pg 84
Gumataotao, Ana S -pg 340
Gumataotao, Andres B -pg 408
Gumataotao, Antonio B -pg 403
Gumataotao, Antonio L -pg 84
Gumataotao, Antonio -pg 340
Gumataotao, Atanasio T -pg 209
Gumataotao, Emilia L -pg 84
Gumataotao, Emiliana P -pg 427
Gumataotao, Eulogio G -pg 201
Gumataotao, Fermin G -pg 201
Gumataotao, Francisco B -pg 427
Gumataotao, Francisco G -pg 201
Gumataotao, Francisco U -pg 261
Gumataotao, Francisco -pg 340
Gumataotao, Ignacio S -pg 261
Gumataotao, Isabel T -pg 209
Gumataotao, Joaquin D -pg 403
Gumataotao, Joaquin M -pg 209
Gumataotao, Jose B -pg 408
Gumataotao, Jose D -pg 403
Gumataotao, Jose S -pg 340
Gumataotao, Jose T -pg 209
Gumataotao, Juan C -pg 408
Gumataotao, Juan L -pg 84
Gumataotao, Juan T -pg 209
Gumataotao, Juana D -pg 226
Gumataotao, Leon D -pg 403
Gumataotao, Lorenzo T -pg 340
Gumataotao, Manuela G -pg 201
Gumataotao, Maria D -pg 403
Gumataotao, Maria S -pg 340
Gumataotao, Maria T -pg 340
Gumataotao, Mariano P -pg 427
Gumataotao, Nicolas D -pg 404

Gumataotao, Oscar D -pg 404
Gumataotao, Paciano G -pg 201
Gumataotao, Pedro D -pg 404
Gumataotao, Rafael L -pg 84
Gumataotao, Ramona T -pg 209
Gumataotao, Rita L -pg 84
Gumataotao, Rita T -pg 340
Gumataotao, Rita U -pg 261
Gumataotao, Rosa D -pg 404
Gumataotao, Soledad S -pg 340
Gumataotao, Teresa B -pg 408
Gumataotao, Teresa G -pg 201
Gumataotao, Vicente T -pg 209
Gumataotao, Virginia U -pg 261
Gusman, Pedro L -pg 497
Gutierez, Ana D -pg 205
Gutierez, Domingo N -pg 205
Gutierez, Esiquiel N -pg 206
Gutierez, Felecita D -pg 205
Gutierez, Filomena D -pg 204
Gutierez, Jesus T -pg 206
Gutierez, Jose D -pg 205
Gutierez, Jose D -pg 205
Gutierez, Juan D -pg 204
Gutierez, Leonila D -pg 205
Gutierez, Luis M -pg 204
Gutierez, Maria D -pg 205
Gutierez, Maria T -pg 206
Gutierez, Maria T jr -pg 206
Gutierez, Rosa D -pg 204
Gutierez, Rosa D -pg 205
Gutierez, Soledad D -pg 205
Gutierez, Tomasa D -pg 205
Gutierrez, Agosto T -pg 301
Gutierrez, Agueda T -pg 300
Gutierrez, Ana T -pg 301
Gutierrez, Angusta T -pg 301
Gutierrez, Antonia T -pg 301
Gutierrez, Carlos T -pg 301
Gutierrez, Frederico T -pg 301
Gutierrez, Grace T -pg 301
Gutierrez, Jane T -pg 301
Gutierrez, Jose T -pg 301
Gutierrez, Julia T -pg 301
Gutierrez, Maria T -pg 300
Gutierrez, Maria T -pg 301
Gutierrez, Rosa T -pg 301
Gutierrez, Tomas C -pg 300
Gutierrez, Tomas T -pg 301
Guzman, Agnes P -pg 213
Guzman, Agueda D -pg 407
Guzman, Agustin F -pg 216

Guzman, Amalia P -pg 213
Guzman, Ana D -pg 405
Guzman, Ana M -pg 192
Guzman, Ana M -pg 282
Guzman, Antonia C -pg 274
Guzman, Antonia C -pg 419
Guzman, Antonia M -pg 216
Guzman, Antonia M -pg 282
Guzman, Antonio LG -pg 54
Guzman, Antonio S -pg 413
Guzman, Caridad I -pg 277
Guzman, Carmen C -pg 312
Guzman, Carmen C -pg 419
Guzman, Dolores C -pg 282
Guzman, Dolores C -pg 413
Guzman, Dolores LG -pg 54
Guzman, Emeliana P -pg 213
Guzman, Ernestina G -pg 413
Guzman, Esperanza I -pg 277
Guzman, Fidela M -pg 192
Guzman, Francisco C -pg 282
Guzman, Francisco C -pg 312
Guzman, Francisco H -pg 213
Guzman, Francisco S -pg 419
Guzman, Francisco -pg 312
Guzman, Gonzalo M -pg 192
Guzman, Gregorio C -pg 312
Guzman, Gregorio M -pg 282
Guzman, Guadalupe C -pg 413
Guzman, Jesus C -pg 282
Guzman, Jesus C -pg 419
Guzman, Jesus M -pg 282
Guzman, Jesusa LG -pg 54
Guzman, Joaquin C -pg 192
Guzman, Joaquin C -pg 419
Guzman, Joaquin U -pg 291
Guzman, Jose C -pg 419
Guzman, Jose LG -pg 54
Guzman, Jose M -pg 54
Guzman, Jose M -pg 192
Guzman, Jose M -pg 296
Guzman, Jose P -pg 213
Guzman, Josefa C -pg 282
Guzman, Josefa C -pg 413
Guzman, Juan A -pg 277
Guzman, Juan C -pg 282
Guzman, Juan C -pg 419
Guzman, Juan D -pg 282
Guzman, Juan D -pg 406
Guzman, Juan LG -pg 54
Guzman, Juan P -pg 213
Guzman, Juan S -pg 407

Guzman, Julio S -pg 192
Guzman, Maria C -pg 419
Guzman, Maria D -pg 405
Guzman, Maria D -pg 406
Guzman, Maria F -pg 332
Guzman, Maria P -pg 213
Guzman, Maria S -pg 407
Guzman, Mercedes P -pg 213
Guzman, Natividad C -pg 282
Guzman, Petronila G -pg 413
Guzman, Pilar P -pg 213
Guzman, Potenciana F -pg 332
Guzman, Rita I -pg 277
Guzman, Tomas -pg 282
Guzman, Trinidad I -pg 277
Guzman, Vicente C -pg 282
Guzman, Vicente D -pg 405
Guzman, Vicente LG -pg 54
Haller, Dolores C -pg 385
Haniu, Asuncion B -pg 190
Haniu, Atanasio B -pg 190
Haniu, Jesus B -pg 190
Haniu, Jose B -pg 191
Haniu, Jose H -pg 190
Haniu, Josefina B -pg 190
Haniu, Juan B -pg 191
Haniu, Maria B -pg 190
Haniu, Pilar B -pg 190
Haniu, Serafina B -pg 191
Hara, Francisca C -pg 553
Hara, Jose C -pg 553
Hara, Jose H -pg 553
Hara, Manuel C -pg 553
Hara, Maria C -pg 553
Hara, Romana C -pg 553
Hataguchi, Okidia -pg 559
Hawamoto, Isematsu -pg 458
Hemeworth, Christopher -pg 426
Hennicker, George C -pg 212
Hennicker, Ignacia LG -pg 212
Hernandez, Ana F -pg 144
Hernandez, Ana F -pg 144
Hernandez, Antonio 0 -pg 161
Hernandez, Antonio B -pg 144
Hernandez, Asuncion F -pg 144
Hernandez, Eugenio P -pg 157
Hernandez, Francisco B -pg 144
Hernandez, Ignacio E -pg 126
Hernandez, Jesus 0 -pg 146
Hernandez, Jesus B -pg 126
Hernandez, Joaquin 0 -pg 161
Hernandez, Joaquin F -pg 144

Hernandez, Joaquina B -pg 126
Hernandez, Jose 0 -pg 161
Hernandez, Jose B -pg 126
Hernandez, Jose B -pg 144
Hernandez, Jose F -pg 144
Hernandez, Jose SA -pg 170
Hernandez, Juan 0 -pg 146
Hernandez, Manuel P -pg 144
Hernandez, Maria 0 -pg 161
Hernandez, Maria B -pg 144
Hernandez, Pedro T -pg 144
Hernandez, Precedes P -pg 144
Hernandez, Ramon E -pg 143
Hernandez, Vicente 0 -pg 161
Hernandez, Yunin B -pg 144
Herrero, Alfredo C -pg 62
Herrero, Alice L -pg 251
Herrero, Angel C -pg 62
Herrero, Caridad C -pg 61
Herrero, Consuelo C -pg 61
Herrero, Edward P -pg 186
Herrero, Edward P -pg 251
Herrero, Edwardo C -pg 62
Herrero, Enrique M -pg 61
Herrero, Fernando P -pg 186
Herrero, Florence B -pg 251
Herrero, Francisco C -pg 61
Herrero, Francisco C -pg 61
Herrero, Francisco LG -pg 26
Herrero, Francisco S -pg 446
Herrero, Helen C -pg 251
Herrero, Henry A -pg 251
Herrero, Jesus S -pg 446
Herrero, Jose C -pg 61
Herrero, Jose S -pg 456
Herrero, Jose SN -pg 26
Herrero, Josefa C -pg 61
Herrero, Josefa SN -pg 26
Herrero, Josefina C -pg 61
Herrero, Julia C -pg 62
Herrero, Leillian J -pg 251
Herrero, Lola C -pg 62
Herrero, Manuel A -pg 447
Herrero, Manuela S -pg 446
Herrero, Maria C -pg 61
Herrero, Maria C -pg 61
Herrero, Rita S -pg 446
Herrero, Rosa SN -pg 186
Herrero, Ruth L -pg 251
Herrero, Soledad SN -pg 26
Herrero, Tomas C -pg 61
Herrero, Vicente P -pg 251

Herrero, Vicente R -pg 186
Hines, Adolofo C -pg 275
Hines, Arturo C -pg 276
Hines, Ascencion C -pg 275
Hines, Cristobal C -pg 275
Hines, Eloise C -pg 275
Hines, Fabian -pg 275
Hines, Lagrimas C -pg 275
Hines, Maria C -pg 275
Hines, Viviana C -pg 276
Hirano, Ai -pg 309
Hirano, Moto -pg 309
Hodge, Francisca C -pg 482
Hodge, James C -pg 481
Hong, Lam 0 -pg 18
Hongyee, Alejandro 0 -pg 139
Hongyee, Isabel P -pg 139
Hongyee, Jesus P -pg 139
Hongyee, Joaquin P -pg 139
Hongyee, Jose P -pg 139
Hongyee, Juan R -pg 139
Hongyee, Nieves P -pg 139
Hongyee, Vicente R -pg 139
Huertas, Tomas 0 -pg 18
Hugolino, Gainca 0 -pg 59
Ibanez, Candelaria SN -pg 160
Ibanez, Jose SN -pg 160
Ibanez, Pedro SN -pg 160
Ibanez, Taitano SN -pg 160
Ibasco, Ana 0 -pg 145
Ibasco, Catalina 0 pg 145
Ibasco, Charlie 0 -pg 145
Ibasco, Enrique 0 -pg 181
Ibasco, Ines S -pg 181
Ibasco, Josefa 0 -pg 145
Ibasco, Magdalena C -pg 181
Ibasco, Maria 0 -pg 145
Ibasco, Maria S -pg 182
Ibasco, Mercedes S -pg 182
Ibasco, Santiago 0 -pg 145
Ichijara, Dolores SM -pg 56
Ichijara, Francisco SM -pg 56
Ichijara, Joaquin SM -pg 56
Ichijara, Jose 0 -pg 56
Ichijara, Jose SM -pg 56
Ichijara, Rita SM -pg 56
Ida, Yoki -pg 265
Idol, Dolores P -pg 265
Idol, Fabian G -pg 265
Iglay, Candido S -pg 122
Iglesias, Ana D -pg 13
Iglesias, Ana F -pg 14

Iglesias, Antonio A -pg 14
Iglesias, Consolacion G -pg 13
Iglesias, Enrique F -pg 14
Iglesias, Ferina G -pg 118
Iglesias, Francisco A -pg 118
Iglesias, Francisco G -pg 14
Iglesias, Francisco Q -pg 392
Iglesias, Jesus F -pg 13
Iglesias, Joaquina G -pg 118
Iglesias, Jose A -pg 135
Iglesias, Jose G -pg 14
Iglesias, Jose G -pg 118
Iglesias, Jose L -pg 13
Iglesias, Jose Q -pg 392
Iglesias, Josefa A -pg 14
Iglesias, Joseph D -pg 13
Iglesias, Juan G -pg 14
Iglesias, Juan Q -pg 392
Iglesias, Magdalena Q -pg 392
Iglesias, Maria A -pg 14
Iglesias, Maria G -pg 118
Iglesias, Rita F -pg 14
Iglesias, Tomas A -pg 14
Ignacio, Ana -pg 248
Ignacio, Antonia C -pg 394
Ignacio, Antonio C -pg 381
Ignacio, Carmen C -pg 394
Ignacio, Concepcion C -pg 394
Ignacio, Concepcion M -pg 380
Ignacio, Consolacion M -pg 211
Ignacio, Embertriz C -pg 381
Ignacio, Enrique M -pg 212
Ignacio, Enrique R -pg 355
Ignacio, Filomina C -pg 248
Ignacio, Francisco C -pg 209
Ignacio, Francisco N -pg 177
Ignacio, Gregorio C -pg 262
Ignacio, Isabel C -pg 381
Ignacio, Jesus C -pg 262
Ignacio, Jesus C -pg 394
Ignacio, Jesus N -pg 177
Ignacio, Jesus R -pg 211
Ignacio, Joaquin C -pg 380
Ignacio, Jose C -pg 380
Ignacio, Jose C -pg 394
Ignacio, Jose N -pg 178
Ignacio, Jose R -pg 212
Ignacio, Josefa C -pg 262
Ignacio, Josefina C -pg 381
Ignacio, Juan C -pg 380
Ignacio, Juana C -pg 380
Ignacio, Leonicio C -pg 394

Ignacio, Luis C -pg 394
Ignacio, Manuel A -pg 273
Ignacio, Manuel A -pg 394
Ignacio, Manuel C -pg 381
Ignacio, Marcela N -pg 177
Ignacio, Maria C -pg 347
Ignacio, Maria C -pg 394
Ignacio, Maria M -pg 212
Ignacio, Maria N -pg 177
Ignacio, Maria -pg 248
Ignacio, Maria -pg 277
Ignacio, Pedro A -pg 177
Ignacio, Placida C -pg 273
Ignacio, Placida C -pg 394
Ignacio, Preciosa N -pg 178
Ignacio, Rafael P -pg 394
Ignacio, Ramon C -pg 273
Ignacio, Regina M -pg 212
Ignacio, Rita C -pg 394
Ignacio, Rosa C -pg 273
Ignacio, Rosa C -pg 394
Ignacio, Rosa C -pg 394
Ignacio, Soledad J -pg 355
Ignacio, Tomasa A -pg 273
Ignacio, Trinidad R -pg 209
Ignacio, Ursula C -pg 347
Ignacio, Vicente A -pg 347
Imbuluqueta, Crispin O -pg 59
Indalecio, Ana -pg 230
Indalecio, Ana -pg 313
Indalecio, Antonio C -pg 219
Indalecio, Carmen -pg 313
Indalecio, Catalina C -pg 219
Indalecio, Dolores -pg 230
Indalecio, Dolores -pg 313
Indalecio, Jose C -pg 219
Indalecio, Jose R -pg 300
Indalecio, Jose -pg 230
Indalecio, Jose -pg 313
Indalecio, Juan C -pg 219
Indalecio, Juan -pg 230
Indalecio, Magdalena -pg 230
Indalecio, Maria C -pg 219
Indalecio, Maria -pg 313
Indalecio, Pedro -pg 219
Indalecio, Rita R -pg 300
Indalecio, Rita -pg 230
Indalecio, Rosa -pg 313
Indalecio, Rosalia C -pg 219
Indalecio, Rufina C -pg 219
Indalecio, Vicente -pg 230
Inoye, Ana S -pg 383

Inoye, Benedicta S -pg 383
Inoye, Joaquin S -pg 383
Inoye, Maria S -pg 383
Iriarte, Agustina D -pg 220
Iriarte, Ana D -pg 232
Iriarte, Ana D -pg 232
Iriarte, Ana -pg 231
Iriarte, Antonio D -pg 232
Iriarte, Cristina D -pg 232
Iriarte, Dolores D -pg 221
Iriarte, Felisa D -pg 232
Iriarte, Francisca J -pg 218
Iriarte, Ignacio D -pg 232
Iriarte, Jesus C -pg 218
Iriarte, Jesus D -pg 221
Iriarte, Jose C -pg 220
Iriarte, Jose D -pg 232
Iriarte, Jose R -pg 83
Iriarte, Juan D -pg 232
Iriarte, Juan D -pg 232
Iriarte, Juana C -pg 220
Iriarte, Juana D -pg 220
Iriarte, Lorenzo -pg 232
Iriarte, Maria D -pg 221
Iriarte, Maria D -pg 232
Iriarte, Monica D -pg 220
Iriarte, Nativiad D -pg 220
Iriarte, Nicolas G -pg 220
Iriarte, Pedro C -pg 220
Iriarte, Tomas D -pg 221
Iriarte, Tomas D -pg 232
Iriarte, Vicente D -pg 232
Isezaki, Francisco M -pg 465
Isezaki, Jesus P -pg 138
Isezaki, Jose P -pg 138
Isezaki, Jose J -pg 465
Isezaki, Marcelina P -pg 138
Isezaki, Maria P -pg 138
Isezaki, Rita M -pg 465
Isezaki, Rosa M -pg 465
Isezaki, Rosia M -pg 465
Isezaki, Vicente P -pg 138
Isezaki, Vicente Y -pg 138
Ishizaki, Agueda P -pg 401
Ishizaki, Filomena P -pg 401
Ishizaki, Francisco -pg 401
Ishizaki, Joaquin P -pg 401
Isidro, Dolores A -pg 318
Isidro, Ursula A -pg 318
Isidro, Victoria A -pg 318
Ito, Amalia S -pg 46
Ito, Genyo O -pg 46

Ito, Sanfiro O -pg 165
Iwatsu, Carmen S -pg 239
Iwatsu, Jose -pg 239
Iwatsu, Juana S -pg 239
Jackson, Altura C -pg 73
Jackson, Arthur W -pg 348
Jackson, Dolores K -pg 73
Jackson, Enrique C -pg 73
Jackson, Frank K -pg 73
Jackson, Lilian K -pg 73
James, Daisy F -pg 261
James, David W R -pg 261
James, Dolores F -pg 260
James, Eugenia F -pg 261
James, Joseph F -pg 261
James, Joseph H -pg 260
James, Lily F -pg 261
James, Pedro F -pg 261
James, William F -pg 261
James, Woodrow F -pg 261
Javier, Dolores A -pg 323
Javier, Francisco G -pg 327
Javier, Isabel A -pg 324
Javier, Jesus P -pg 327
Javier, Joaquina G -pg 411
Javier, Jose P -pg 327
Javier, Josefa P -pg 327
Javier, Julia P -pg 327
Javier, Maria A -pg 324
Javier, Maria P -pg 327
Javier, Rosa P -pg 327
Jesus, Ana C -pg 92
Jesus, Ana S -pg 434
Jesus, Angela C -pg 92
Jesus, Antonio C -pg 335
Jesus, Caridad C -pg 335
Jesus, Concepcion C -pg 92
Jesus, Concepcion L -pg 355
Jesus, Derfina S -pg 437
Jesus, Eufemia G -pg 364
Jesus, Felix J -pg 398
Jesus, Francisca B -pg 455
Jesus, Francisco C -pg 335
Jesus, Joaquin L -pg 364
Jesus, Joaquin SN -pg 366
Jesus, Jose C -pg 335
Jesus, Jose J -pg 398
Jesus, Josefa C -pg 335
Jesus, Josefa G -pg 364
Jesus, Lucas F -pg 130
Jesus, Luis F -pg 92
Jesus, Magdalena S -pg 437

Jesus, Marcelo B -pg 455
Jesus, Maria C -pg 130
Jesus, Maria H -pg 173
Jesus, Natividad J -pg 398
Jesus, Rita C -pg 335
Jesus, Rosalia C -pg 335
Jesus, Vicenta C -pg 335
Jesus, Vicenta C -pg 366
Jesus, Yrestina B -pg 455
Jococ, Bartola C -pg 444
Johnson, Andrew P -pg 327
Johnson, Ignacia P -pg 327
Johnson, Olga P -pg 327
Johnson, Patrick P -pg 327
Jota, Toyoki 0 -pg 180
Juan, Camilo C -pg 263
Juan, Isabel M -pg 263
Kamikabya, K 0 -pg 157
Kamikabya, Lai 0 -pg 157
Kamminga, Felicidad T -pg 525
Kamminga, Felicita SN -pg 373
Kamminga, Felix R -pg 373
Kamminga, Frank R -pg 373
Kamminga, Gale F -pg 88
Kamminga, George SN -pg 374
Kamminga, Guele R -pg 373
Kamminga, Joaquina F -pg 88
Kamminga, Joaquina H -pg 42
Kamminga, Joaquina H -pg 42
Kamminga, John S -pg 373
Kamminga, Jose 0 -pg 88
Kamminga, Jose F -pg 88
Kamminga, Jose H -pg 351
Kamminga, Jose K -pg 73
Kamminga, Juana R -pg 373
Kamminga, Juana SN -pg 373
Kamminga, Lolkie H -pg 373
Kamminga, Lorenzo F -pg 88
Kamminga, Magdalena F -pg 88
Kamminga, Maria F -pg 88
Kamminga, Maria F jr -pg 88
Kamminga, Maria H -pg 373
Kamminga, Pilar SN -pg 374
Kamminga, Rita 0 -pg 88
Kamminga, Simeon H -pg 525
Kamminga, Simon -pg 373
Kamo, Antonio I -pg 514
Kamo, Carmen C -pg 514
Kamo, Teodora C -pg 514
Kemp, Robert -pg 426
Keven, Raymund J -pg 426
Kiga, Jesus -pg 541

Kiga, Y -pg 541
Kiga, Yioshi -pg 541
Kitamura, Naoshi -pg 251
Kitamura, Toyoye -pg 309
Kochi, K -pg 246
Kukuri, Manuel L -pg 87
Kumiyama, Juan M -pg 514
Kumiyama, Margarita M -pg 514
Kumiyama, Maria M -pg 514
Kumiyama, Rita M -pg 514
Kurokawa, G -pg 240
La Rosa, Joaquin R -pg 91
La Rosa, Teodora T -pg 91
La Torre, Apolonia A -pg 141
La Torre, Consolasion C -pg 121
La Torre, Felicita A -pg 141
La Torre, Francisco C -pg 121
La Torre, Gregorio A -pg 121
La Torre, Jesus C -pg 121
La Torre, Joaquina C -pg 121
La Torre, Jose C -pg 121
La Torre, Josefa A -pg 141
La Torre, Juan A -pg 140
La Torre, Juan A -pg 141
La Torre, Maria C -pg 121
La Torre, Maria C -pg 121
La Torre, Soledad A -pg 141
La Torre, Vicenta A -pg 141
Laguana, Felicidad P -pg 189
Laguana, Ignacia C -pg 210
Laguana, Ignacia P -pg 189
Laguana, Joaquin P -pg 188
Laguana, Jose P -pg 189
Laguana, Natividad P -pg 189
Laguana, Rosa P -pg 188
Laguana, Soledad P -pg 189
Lalae, Florentino 0 -pg 72
Lalae, Manuel U -pg 72
Lalae, Martina LG -pg 72
Lalae, Terasa G -pg 72
Larrasoana, Vicente M -pg 457
Lazaro, Antonia U -pg 198
Lazaro, Ernesto U -pg 198
Lazaro, Josefa U -pg 198
Lazaro, Juan U -pg 198
Lazaro, Nicolas R -pg 198
Leddy, Daniel B -pg 346
Leddy, Elsie B -pg 346
Leddy, Henry V -pg 346
Leddy, John B -pg 346
Leddy, Lucy B -pg 346
Leon, Ascencion P -pg 305

Leon, Eziquel I -pg 13
Leon, Francisca I -pg 13
Leon, Francisco I -pg 13
Leon, Jesus I -pg 13
Leon, Joaquin -pg 305
Leon, Jose M -pg 13
Leon, Juan M -pg 305
Leon, Maria M -pg 305
Leon Guerrero, Agapito C -pg 275
Leon Guerrero, Agueda C -pg 194
Leon Guerrero, Ana A -pg 521
Leon Guerrero, Ana B -pg 59
Leon Guerrero, Ana C -pg 60
Leon Guerrero, Ana C -pg 95
Leon Guerrero, Ana C -pg 194
Leon Guerrero, Ana C -pg 289
Leon Guerrero, Ana D -pg 509
Leon Guerrero, Ana M -pg 44
Leon Guerrero, Ana M -pg 162
Leon Guerrero, Ana M -pg 218
Leon Guerrero, Ana M -pg 275
Leon Guerrero, Ana N -pg 523
Leon Guerrero, Ana P -pg 136
Leon Guerrero, Ana P -pg 215
Leon Guerrero, Ana P -pg 281
Leon Guerrero, Ana P -pg 308
Leon Guerrero, Ana R -pg 60
Leon Guerrero, Ana R -pg 163
Leon Guerrero, Ana R -pg 164
Leon Guerrero, Ana S -pg 35
Leon Guerrero, Ana S -pg 35
Leon Guerrero, Ana S -pg 82
Leon Guerrero, Ana T -pg 306
Leon Guerrero, Ana -pg 215
Leon Guerrero, Ana -pg 329
Leon Guerrero, Ana de 0 -pg 35
Leon Guerrero, Angelina S -pg 26
Leon Guerrero, Antonia B -pg 59
Leon Guerrero, Antonia B -pg 126
Leon Guerrero, Antonia D -pg 510
Leon Guerrero, Antonia S -pg 82
Leon Guerrero, Antonia T -pg 429
Leon Guerrero, Antonio C -pg 184
Leon Guerrero, Antonio C -pg 275
Leon Guerrero, Ascension R -pg
164
Leon Guerrero, Asuncion I -pg 148
Leon Guerrero, Balbino D -pg 156
Leon Guerrero, Bernada C -pg 383
Leon Guerrero, Brijida S -pg 58
Leon Guerrero, Caridad A -pg 59
Leon Guerrero, Carlos B -pg 59

Leon Guerrero, Carlotta T -pg 531

Leon Guerrero, Carmen C -pg 383

Leon Guerrero, Carmen D -pg 510

Leon Guerrero, Carmen P -pg 308

Leon Guerrero, Carmen R -pg 486

Leon Guerrero, Carmen S -pg 26

Leon Guerrero, Carmen S -pg 35

Leon Guerrero, Catalina -pg 214

Leon Guerrero, Concepcion B -pg 20

Leon Guerrero, Concepcion D -pg 156

Leon Guerrero, Concepcion I -pg 187

Leon Guerrero, Concepcion M -pg 162

Leon Guerrero, Concepcion P -pg 184

Leon Guerrero, Delfin P -pg 281

Leon Guerrero, Dolores A -pg 26

Leon Guerrero, Dolores F -pg 31

Leon Guerrero, Dolores I -pg 187

Leon Guerrero, Dolores P -pg 308

Leon Guerrero, Dolores U -pg 48

Leon Guerrero, Dolores U -pg 261

Leon Guerrero, Dolores -pg 224

Leon Guerrero, Efrain C -pg 289

Leon Guerrero, Eliza P -pg 184

Leon Guerrero, Emeliana B -pg 274

Leon Guerrero, Emilia C -pg 153

Leon Guerrero, Emogines C -pg 275

Leon Guerrero, Enrique C -pg 153

Leon Guerrero, Enrique P -pg 95

Leon Guerrero, Ested R -pg 60

Leon Guerrero, Estefania R -pg 486

Leon Guerrero, Experancia B -pg 59

Leon Guerrero, Ezeqiel C -pg 275

Leon Guerrero, Felipe P -pg 281

Leon Guerrero, Felix P -pg 318

Leon Guerrero, Filomena A -pg 150

Leon Guerrero, Francisca T -pg 48

Leon Guerrero, Francisco B -pg 152

Leon Guerrero, Francisco B -pg 153

Leon Guerrero, Francisco B -pg 184

Leon Guerrero, Francisco C -pg 194

Leon Guerrero, Francisco LG -pg 156

Leon Guerrero, Francisco P -pg 95

Leon Guerrero, Francisco P -pg 184

Leon Guerrero, Francisco R -pg 82

Leon Guerrero, Francisco S -pg 136

Leon Guerrero, Gonzalo A -pg 59

Leon Guerrero, Gonzalo B -pg 59

Leon Guerrero, Gregorio S -pg 57

Leon Guerrero, Gregorio -pg 337

Leon Guerrero, Ignacia LG -pg 238

Leon Guerrero, Ignacia S -pg 82

Leon Guerrero, Ignacio P -pg 308

Leon Guerrero, Ignacio R -pg 164

Leon Guerrero, Ignacio S -pg 35

Leon Guerrero, Inocencio -pg 531

Leon Guerrero, Isabel D -pg 156

Leon Guerrero, Isabel T -pg 165

Leon Guerrero, Isabel -pg 337

Leon Guerrero, Jesus A -pg 521

Leon Guerrero, Jesus D -pg 510

Leon Guerrero, Jesus I -pg 187

Leon Guerrero, Jesus P -pg 148

Leon Guerrero, Jesus P -pg 281

Leon Guerrero, Jesus P -pg 308

Leon Guerrero, Jesus R -pg 164

Leon Guerrero, Jesus R -pg 486

Leon Guerrero, Jesus S -pg 214

Leon Guerrero, Jesus U -pg 261

Leon Guerrero, Jesus -pg 337

Leon Guerrero, Joaquin A -pg 146

Leon Guerrero, Joaquin B -pg 60

Leon Guerrero, Joaquin B -pg 153

Leon Guerrero, Joaquin C -pg 59

Leon Guerrero, Joaquin D -pg 510

Leon Guerrero, Joaquin I -pg 187

Leon Guerrero, Joaquin LG -pg 140

Leon Guerrero, Joaquin M -pg 162

Leon Guerrero, Joaquin P -pg 95

Leon Guerrero, Joaquin R -pg 163

Leon Guerrero, Joaquin R -pg 164

Leon Guerrero, Joaquin S -pg 521

Leon Guerrero, Joaquina B -pg 153

Leon Guerrero, Joaquina I -pg 148

Leon Guerrero, Joaquina N -pg 531

Leon Guerrero, Joaquina S -pg 46

Leon Guerrero, Jose A -pg 150

Leon Guerrero, Jose C -pg 194

Leon Guerrero, Jose D -pg 218

Leon Guerrero, Jose D -pg 429

Leon Guerrero, Jose D -pg 510

Leon Guerrero, Jose I -pg 187

Leon Guerrero, Jose LG -pg 238

Leon Guerrero, Jose M -pg 344

Leon Guerrero, Jose P -pg 95

Leon Guerrero, Jose P -pg 148

Leon Guerrero, Jose P -pg 281

Leon Guerrero, Jose P -pg 301

Leon Guerrero, Jose P -pg 308

Leon Guerrero, Jose P -pg 318

Leon Guerrero, Jose R -pg 164

Leon Guerrero, Jose R -pg 344

Leon Guerrero, Jose R -pg 486

Leon Guerrero, Jose S -pg 35

Leon Guerrero, Jose S -pg 82

Leon Guerrero, Jose S -pg 214

Leon Guerrero, Jose -pg 337

Leon Guerrero, Josefa M -pg 218

Leon Guerrero, Josefina 0 -pg 46

Leon Guerrero, Josefina M -pg 218

Leon Guerrero, Josefina M -pg 275

Leon Guerrero, Juan 0 -pg 46

Leon Guerrero, Juan C -pg 60

Leon Guerrero, Juan C -pg 177

Leon Guerrero, Juan D -pg 156

Leon Guerrero, Juan D? -pg 136

Leon Guerrero, Juan I -pg 187

Leon Guerrero, Juan LG -pg 176

Leon Guerrero, Juan P -pg 308

Leon Guerrero, Juan P -pg 318

Leon Guerrero, Juan R -pg 164

Leon Guerrero, Juan S -pg 20

Leon Guerrero, Juan S -pg 136

Leon Guerrero, Juan T -pg 238

Leon Guerrero, Juan U -pg 261

Leon Guerrero, Juan -pg 337

Leon Guerrero, Juana C -pg 194

Leon Guerrero, Juana S -pg 35

Leon Guerrero, Justa B -pg 152

Leon Guerrero, Justo C -pg 289

Leon Guerrero, Lagrimas N -pg 531

Leon Guerrero, Lagrimas P -pg 184

Leon Guerrero, Linia A -pg 59

Leon Guerrero, Lorenzo M -pg 153

Leon Guerrero, Lorenzo M -pg 218

Leon Guerrero, Lourdes P -pg 308

Leon Guerrero, Luis A -pg 521

Leon Guerrero, Luis P -pg 148

Leon Guerrero, Luis T -pg 165

Leon Guerrero, Luisa U -pg 48

Leon Guerrero, Magdalena P -pg 148

Leon Guerrero, Manuel R -pg 164

Leon Guerrero, Manuel T -pg 48

Leon Guerrero, Manuel -pg 215

Leon Guerrero, Manuela S -pg 136

Leon Guerrero, Margarita D -pg 509

Leon Guerrero, Margarita P -pg 318

Leon Guerrero, Maria A -pg 59

Leon Guerrero, Maria A -pg 521
Leon Guerrero, Maria B -pg 20
Leon Guerrero, Maria B -pg 59
Leon Guerrero, Maria B -pg 126
Leon Guerrero, Maria C -pg 95
Leon Guerrero, Maria C -pg 126
Leon Guerrero, Maria C -pg 153
Leon Guerrero, Maria C -pg 176
Leon Guerrero, Maria C -pg 177
Leon Guerrero, Maria D -pg 510
Leon Guerrero, Maria F -pg 31
Leon Guerrero, Maria I -pg 148
Leon Guerrero, Maria I -pg 187
Leon Guerrero, Maria LG -pg 140
Leon Guerrero, Maria M -pg 275
Leon Guerrero, Maria M -pg 344
Leon Guerrero, Maria M -pg 344
Leon Guerrero, Maria P -pg 148
Leon Guerrero, Maria P -pg 184
Leon Guerrero, Maria P -pg 281
Leon Guerrero, Maria P -pg 301
Leon Guerrero, Maria P -pg 318
Leon Guerrero, Maria R -pg 82
Leon Guerrero, Maria R -pg 164
Leon Guerrero, Maria R -pg 238
Leon Guerrero, Maria S -pg 57
Leon Guerrero, Maria S -pg 58
Leon Guerrero, Maria S -pg 82
Leon Guerrero, Maria S -pg 136
Leon Guerrero, Maria S -pg 214
Leon Guerrero, Maria U -pg 48
Leon Guerrero, Maria U -pg 261
Leon Guerrero, Maria de 0 -pg 34
Leon Guerrero, Mariana M -pg 275
Leon Guerrero, Mariana P -pg 184
Leon Guerrero, Mariano D -pg 510
Leon Guerrero, Mariano I -pg 148
Leon Guerrero, Mariano R -pg 509
Leon Guerrero, Mariano S -pg 214
Leon Guerrero, Matias T -pg 275
Leon Guerrero, Matias -pg 318
Leon Guerrero, Maximimo R -pg 486
Leon Guerrero, Miguel A -pg 306
Leon Guerrero, Pedro B -pg 152
Leon Guerrero, Pedro C -pg 177
Leon Guerrero, Pedro C -pg 194
Leon Guerrero, Pedro C -pg 286
Leon Guerrero, Pedro LG -pg 238
Leon Guerrero, Pedro P -pg 194
Leon Guerrero, Pedro P -pg 281
Leon Guerrero, Pedro R -pg 486

Leon Guerrero, Ramon B -pg 26
Leon Guerrero, Regina P -pg 308
Leon Guerrero, Remedios C -pg 60
Leon Guerrero, Remedios P -pg 184
Leon Guerrero, Rita A -pg 148
Leon Guerrero, Rita C -pg 194
Leon Guerrero, Rita C -pg 275
Leon Guerrero, Rita C -pg 289
Leon Guerrero, Roberto C -pg 194
Leon Guerrero, Rosa C -pg 177
Leon Guerrero, Rosa D -pg 510
Leon Guerrero, Rosa P -pg 148
Leon Guerrero, Rosa P -pg 308
Leon Guerrero, Rosa S -pg 26
Leon Guerrero, Rosalia C -pg 194
Leon Guerrero, Rosalia S -pg 57
Leon Guerrero, Rosario A -pg 521
Leon Guerrero, Rosario B -pg 153
Leon Guerrero, Rosario C -pg 95
Leon Guerrero, Rosario C -pg 194
Leon Guerrero, Rosario C -pg 275
Leon Guerrero, Rosario D -pg 510
Leon Guerrero, Rosario M -pg 344
Leon Guerrero, Rufina A -pg 26
Leon Guerrero, Segundo P -pg 184
Leon Guerrero, Silvestre B -pg 59
Leon Guerrero, Silvestre C -pg 60
Leon Guerrero, Soledad LG -pg 238
Leon Guerrero, Soledad S -pg 214
Leon Guerrero, Susana I -pg 187
Leon Guerrero, Teresa D -pg 510
Leon Guerrero, Tomasa C -pg 184
Leon Guerrero, Tomasa P -pg 184
Leon Guerrero, Trinidad P -pg 95
Leon Guerrero, Trinidad S -pg 35
Leon Guerrero, Vicenta C -pg 95
Leon Guerrero, Vicenta N -pg 531
Leon Guerrero, Vicenta P -pg 215
Leon Guerrero, Vicenta S -pg 35
Leon Guerrero, Vicenta S -pg 522
Leon Guerrero, Vicenta de 0 -pg 34
Leon Guerrero, Vicente A -pg 150
Leon Guerrero, Vicente A -pg 275
Leon Guerrero, Vicente B -pg 126
Leon Guerrero, Vicente C -pg 59
Leon Guerrero, Vicente C -pg 95
Leon Guerrero, Vicente C -pg 351
Leon Guerrero, Vicente D -pg 510
Leon Guerrero, Vicente F -pg 289
Leon Guerrero, Vicente LG -pg 31
Leon Guerrero, Vicente M -pg 238

Leon Guerrero, Vicente M -pg 275
Leon Guerrero, Vicente P -pg 136
Leon Guerrero, Vicente P -pg 148
Leon Guerrero, Vicente P -pg 301
Leon Guerrero, Vicente R -pg 486
Leon Guerrero, Vicente S -pg 35
Leon Guerrero, Vicente S -pg 82
Leon Guerrero, Vicente S -pg 531
Leon Guerrero, Victoria C -pg 153
Limtiaco, Adela A -pg 364
Limtiaco, Ana A -pg 364
Limtiaco, Ana SN -pg 363
Limtiaco, Ana T -pg 355
Limtiaco, Angela C -pg 358
Limtiaco, Antonia A -pg 364
Limtiaco, Antonio A -pg 360
Limtiaco, Antonio T -pg 364
Limtiaco, Carlina A -pg 360
Limtiaco, Dolores M -pg 416
Limtiaco, Francisco A -pg 360
Limtiaco, Joaquin A -pg 364
Limtiaco, Joaquina A -pg 360
Limtiaco, Jose A -pg 360
Limtiaco, Jose L -pg 358
Limtiaco, Josefina SN -pg 363
Limtiaco, Juan A -pg 364
Limtiaco, Maria A -pg 360
Limtiaco, Maria A -pg 364
Limtiaco, Matilde SN -pg 363
Limtiaco, Rosa A -pg 364
Limtiaco, Santiago A -pg 363
Limtiaco, Sebastian A -pg 364
Limtiaco, Vicente A -pg 364
Lizama, Ana C -pg 339
Lizama, Ana F -pg 310
Lizama, Ana Q -pg 355
Lizama, Ana S -pg 270
Lizama, Ana S -pg 278
Lizama, Augustin A -pg 453
Lizama, Benedicto F -pg 410
Lizama, Benito S -pg 537
Lizama, Candelaria C -pg 405
Lizama, Caridad -pg 203
Lizama, Carmelo L -pg 447
Lizama, Carmen A -pg 334
Lizama, Carmen S -pg 278
Lizama, Catalina P -pg 278
Lizama, Catalina S -pg 270
Lizama, Cecilia Q -pg 420
Lizama, Concepcion C -pg 338
Lizama, Conception S -pg 458
Lizama, Cristina C -pg 453

Lizama, Cristina S -pg 458
Lizama, Cristobal A -pg 334
Lizama, Daniel Q -pg 420
Lizama, Dolores C -pg 332
Lizama, Dolores Q -pg 420
Lizama, Dolores S -pg 270
Lizama, Dolores S -pg 278
Lizama, Emilia -pg 203
Lizama, Esiquiel -pg 405
Lizama, Felicita G -pg 339
Lizama, Felipe A -pg 334
Lizama, Felix F -pg 310
Lizama, Felix F -pg 412
Lizama, Felix -pg 207
Lizama, Feliza 0 -pg 86
Lizama, Filomena Q -pg 355
Lizama, Florencia C -pg 339
Lizama, Francisca A -pg 449
Lizama, Francisca Q -pg 419
Lizama, Francisco A -pg 207
Lizama, Francisco D -pg 412
Lizama, Francisco F -pg 310
Lizama, Francisco P -pg 278
Lizama, Ignacio C -pg 553
Lizama, Ignacio F -pg 310
Lizama, Ignacio L -pg 208
Lizama, Isabel C -pg 447
Lizama, Jesus G -pg 339
Lizama, Jesus Q -pg 376
Lizama, Joaquin A -pg 458
Lizama, Joaquin G -pg 339
Lizama, Joaquin Q -pg 376
Lizama, Joaquina C -pg 339
Lizama, Jose A -pg 207
Lizama, Jose B -pg 192
Lizama, Jose C -pg 339
Lizama, Jose D -pg 420
Lizama, Jose F -pg 310
Lizama, Jose G -pg 339
Lizama, Jose L -pg 86
Lizama, Jose L -pg 393
Lizama, Jose P -pg 270
Lizama, Jose Q -pg 355
Lizama, Jose Q -pg 376
Lizama, Jose S -pg 278
Lizama, Jose SN -pg 459
Lizama, Josefina B -pg 355
Lizama, Juan B -pg 339
Lizama, Juan C -pg 106
Lizama, Juan C -pg 339
Lizama, Juan C -pg 405
Lizama, Juan F -pg 310

Lizama, Juan G -pg 339
Lizama, Juan L -pg 86
Lizama, Juan P -pg 278
Lizama, Juan P -pg 310
Lizama, Juan S -pg 278
Lizama, Juan SN -pg 206
Lizama, Juliana P -pg 278
Lizama, Justo P -pg 278
Lizama, Luisa G -pg 106
Lizama, Magdalena -pg 334
Lizama, Manuel D -pg 412
Lizama, Manuel Q -pg 376
Lizama, Marcelino B -pg 334
Lizama, Maria A -pg 207
Lizama, Maria D -pg 412
Lizama, Maria F -pg 310
Lizama, Maria F -pg 310
Lizama, Maria M -pg 203
Lizama, Maria Q -pg 355
Lizama, Maria Q -pg 375
Lizama, Maria S -pg 270
Lizama, Maria S -pg 278
Lizama, Milagro Q -pg 355
Lizama, Nicolas S -pg 458
Lizama, Oliva G -pg 339
Lizama, Paula D -pg 537
Lizama, Pedro C -pg 405
Lizama, Pedro F -pg 553
Lizama, Raymundo L -pg 553
Lizama, Regina F -pg 553
Lizama, Remedios C -pg 339
Lizama, Rita N -pg 187
Lizama, Rita P -pg 270
Lizama, Rita S -pg 270
Lizama, Rodovico C -pg 355
Lizama, Rosa C -pg 339
Lizama, Rosa C -pg 405
Lizama, Rosa C -pg 453
Lizama, Rosa D -pg 412
Lizama, Rosa G -pg 339
Lizama, Rosa L -pg 86
Lizama, Rosa Q -pg 376
Lizama, Rosa S -pg 278
Lizama, Saturnina A -pg 334
Lizama, Simeon F -pg 310
Lizama, Soledad C -pg 405
Lizama, Soledad S -pg 393
Lizama, Vicenta F -pg 553
Lizama, Vicenta Q -pg 375
Lizama, Vicente C -pg 331
Lizama, Vicente D -pg 412
Lizama, Vicente L -pg 187

Lizama, Vicente L -pg 375
Lizama, Vicente Q -pg 355
Lizama, Vicente S -pg 270
Lizama, Vicente -pg 203
Lizama, Victorina T -pg 421
Logan, Arthur U -pg 311
Logan, David E -pg 311
Logan, Edith C -pg 311
Logan, John P -pg 311
Logan, William A -pg 311
Lorenzo, Cleotilde A -pg 211
Lorenzo, Estanislao SN -pg 211
Lorenzo, Gutierez A -pg 211
Lorenzo, Prudencia A -pg 211
Lorenzo, Rosa A -pg 211
Losongco, Ana D -pg 49
Losongco, Antonio D -pg 49
Losongco, Antonio M -pg 49
Losongco, Dolores D -pg 49
Losongco, Joaquin D -pg 49
Losongco, Luis D -pg 49
Losongco, Rosa D -pg 49
Lucero, Fidela C -pg 194
Lucero, Maria C -pg 194
Lujan, Ana C -pg 153
Lujan, Ana F -pg 206
Lujan, Ana G -pg 215
Lujan, Andres C -pg 506
Lujan, Antonio U -pg 543
Lujan, Anunsacion C -pg 506
Lujan, Ascemcion E -pg 489
Lujan, Atanasio -pg 254
Lujan, Carmen G -pg 215
Lujan, Carmen SN -pg 43
Lujan, Carmen U -pg 543
Lujan, Catalina C -pg 85
Lujan, Catalina F -pg 507
Lujan, Celidonia E -pg 489
Lujan, Concepcion C -pg 85
Lujan, Concepcion C jr -pg 85
Lujan, Crecencia E -pg 489
Lujan, Dolores C -pg 153
Lujan, Dolores F -pg 507
Lujan, Dolores G -pg 75
Lujan, Dolores T -pg 41
Lujan, Dometrio E -pg 486
Lujan, Dominga B -pg 58
Lujan, Engracia G -pg 75
Lujan, Enrique M -pg 80
Lujan, Filomena C -pg 238
Lujan, Florencia C -pg 85
Lujan, Francisco G -pg 75

Lujan, Francisco U -pg 543
Lujan, Guardalupe -pg 254
Lujan, Henry U -pg 543
Lujan, Ignacio C -pg 506
Lujan, Irene T -pg 41
Lujan, Isabel C -pg 85
Lujan, Isabel M -pg 80
Lujan, Jesus B -pg 58
Lujan, Jesus G -pg 238
Lujan, Jesus S -pg 75
Lujan, Jesus SN -pg 43
Lujan, Joaquin D -pg 238
Lujan, Joaquin E -pg 489
Lujan, Joaquin G -pg 75
Lujan, Joaquin M -pg 80
Lujan, Joaquin SN -pg 43
Lujan, Jose B -pg 506
Lujan, Jose G -pg 75
Lujan, Jose G -pg 85
Lujan, Jose R -pg 486
Lujan, Jose S -pg 87
Lujan, Jose SN -pg 58
Lujan, Juan E -pg 489
Lujan, Juan G -pg 75
Lujan, Juan G -pg 215
Lujan, Juan M -pg 80
Lujan, Juan R -pg 153
Lujan, Juan R -pg 486
Lujan, Juliana G -pg 252
Lujan, Lorenzo N -pg 58
Lujan, Luis T -pg 291
Lujan, Luisa G -pg 231
Lujan, Magdalena C -pg 238
Lujan, Manuel M -pg 80
Lujan, Manuel N -pg 58
Lujan, Manuel O -pg 543
Lujan, Manuel U -pg 543
Lujan, Manuela E -pg 489
Lujan, Marcela G -pg 69
Lujan, Margarita C -pg 239
Lujan, Maria C -pg 85
Lujan, Maria C -pg 239
Lujan, Maria C -pg 506
Lujan, Maria C -pg 506
Lujan, Maria F -pg 507
Lujan, Maria G -pg 75
Lujan, Maria G -pg 215
Lujan, Maria G Jr -pg 75
Lujan, Maria R -pg 486
Lujan, Maria S -pg 80
Lujan, Maria SN -pg 40
Lujan, Maria SN -pg 169

Lujan, Maria T -pg 291
Lujan, Mariano LG -pg 206
Lujan, Nicolasa C -pg 239
Lujan, Nieves SA -pg 87
Lujan, Nieves SN -pg 43
Lujan, Paz M -pg 80
Lujan, Pedro C -pg 238
Lujan, Pepeto C -pg 239
Lujan, Ramona C -pg 238
Lujan, Rita R -pg 486
Lujan, Rosa G -pg 75
Lujan, Rosa G -pg 252
Lujan, Rosalia L -pg 425
Lujan, Rosalia -pg 254
Lujan, Rufina C -pg 239
Lujan, Soledad C -pg 238
Lujan, Soledad G -pg 215
Lujan, Trinidad C -pg 239
Lujan, Vicenta T -pg 41
Lujan, Vicente N -pg 58
Lujan, Vicente R -pg 58
Lujan, Victor G -pg 215
Lujan, William U -pg 543
Maanao, Artemio I -pg 298
Maanao, Dolores I -pg 298
Maanao, Gregorio I -pg 298
Maanao, Jose A -pg 359
Maanao, Jose I -pg 298
Maanao, Manuel A -pg 359
Maanao, Maria A -pg 359
Maanao, Maria I -pg 298
Maanao, Martina A -pg 359
Maanao, Ramona M -pg 354
Maanao, Rosalia I -pg 298
Maanao, Vicente A -pg 359
Machignia, Carmen M -pg 383
Machignia, Jesus M -pg 383
Machignia, Jose M -pg 383
Machignia, Josefina M -pg 383
Machignia, Maria M -pg 383
Machignia, Rafael C -pg 383
Maekawa, Aurelia T -pg 417
Maekawa, Regina T -pg 424
Maekawa, Rosa T -pg 417
Mafnas, Ana A -pg 343
Mafnas, Ana B -pg 269
Mafnas, Ana C -pg 240
Mafnas, Ana F -pg 138
Mafnas, Andres F -pg 138
Mafnas, Antonia A -pg 343
Mafnas, Antonia C -pg 115
Mafnas, Antonia C -pg 240

Mafnas, Antonio A -pg 343
Mafnas, Antonio B -pg 269
Mafnas, Antonio C -pg 242
Mafnas, Antonio C -pg 280
Mafnas, Antonio L -pg 331
Mafnas, Benancio C -pg 232
Mafnas, Carmen C -pg 241
Mafnas, Carmen R -pg 269
Mafnas, Concepcion A -pg 343
Mafnas, Elena A -pg 99
Mafnas, Felipe M -pg 270
Mafnas, Filomena R -pg 269
Mafnas, Francisco C -pg 242
Mafnas, Francisco L -pg 331
Mafnas, Ignacia C -pg 269
Mafnas, Ignacia R -pg 269
Mafnas, Ignacia R -pg 280
Mafnas, Ignacio M -pg 269
Mafnas, Jesus F -pg 214
Mafnas, Jesus M -pg 269
Mafnas, Joaquin C -pg 240
Mafnas, Joaquin C -pg 241
Mafnas, Joaquin F -pg 99
Mafnas, Joaquin R -pg 242
Mafnas, Joaquin R -pg 269
Mafnas, Jose C -pg 269
Mafnas, Jose C -pg 281
Mafnas, Jose C -pg 331
Mafnas, Jose F -pg 138
Mafnas, Jose P -pg 231
Mafnas, Jose R -pg 269
Mafnas, Jose -pg 281
Mafnas, Jose -pg 281
Mafnas, Juan A -pg 351
Mafnas, Juan C -pg 242
Mafnas, Juan C -pg 281
Mafnas, Juan C -pg 544
Mafnas, Juan R -pg 240
Mafnas, Juana T -pg 232
Mafnas, Lucia R -pg 280
Mafnas, Luis C -pg 138
Mafnas, Magdalena M -pg 270
Mafnas, Magdalena P -pg 231
Mafnas, Manuel P -pg 231
Mafnas, Manuel R -pg 195
Mafnas, Maria B -pg 269
Mafnas, Maria C -pg 240
Mafnas, Maria C -pg 242
Mafnas, Maria C -pg 544
Mafnas, Maria C -pg 544
Mafnas, Maria P -pg 232
Mafnas, Maria P -pg 232

Mafnas, Maria R -pg 269
Mafnas, Placida C -pg 240
Mafnas, Regina L -pg 331
Mafnas, Remedios M -pg 269
Mafnas, Rosa C -pg 281
Mafnas, Rosa L -pg 331
Mafnas, Rosa R -pg 158
Mafnas, Rosa R -pg 280
Mafnas, Rosa T -pg 233
Mafnas, Rosario C -pg 242
Mafnas, Santiago C -pg 269
Mafnas, Serafin B -pg 544
Mafnas, Tomasa R -pg 280
Mafnas, Vicenta B -pg 544
Mafnas, Vicenta C -pg 241
Mafnas, Vicente C -pg 115
Mafnas, Vicente P -pg 269
Mafnas, Vicente R -pg 280
Mafnas, Vicente -pg 343
Maguadoc, Adela N -pg 498
Maguadoc, Antonia B -pg 486
Maguadoc, Luis N -pg 498
Maguadoc, Maria F -pg 498
Maguadoc, Moises N -pg 485
Magudoc, Elario N -pg 480
Magudoc, Victorila N -pg 480
Malijan, Jose A -pg 471
Malijan, Lourdes A -pg 471
Manalisay, Alexjandra B -pg 492
Manalisay, Antonia S -pg 163
Manalisay, Beatris C -pg 487
Manalisay, Carmen C -pg 487
Manalisay, Dolores N -pg 497
Manalisay, Felix C -pg 491
Manalisay, Francisco T -pg 497
Manalisay, Gregorio B -pg 492
Manalisay, Isidro C -pg 487
Manalisay, Jesus S -pg 163
Manalisay, Jose C -pg 474
Manalisay, Juan C -pg 487
Manalisay, Julian C -pg 497
Manalisay, Manuel LG -pg 163
Manalisay, Maria C -pg 474
Manalisay, Nieves C -pg 487
Manalisay, Soledad C -pg 474
Manalisay, Venancio C -pg 487
Manglona, Ana L -pg 335
Manglona, Ana M -pg 162
Manglona, Ana S -pg 335
Manglona, Antonio C -pg 334
Manglona, Carmen L -pg 335
Manglona, Dolores C -pg 334

Manglona, Felix C -pg 335
Manglona, Francisco C -pg 335
Manglona, Gregorio L -pg 335
Manglona, Isabel S -pg 335
Manglona, Jesus C -pg 530
Manglona, Juan S -pg 334
Manglona, Leoncia C -pg 530
Manglona, Luisa L -pg 335
Manglona, Maria L -pg 335
Manglona, Maria S -pg 335
Manglona, Paulino S -pg 529
Manglona, Raimundo L -pg 335
Manglona, Susana S -pg 335
Manglona, Vicente S -pg 195
Manglona, Vicente S -pg 335
Manglona, Virginia L -pg 335
Manibusan, Adela C -pg 389
Manibusan, Ana C -pg 33
Manibusan, Ana C -pg 224
Manibusan, Ana C -pg 224
Manibusan, Ana C -pg 389
Manibusan, Ana C jr -pg 389
Manibusan, Ana F -pg 384
Manibusan, Ana L -pg 191
Manibusan, Ana LG -pg 270
Manibusan, Ana M -pg 34
Manibusan, Ana N C -pg 14
Manibusan, Ana P -pg 97
Manibusan, Antonia D -pg 415
Manibusan, Antonia F -pg 290
Manibusan, Antonio F -pg 289
Manibusan, Antonio M -pg 118
Manibusan, Antonio M -pg 296
Manibusan, Antonio P -pg 97
Manibusan, Ascencion LG -pg 270
Manibusan, Benigno C -pg 118
Manibusan, Dolores B -pg 92
Manibusan, Dolores L -pg 191
Manibusan, Dolores M -pg 34
Manibusan, Dolores S -pg 181
Manibusan, Emeterio C -pg 224
Manibusan, Felicita M -pg 296
Manibusan, Felix M -pg 191
Manibusan, Felomena T -pg 52
Manibusan, Filomena A -pg 90
Manibusan, Francisco B -pg 33
Manibusan, Francisco C -pg 371
Manibusan, Francisco L -pg 339
Manibusan, Francisco Q -pg 171
Manibusan, Francisco Q -pg 350
Manibusan, Herminia C -pg 371
Manibusan, Ignacia A -pg 90

Manibusan, Ignacio C -pg 389
Manibusan, Isabel C -pg 33
Manibusan, Isabel M -pg 34
Manibusan, Jesus B -pg 118
Manibusan, Jesus L -pg 108
Manibusan, Jesus LG -pg 270
Manibusan, Jesus M -pg 34
Manibusan, Joaquin F -pg 270
Manibusan, Joaquin L -pg 191
Manibusan, Joaquin M -pg 34
Manibusan, Joaquin P -pg 44
Manibusan, Joaquin R -pg 181
Manibusan, Joaquin T -pg 118
Manibusan, Joaquina B -pg 118
Manibusan, Joe -pg 191
Manibusan, Jose A -pg 34
Manibusan, Jose A -pg 41
Manibusan, Jose C -pg 33
Manibusan, Jose C -pg 96
Manibusan, Jose C -pg 224
Manibusan, Jose D -pg 14
Manibusan, Jose G -pg 108
Manibusan, Jose LG -pg 270
Manibusan, Jose M -pg 118
Manibusan, Jose M -pg 296
Manibusan, Jose P -pg 15
Manibusan, Jose P -pg 90
Manibusan, Jose R -pg 289
Manibusan, Jose T -pg 92
Manibusan, Josefa A -pg 41
Manibusan, Josefina LG -pg 270
Manibusan, Juan A -pg 34
Manibusan, Juan B -pg 118
Manibusan, Juan D -pg 452
Manibusan, Juan M -pg 34
Manibusan, Juan M -pg 118
Manibusan, Juan M -pg 339
Manibusan, Juan P -pg 96
Manibusan, Juan P -pg 168
Manibusan, Juan P -pg 191
Manibusan, Juan R -pg 33
Manibusan, Juan SN -pg 384
Manibusan, Juana G -pg 289
Manibusan, Juana L -pg 108
Manibusan, Juana M -pg 96
Manibusan, Lorenzo A -pg 34
Manibusan, Lorenzo M -pg 34
Manibusan, Luis P -pg 97
Manibusan, Luisa LG -pg 270
Manibusan, Magdalena M -pg 296
Manibusan, Manuel G -pg 108
Manibusan, Manuel M -pg 118

Manibusan, Manuel M -pg 191
Manibusan, Manuel SN -pg 371
Manibusan, Maria 0 -pg 90
Manibusan, Maria C -pg 14
Manibusan, Maria C -pg 33
Manibusan, Maria C -pg 371
Manibusan, Maria C -pg 389
Manibusan, Maria L -pg 191
Manibusan, Maria L jr -pg 191
Manibusan, Maria LG -pg 270
Manibusan, Maria M -pg 34
Manibusan, Maria M -pg 119
Manibusan, Maria M -pg 293
Manibusan, Maria M -pg 296
Manibusan, Maria P -pg 96
Manibusan, Maria P -pg 168
Manibusan, Maria P -pg 168
Manibusan, Maria P jr -pg 97
Manibusan, Maria -pg 191
Manibusan, Mary D -pg 191
Manibusan, Matias P -pg 97
Manibusan, Miguel C -pg 371
Manibusan, Nicolas C -pg 296
Manibusan, Nicolasa P -pg 168
Manibusan, Nicolasa S -pg 94
Manibusan, Oscar C -pg 224
Manibusan, Oscarl L -pg 191
Manibusan, Pedro F -pg 290
Manibusan, Ramon P -pg 96
Manibusan, Regina A -pg 34
Manibusan, Regina L -pg 191
Manibusan, Rosa A -pg 41
Manibusan, Rosa P -pg 168
Manibusan, Rosa T -pg 52
Manibusan, Rosario L -pg 191
Manibusan, Rosario S -pg 182
Manibusan, Rufina C -pg 389
Manibusan, Soledad G -pg 339
Manibusan, Trinidad M -pg 34
Manibusan, Veronica L -pg 108
Manibusan, Vicenta R -pg 293
Manibusan, Vicente A -pg 34
Manibusan, Vicente C -pg 371
Manibusan, Vicente C -pg 389
Manibusan, Vicente P -pg 97
Manibusan, Vicente P -pg 168
Manibusan, Vicente T -pg 34
Mansapit, Clemente U -pg 491
Mansapit, Cristina N -pg 496
Mansapit, Cristobal M -pg 495
Mansapit, Dolores C -pg 442
Mansapit, Emelia N -pg 496

Mansapit, Felix C -pg 495
Mansapit, Filipe B -pg 496
Mansapit, Filomena M -pg 495
Mansapit, Gregorio C -pg 439
Mansapit, Inez U -pg 491
Mansapit, Jesus M -pg 495
Mansapit, Joaquin M -pg 495
Mansapit, Jose M -pg 495
Mansapit, Juan C -pg 442
Mansapit, Manuel N -pg 496
Mansapit, Maria C -pg 442
Mansapit, Nicolasa C -pg 491
Mansapit, Pedro N -pg 496
Mansapit, Rosalia C -pg 442
Mansapit, Santiago N -pg 496
Mansapit, Venancio N -pg 496
Mantanona, Ana M -pg 517
Mantanona, Ana P -pg 518
Mantanona, Andrea C -pg 524
Mantanona, Angelina P -pg 518
Mantanona, Antonia C -pg 517
Mantanona, Antonia P -pg 539
Mantanona, Asuncion M -pg 513
Mantanona, Atanasio I -pg 554
Mantanona, Baldomero C -pg 513
Mantanona, Benito M -pg 554
Mantanona, Carmen L -pg 512
Mantanona, Carmen P -pg 539
Mantanona, Casiano A -pg 511
Mantanona, Catlina M -pg 521
Mantanona, Ceclllo C -pg 513
Mantanona, Dolores L -pg 511
Mantanona, Dolores M -pg 517
Mantanona, Dometila M -pg 517
Mantanona, Felicitas P -pg 517
Mantanona, Francisco M -pg 524
Mantanona, Froilan M -pg 513
Mantanona, Genoveva M -pg 517
Mantanona, Ignacia M -pg 517
Mantanona, Ignacio L -pg 511
Mantanona, Isaac C -pg 523
Mantanona, Jesus C -pg 513
Mantanona, Joaquin C -pg 524
Mantanona, Joaquina M -pg 554
Mantanona, Jose C -pg 521
Mantanona, Jose L -pg 512
Mantanona, Jose M -pg 517
Mantanona, Jose M -pg 521
Mantanona, Jose M -pg 524
Mantanona, Jose N -pg 517
Mantanona, Jose C F -pg 517
Mantanona, Josefa M -pg 517

Mantanona, Juan M -pg 523
Mantanona, Juan P -pg 529
Mantanona, Juan P -pg 539
Mantanona, Luis C -pg 513
Mantanona, Manuel L -pg 512
Mantanona, Manuel P -pg 517
Mantanona, Manuel P -pg 539
Mantanona, Manuela M -pg 523
Mantanona, Margarita L -pg 511
Mantanona, Maria T -pg 554
Mantanona, Mariano SN -pg 514
Mantanona, Martina M -pg 524
Mantanona, Milagros P -pg 539
Mantanona, Natividad T -pg 554
Mantanona, Oliva C -pg 524
Mantanona, Pedro M -pg 517
Mantanona, Petronila M -pg 524
Mantanona, Ramon M -pg 517
Mantanona, Remedios P -pg 518
Mantanona, Rita C -pg 513
Mantanona, Rita L -pg 511
Mantanona, Rosa M -pg 521
Mantanona, Rosalia M -pg 524
Mantanona, Rumio P -pg 518
Mantanona, Silvestre M -pg 517
Mantanona, Silvestre N -pg 517
Mantanona, Silvina P -pg 518
Mantanona, Teresa P -pg 539
Marcelo, Julian -pg 208
Mariano, Amalia F -pg 328
Marlano, Ana F -pg 328
Mariano, Ana Q -pg 326
Mariano, Antonia F -pg 329
Mariano, Antonio Q -pg 326
Mariano, Candalaria F -pg 328
Mariano, Juan Q -pg 328
Mariano, Maria Q -pg 326
Mariano, Nicolas F -pg 329
Mariano, Soledad Q -pg 61
Mariano, Vicente F -pg 328
Mariyan, Luisa A -pg 465
Marron, Eduardo B -pg 171
Marron, Geronimo B -pg 171
Marron, Lorenso B -pg 171
Marron, Rita B -pg 171
Martinez, Ana C -pg 257
Martinez, Ana L -pg 237
Martinez, Ana M -pg 110
Martinez, Angel W -pg 61
Martinez, Angelina C -pg 257
Martinez, Antonia C -pg 309
Martinez, Antonia F -pg 142

Martinez, Antonia I -pg 237
Martinez, Antonio K -pg 61
Martinez, Antonio P -pg 257
Martinez, Caridad R -pg 529
Martinez, Carmen C -pg 123
Martinez, Carmen R -pg 529
Martinez, Carmen V -pg 123
Martinez, Clemente R -pg 529
Martinez, Concepcion M -pg 292
Martinez, Concepcion P -pg 257
Martinez, Concepcion R -pg 529
Martinez, Dolores LG -pg 245
Martinez, Dolores M -pg 110
Martinez, Dolores V -pg 120
Martinez, Eduvegis P -pg 257
Martinez, Eduvegis P -pg 257
Martinez, Emelia K -pg 61
Martinez, Enrique -pg 530
Martinez, Francisca M -pg 161
Martinez, Francisco G -pg 245
Martinez, Francisco P -pg 245
Martinez, Francisco V -pg 123
Martinez, Glen D -pg 189
Martinez, Grace J -pg 189
Martinez, Ignacia C -pg 123
Martinez, Ignacio C -pg 161
Martinez, Ignacio M -pg 292
Martinez, Isabel SA -pg 124
Martinez, Isabel V -pg 123
Martinez, Jesus 0 -pg 124
Martinez, Jesus M -pg 162
Martinez, Jesus P -pg 245
Martinez, Jesus R -pg 507
Martinez, Jesus SA -pg 124
Martinez, Joaquin C -pg 291
Martinez, Joaquin P -pg 245
Martinez, Joaquin R -pg 529
Martinez, Joaquina C -pg 123
Martinez, Jose B -pg 378
Martinez, Jose C -pg 110
Martinez, Jose C -pg 124
Martinez, Jose F -pg 142
Martinez, Jose P -pg 257
Martinez, Jose R -pg 529
Martinez, Jose V -pg 120
Martinez, Josefa R -pg 529
Martinez, Juan C -pg 256
Martinez, Juan L -pg 237
Martinez, Juan P -pg 245
Martinez, Juan P -pg 257
Martinez, Juan V -pg 124
Martinez, Juana P -pg 245

Martinez, Julia M -pg 309
Martinez, Lucy R -pg 189
Martinez, Manuel C -pg 257
Martinez, Manuel M -pg 92
Martinez, Manuel M -pg 292
Martinez, Manuel P -pg 245
Martinez, Manuel R -pg 530
Martinez, Manuela J -pg 245
Martinez, Manuela R -pg 92
Martinez, Marcus C -pg 124
Martinez, Maria F -pg 142
Martinez, Maria P -pg 245
Martinez, Maria R -pg 509
Martinez, Maria T -pg 237
Martinez, Maria V -pg 123
Martinez, Mariano C -pg 123
Martinez, Mary R -pg 189
Martinez, Nieves P -pg 257
Martinez, Oliva M -pg 110
Martinez, Pedro M -pg 237
Martinez, Pedro P -pg 237
Martinez, Pilar M -pg 292
Martinez, Ramon C -pg 142
Martinez, Remedios C -pg 257
Martinez, Rita C -pg 189
Martinez, Rita M -pg 309
Martinez, Rita P -pg 256
Martinez, Rosa M -pg 161
Martinez, Rosa P -pg 245
Martinez, Rosa V -pg 123
Martinez, Rosalia M -pg 162
Martinez, Rosario M -pg 292
Martinez, Soledad M -pg 291
Martinez, Susana B -pg 378
Martinez, Teodora V -pg 120
Martinez, Vicente B -pg 189
Martinez, Vicente C -pg 123
Martinez, Vicente M -pg 110
Martinez, Vicente P -pg 245
Martinez, Vicente V -pg 123
Mata, Ana C -pg 498
Mata, Blas C -pg 498
Mata, Carmen C -pg 498
Mata, Ignacio C -pg 498
Mata, Jose C -pg 498
Mata, Maria C -pg 498
Mata, Martina C -pg 498
Mata, Milagro C -pg 498
Mata, Nieves C -pg 498
Mata, Vicente C -pg 498
Matanane, Ana B -pg 159
Matanane, Ana C -pg 85

Matanane, Ana Q -pg 167
Matanane, Catalina Q -pg 167
Matanane, Dolores B -pg 159
Matanane, Dolores B jr -pg 159
Matanane, Engracia B -pg 159
Matanane, Ignacio M -pg 249
Matanane, Jesus C -pg 85
Matanane, Jose C -pg 85
Matanane, Jose -pg 232
Matanane, Juan C -pg 85
Matanane, Juan M -pg 85
Matanane, Manuel M -pg 167
Matanane, Maria A -pg 232
Matanane, Maria Q -pg 167
Matanane, Vicente B -pg 159
Matanane, Victorina F -pg 249
Mateo, Antonio C -pg 17
Mateo, Jose C -pg 17
Mateo, Pedro C -pg 17
Mateo, Tomasa C -pg 17
Materne, Ana P -pg 200
Materne, Andres D -pg 542
Materne, Antonio M -pg 294
Materne, Antonio -pg 305
Materne, Antonio -pg 313
Materne, Dolores D -pg 142
Materne, Dolores M -pg 305
Materne, Dolores -pg 305
Materne, Domingo C -pg 208
Materne, Eduvegis M -pg 305
Materne, Francisca M -pg 96
Materne, Francisca M -pg 208
Materne, Francisco D -pg 141
Materne, Joaquin P -pg 200
Materne, Jose S -pg 538
Materne, Juan D -pg 542
Materne, Juan -pg 208
Materne, Manuel D -pg 141
Materne, Maria P -pg 200
Materne, Mariana P -pg 200
Materne, Mariano M -pg 200
Materne, Mercedes C -pg 208
Materne, Nieves D -pg 141
Materne, Pedro D -pg 141
Materne, Potenciana C -pg 208
Materne, Teresa C -pg 208
Materne, Ynes S -pg 538
Megofna, Carmen C -pg 371
Megofna, Engracia C -pg 371
Megofna, Maria C -pg 384
Megofna, Rita C -pg 371
Mendiola, Ana A -pg 283

Mendiola, Ana A -pg 423
Mendiola, Ana C -pg 246
Mendiola, Ana C -pg 284
Mendiola, Ana G -pg 256
Mendiola, Ana M -pg 196
Mendiola, Ana M -pg 309
Mendiola, Ana P -pg 224
Mendiola, Ana Q -pg 192
Mendiola, Ana Q -pg 417
Mendiola, Ana S -pg 62
Mendiola, Ana S -pg 350
Mendiola, Ana S -pg 413
Mendiola, Andres R -pg 216
Mendiola, Antonia B -pg 18
Mendiola, Antonia P -pg 151
Mendiola, Antonia P -pg 233
Mendiola, Antonina M -pg 196
Mendiola, Antonio C -pg 314
Mendiola, Antonio P -pg 55
Mendiola, Antonio Q -pg 192
Mendiola, Antonio R -pg 417
Mendiola, Ascencion M -pg 319
Mendiola, Asuncion P -pg 151
Mendiola, Auria G -pg 439
Mendiola, Barbara S -pg 440
Mendiola, Beatris S -pg 414
Mendiola, Benigno C -pg 24
Mendiola, Candelaria B -pg 18
Mendiola, Candelaria P -pg 203
Mendiola, Caridad B -pg 402
Mendiola, Carlos C -pg 73
Mendiola, Carmen C -pg 285
Mendiola, Carmen C -pg 317
Mendiola, Carmen S -pg 188
Mendiola, Carmen S -pg 458
Mendiola, Catalino Q -pg 417
Mendiola, Celia P -pg 203
Mendiola, Concepcion Q -pg 192
Mendiola, Concepcion S -pg 133
Mendiola, Concepcion S -pg 246
Mendiola, Concepcion U -pg 403
Mendiola, Consolacion B -pg 55
Mendiola, Consolacion F -pg 24
Mendiola, Consolacion G -pg 314
Mendiola, Consolacion H -pg 256
Mendiola, Consolacion S -pg 413
Mendiola, Cristina U -pg 403
Mendiola, Demetrio P -pg 203
Mendiola, Dolores P -pg 151
Mendiola, Dolores P -pg 233
Mendiola, Dolores Q -pg 417
Mendiola, Dolores S -pg 414

Mendiola, Dolores S -pg 458
Mendiola, Dolores -pg 229
Mendiola, Engracia M -pg 319
Mendiola, Enrique C -pg 285
Mendiola, Filomena C -pg 125
Mendiola, Filomena U -pg 55
Mendiola, Francisca C -pg 284
Mendiola, Francisca M -pg 319
Mendiola, Francisca M -pg 319
Mendiola, Francisco G -pg 108
Mendiola, Francisco G -pg 314
Mendiola, Francisco M -pg 125
Mendiola, Francisco P -pg 151
Mendiola, Francisco U -pg 403
Mendiola, Francisco U jr -pg 403
Mendiola, Geronimo C -pg 423
Mendiola, Gonzalo A -pg 283
Mendiola, Graviel C -pg 423
Mendiola, Graviel S -pg 439
Mendiola, Ignacio B -pg 208
Mendiola, Ignacio G -pg 439
Mendiola, Ignacio P -pg 278
Mendiola, Ignacio Q -pg 414
Mendiola, Ignacio Q -pg 418
Mendiola, Ignacio R -pg 216
Mendiola, Ignacio R -pg 458
Mendiola, Ignacio S -pg 133
Mendiola, Ignacio S -pg 414
Mendiola, Isabel G -pg 314
Mendiola, Isabel S -pg 188
Mendiola, Jesus A -pg 283
Mendiola, Jesus B -pg 149
Mendiola, Jesus C -pg 73
Mendiola, Jesus C -pg 285
Mendiola, Jesus G -pg 417
Mendiola, Jesus P -pg 96
Mendiola, Jesus Q -pg 192
Mendiola, Jesus S -pg 62
Mendiola, Jesusa B -pg 402
Mendiola, Joaquin B -pg 55
Mendiola, Joaquin F -pg 351
Mendiola, Joaquin G -pg 256
Mendiola, Joaquin L -pg 188
Mendiola, Joaquin P -pg 224
Mendiola, Joaquina C -pg 423
Mendiola, Joaquina G -pg 439
Mendiola, Joaquina M -pg 65
Mendiola, Joaquina U -pg 56
Mendiola, Jose A -pg 283
Mendiola, Jose B -pg 65
Mendiola, Jose B -pg 73
Mendiola, Jose B -pg 149

Mendiola, Jose C -pg 62
Mendiola, Jose C -pg 224
Mendiola, Jose C -pg 284
Mendiola, Jose C -pg 319
Mendiola, Jose F -pg 24
Mendiola, Jose G -pg 125
Mendiola, Jose G -pg 133
Mendiola, Jose G -pg 314
Mendiola, Jose G -pg 417
Mendiola, Jose L -pg 188
Mendiola, Jose M -pg 66
Mendiola, Jose M -pg 319
Mendiola, Jose P -pg 203
Mendiola, Jose P -pg 224
Mendiola, Jose Q -pg 203
Mendiola, Jose S -pg 188
Mendiola, Josefa C -pg 246
Mendiola, Josefa S -pg 62
Mendiola, Josefa U -pg 403
Mendiola, Josefina M -pg 319
Mendiola, Juan A -pg 283
Mendiola, Juan B -pg 149
Mendiola, Juan B -pg 209
Mendiola, Juan C -pg 216
Mendiola, Juan C -pg 284
Mendiola, Juan C -pg 319
Mendiola, Juan C -pg 336
Mendiola, Juan C -pg 423
Mendiola, Juan H -pg 256
Mendiola, Juan L -pg 283
Mendiola, Juan M -pg 319
Mendiola, Juan P -pg 151
Mendiola, Juan P -pg 224
Mendiola, Juan Q -pg 417
Mendiola, Juan S -pg 133
Mendiola, Juan S -pg 350
Mendiola, Juan S -pg 440
Mendiola, Juan U -pg 403
Mendiola, Juan -pg 319
Mendiola, Juliana G -pg 125
Mendiola, Juliana P -pg 278
Mendiola, Luis A -pg 61
Mendiola, Luis S -pg 413
Mendiola, Luisa G -pg 314
Mendiola, Magdalena H -pg 256
Mendiola, Manuel B -pg 150
Mendiola, Manuel P -pg 224
Mendiola, Manuel Q -pg 417
Mendiola, Manuel S -pg 62
Mendiola, Manuel S -pg 188
Mendiola, Manuel S -pg 458
Mendiola, Margarita M -pg 196

Mendiola, Margarita M -pg 320
Mendiola, Maria A -pg 283
Mendiola, Maria B -pg 18
Mendiola, Maria B -pg 149
Mendiola, Maria C -pg 284
Mendiola, Maria C -pg 319
Mendiola, Maria C -pg 377
Mendiola, Maria F -pg 24
Mendiola, Maria G -pg 256
Mendiola, Maria G -pg 439
Mendiola, Maria G -pg 439
Mendiola, Maria M -pg 196
Mendiola, Maria P -pg 55
Mendiola, Maria P -pg 96
Mendiola, Maria P -pg 151
Mendiola, Maria P -pg 224
Mendiola, Maria P -pg 411
Mendiola, Maria Q -pg 414
Mendiola, Maria Q -pg 418
Mendiola, Maria R -pg 216
Mendiola, Maria R -pg 402
Mendiola, Maria S -pg 69
Mendiola, Maria S -pg 133
Mendiola, Maria T -pg 299
Mendiola, Maria U -pg 403
Mendiola, Maria -pg 184
Mendiola, Mariano C -pg 284
Mendiola, Mariano C -pg 285
Mendiola, Mariano R -pg 403
Mendiola, Martina C -pg 246
Mendiola, Martina S -pg 413
Mendiola, Miguela V -pg 233
Mendiola, Nicolas C -pg 413
Mendiola, Nicolasa B -pg 402
Mendiola, Nicolasa P -pg 152
Mendiola, Nieves R -pg 110
Mendiola, Paula L -pg 187
Mendiola, Pedro B -pg 296
Mendiola, Pedro D -pg 69
Mendiola, Pedro M -pg 196
Mendiola, Pedro P -pg 55
Mendiola, Pedro S -pg 62
Mendiola, Preciosa G -pg 417
Mendiola, Purification Q -pg 192
Mendiola, Regina S -pg 440
Mendiola, Regino Q -pg 233
Mendiola, Rita C -pg 247
Mendiola, Rita C -pg 318
Mendiola, Rita Q -pg 188
Mendiola, Rosa C -pg 73
Mendiola, Rosa C -pg 244
Mendiola, Rosa C -pg 247

Mendiola, Rosa C -pg 318
Mendiola, Rosa F -pg 24
Mendiola, Rosa M -pg 306
Mendiola, Rosa M -pg 319
Mendiola, Rosa M -pg 319
Mendiola, Rosa Q -pg 417
Mendiola, Rosario S -pg 133
Mendiola, Rufina M -pg 66
Mendiola, Rufina P -pg 224
Mendiola, Satrunino Q -pg 417
Mendiola, Soledad P -pg 55
Mendiola, Soledad S -pg 62
Mendiola, Teresa C -pg 224
Mendiola, Tomas S -pg 440
Mendiola, Tomas U -pg 403
Mendiola, Ursula A -pg 283
Mendiola, Venancio P -pg 149
Mendiola, Veronica C -pg 285
Mendiola, Vicenta B -pg 149
Mendiola, Vicenta C -pg 73
Mendiola, Vicente A -pg 440
Mendiola, Vicente B -pg 112
Mendiola, Vicente F -pg 24
Mendiola, Vicente G -pg 125
Mendiola, Vicente G -pg 256
Mendiola, Vicente L -pg 187
Mendiola, Vicente M -pg 125
Mendiola, Vicente Q -pg 414
Mendiola, Vicente S -pg 62
Mendosa, Ana M -pg 84
Meno, Alexandra C -pg 507
Meno, Amparo B -pg 154
Meno, Ana B -pg 154
Meno, Ana C -pg 163
Meno, Ana C -pg 504
Meno, Ana C -pg 524
Meno, Ana L -pg 507
Meno, Ana LG -pg 520
Meno, Ana M -pg 520
Meno, Ana N -pg 378
Meno, Ana T -pg 521
Meno, Angel C -pg 484
Meno, Antonio C -pg 485
Meno, Antonio M -pg 514
Meno, Antonio N -pg 504
Meno, Antonio P -pg 93
Meno, Asuncion P -pg 93
Meno, Baltazara -pg 336
Meno, Candelaria C -pg 478
Meno, Candelaria D -pg 504
Meno, Candelaria LG -pg 520
Meno, Carmen C -pg 163

Meno, Carmen C -pg 479
Meno, Carmen C -pg 484
Meno, Concepcion L -pg 507
Meno, Consolacion N -pg 524
Meno, Cornelia C -pg 524
Meno, Dolores C -pg 478
Meno, Dolores C -pg 484
Meno, Dolores C -pg 504
Meno, Dolores LG -pg 520
Meno, Dolores M -pg 521
Meno, Dolores P -pg 93
Meno, Dolores Q -pg 518
Meno, Dometrio Q -pg 488
Meno, Dominga SN -pg 521
Meno, Eduvijes LG -pg 520
Meno, Encarnacion M -pg 525
Meno, Engracia T -pg 514
Meno, Fabiana S -pg 336
Meno, Felipe N -pg 503
Meno, Felipe Q -pg 518
Meno, Felix P -pg 93
Meno, Feliza T -pg 521
Meno, Fidela C -pg 518
Meno, Filipe C -pg 484
Meno, Florentino S -pg 434
Meno, Fraim C -pg 514
Meno, Francisca C -pg 485
Meno, Francisca N -pg 527
Meno, Francisco D -pg 507
Meno, Francisco P -pg 93
Meno, Genoveva N -pg 504
Meno, Geronimo SN -pg 521
Meno, Gertrudes M -pg 514
Meno, Ignacia C -pg 484
Meno, Ignacio C -pg 479
Meno, Isabel C -pg 478
Meno, Isabel C -pg 518
Meno, Isabel C -pg 550
Meno, Isidro M -pg 163
Meno, Javiel D -pg 527
Meno, Jesus C -pg 485
Meno, Jesus C -pg 524
Meno, Jesus L -pg 507
Meno, Jesus LG -pg 520
Meno, Jesus N -pg 524
Meno, Jesus P -pg 93
Meno, Jesus P -pg 93
Meno, Joaquin B -pg 154
Meno, Joaquin C -pg 478
Meno, Joaquin C -pg 529
Meno, Joaquin L -pg 507
Meno, Joaquin LG -pg 520

Meno, Joaquina C -pg 484
Meno, Joaquina N -pg 527
Meno, Jose B -pg 154
Meno, Jose C -pg 478
Meno, Jose C -pg 479
Meno, Jose C -pg 484
Meno, Jose C -pg 485
Meno, Jose C -pg 514
Meno, Jose C -pg 527
Meno, Jose D -pg 504
Meno, Jose J -pg 550
Meno, Jose L -pg 507
Meno, Jose LG -pg 520
Meno, Jose M -pg 525
Meno, Jose M -pg 539
Meno, Jose N -pg 524
Meno, Jose P -pg 93
Meno, Jose Q -pg 488
Meno, Jose Q -pg 518
Meno, Jose T -pg 514
Meno, Josefa B -pg 154
Meno, Josefa Q -pg 518
Meno, Juan C -pg 479
Meno, Juan LG -pg 520
Meno, Juan M -pg 93
Meno, Juan P -pg 514
Meno, Juan T -pg 521
Meno, Justa P -pg 93
Meno, Justina LG -pg 520
Meno, Luis N -pg 528
Meno, Manuel C -pg 507
Meno, Margarita T -pg 529
Meno, Maria B -pg 154
Meno, Maria C -pg 479
Meno, Maria C -pg 484
Meno, Maria C -pg 484
Meno, Maria C -pg 518
Meno, Maria C -pg 524
Meno, Maria G -pg 384
Meno, Maria L -pg 507
Meno, Maria L Grro -pg 405
Meno, Maria M -pg 521
Meno, Maria N -pg 524
Meno, Maria P -pg 93
Meno, Maria P -pg 507
Meno, Maria P -pg 507
Meno, Maria Q -pg 475
Meno, Maria Q -pg 518
Meno, Maria S -pg 336
Meno, Maria T -pg 521
Meno, Nieves M -pg 549
Meno, Patricio C -pg 479

Meno, Patrona C -pg 514
Meno, Pedro C -pg 485
Meno, Pedro C -pg 525
Meno, Petra T -pg 521
Meno, Ramon LG -pg 520
Meno, Ramon M -pg 514
Meno, Ramon M -pg 525
Meno, Ramon T -pg 529
Meno, Regina N -pg 524
Meno, Regino C -pg 524
Meno, Rita C -pg 550
Meno, Rosa B -pg 154
Meno, Rosa C -pg 478
Meno, Rosa C -pg 479
Meno, Rosa N -pg 504
Meno, Rosa T -pg 529
Meno, Rosario N -pg 527
Meno, Sabina C -pg 485
Meno, Sebastian N -pg 520
Meno, Sibera M -pg 475
Meno, Soledad D -pg 527
Meno, Soledad P -pg 503
Meno, Tedora C -pg 484
Meno, Teodora S -pg 336
Meno, Teresa LG -pg 520
Meno, Ursula N -pg 527
Meno, Vicenta C -pg 478
Meno, Vicenta P -pg 93
Meno, Vicente C -pg 479
Meno, Vicente C -pg 485
Meno, Vicente C -pg 504
Meno, Vicente C -pg 513
Meno, Vicente C -pg 524
Meno, Vicente C -pg 550
Meno, Vicente M -pg 93
Meno, Vicente M -pg 524
Meno, Vicente T -pg 520
Meno, Vicitacion C -pg 484
Meno, Virginia P -pg 507
Meno, Visitacion C -pg 384
Merfalen, Antonio M -pg 307
Merfalen, Concepcion M -pg 307
Merfalen, Joaquin P -pg 307
Merfalen, Jose M -pg 307
Merfalen, Juan P -pg 196
Merfalen, Lourdes M -pg 307
Merfalen, Maria M -pg 307
Merfalen, Rosa Q -pg 212
Mesa, Adriano C -pg 337
Mesa, Ana C -pg 457
Mesa, Ana dela R -pg 239
Mesa, Ana F -pg 252

Mesa, Ana F -pg 295
Mesa, Ana L -pg 287
Mesa, Ana M -pg 186
Mesa, Ana P -pg 216
Mesa, Ana P -pg 287
Mesa, Ana P -pg 451
Mesa, Ana T -pg 197
Mesa, Ana -pg 235
Mesa, Antonia C -pg 456
Mesa, Antonia M -pg 264
Mesa, Antonia P -pg 179
Mesa, Antonio A -pg 71
Mesa, Antonio M -pg 292
Mesa, Antonio T -pg 293
Mesa, Antonio -pg 235
Mesa, Ascencion R -pg 304
Mesa, Bartolome -pg 372
Mesa, Benigna R -pg 304
Mesa, Carmen C -pg 457
Mesa, Carmen F -pg 252
Mesa, Carmen M -pg 186
Mesa, Concepcion F -pg 252
Mesa, Concepcion P -pg 288
Mesa, Consolacion T -pg 387
Mesa, Dolores A -pg 71
Mesa, Dolores A -pg 240
Mesa, Dolores C -pg 173
Mesa, Dolores C -pg 231
Mesa, Dolores C -pg 457
Mesa, Dolores R -pg 303
Mesa, Dolores R -pg 387
Mesa, Dolores SN -pg 446
Mesa, Eduardo C -pg 300
Mesa, Engracia C -pg 372
Mesa, Enrique A -pg 240
Mesa, Enrique P -pg 451
Mesa, Felisa A -pg 70
Mesa, Felix C -pg 439
Mesa, Felix P -pg 288
Mesa, Francisco A -pg 240
Mesa, Francisco C -pg 298
Mesa, Francisco G -pg 299
Mesa, Francisco P -pg 288
Mesa, Francisco P -pg 451
Mesa, Geronimo R -pg 252
Mesa, Gloria F -pg 252
Mesa, Gonzalo P -pg 178
Mesa, Hester M -pg 176
Mesa, Ignacio A -pg 71
Mesa, Ignacio C -pg 457
Mesa, Ignacio M -pg 197
Mesa, Jesus C -pg 173

Mesa, Jesus C -pg 216
Mesa, Jesus G -pg 303
Mesa, Joaquin 0 -pg 176
Mesa, Joaquin C -pg 173
Mesa, Joaquin P -pg 288
Mesa, Joaquin T -pg 197
Mesa, Jose C -pg 173
Mesa, Jose C jr -pg 173
Mesa, Jose dela R -pg 239
Mesa, Jose F -pg 252
Mesa, Jose M -pg 176
Mesa, Jose M -pg 186
Mesa, Jose M -pg 264
Mesa, Jose M -pg 451
Mesa, Jose P -pg 288
Mesa, Jose P -pg 452
Mesa, Jose T -pg 293
Mesa, Jose T -pg 387
Mesa, Jose -pg 263
Mesa, Josefa L -pg 287
Mesa, Josefina R -pg 304
Mesa, Juan A -pg 71
Mesa, Juan C -pg 298
Mesa, Juan C -pg 456
Mesa, Juan D -pg 90
Mesa, Juan F -pg 252
Mesa, Juan G -pg 298
Mesa, Juan LG -pg 445
Mesa, Juan M -pg 439
Mesa, Juan T -pg 391
Mesa, Juan -pg 240
Mesa, Juana C -pg 216
Mesa, Juana G -pg 303
Mesa, Luis C -pg 173
Mesa, Manuel A -pg 71
Mesa, Manuel P -pg 288
Mesa, Manuela M -pg 173
Mesa, Maria C -pg 298
Mesa, Maria dela R -pg 239
Mesa, Maria F -pg 252
Mesa, Maria G -pg 303
Mesa, Maria M -pg 176
Mesa, Maria P -pg 216
Mesa, Maria P -pg 288
Mesa, Maria P -pg 452
Mesa, Maria T -pg 292
Mesa, Mariano C -pg 457
Mesa, Matilde -pg 303
Mesa, Nicolasa C -pg 372
Mesa, Nicolasa dela R -pg 239
Mesa, Nicolasa -pg 295
Mesa, Pedro -pg 216

Mesa, Remedios P -pg 216
Mesa, Rita C -pg 439
Mesa, Rita M -pg 176
Mesa, Rita P -pg 216
Mesa, Rosa 0 -pg 90
Mesa, Rosa C -pg 457
Mesa, Rosa F -pg 252
Mesa, Rosa T -pg 197
Mesa, Rosalia dela R -pg 239
Mesa, Rosalia P -pg 452
Mesa, Rosario C -pg 299
Mesa, Rufina S -pg 235
Mesa, Simmade dela R -pg 239
Mesa, Soledad F -pg 252
Mesa, Susana B -pg 337
Mesa, Tomas R -pg 304
Mesa, Tomas S -pg 173
Mesa, Tomasa C -pg 439
Mesa, Tomasa M -pg 176
Mesa, Trinidad -pg 235
Mesa, Vicenta F -pg 252
Mesa, Vicente A -pg 71
Mesa, Vicente C -pg 70
Mesa, Vicente C -pg 300
Mesa, Vicente de la R -pg 303
Mesa, Vicente F -pg 252
Mesa, Vicente M -pg 264
Mesa, Vicente M -pg 456
Mesa, Vicente S -pg 231
Mesa, Vicente T -pg 387
Mesa, Vicente -pg 287
Meza, Caridad M -pg 513
Meza, Dolores R -pg 50
Meza, Francisco M -pg 513
Meza, Jose M -pg 50
Meza, Jose P -pg 513
Meza, Jose S -pg 40
Meza, Juliana A -pg 506
Meza, Juliana B -pg 40
Meza, Manuel R -pg 50
Meza, Maria M -pg 50
Meza, Maria R -pg 50
Meza, Vicente B -pg 40
Meza, Vicente S -pg 50
Miasaki, Tomagoro -pg 311
Migofna, Ana A -pg 142
Migofna, Anatasio 0 -pg 142
Migofna, Antonio A -pg 41
Migofna, Antonio G -pg 163
Migofna, Carmen A -pg 41
Migofna, Dolores G -pg 163
Migofna, Felicidad A -pg 142

Migofna, Ignacio A -pg 143
Migofna, Jose A -pg 143
Migofna, Juan A -pg 143
Migofna, Pedro A -pg 143
Migofna, Vicente A -pg 143
Millenchamp, Enrique T -pg 189
Millenchamp, Henry T -pg 84
Millenchamp, Maria B -pg 189
Miner, Ana U -pg 137
Miner, Baldomero P -pg 137
Miner, Benectde A -pg 60
Miner, Clara A -pg 60
Miner, Joaquina A -pg 60
Miner, Jose P -pg 60
Miner, Jose U -pg 137
Miner, Juan A -pg 60
Mizushima, Umikidi -pg 351
Montales, Eduardo R -pg 348
Morcilla, Jesus D -pg 133
Morcilla, Vicenta D -pg 133
Muna, Ana F -pg 18
Muna, Ana G -pg 286
Muna, Ana G -pg 332
Muna, Ana P -pg 449
Muna, Ana S -pg 430
Muna, Antonio C -pg 332
Muna, Asemcion S -pg 431
Muna, Carmen P -pg 449
Muna, Clarita C -pg 393
Muna, Dolores F -pg 18
Muna, Felipe G -pg 332
Muna, Felisitas D -pg 169
Muna, Francisco D -pg 169
Muna, Francisco F -pg 18
Muna, Gabina A -pg 135
Muna, Gregorio D -pg 169
Muna, Gregorio D -pg 430
Muna, Ignacio D -pg 169
Muna, Isabel S -pg 431
Muna, Joaquin C -pg 393
Muna, Jose C -pg 332
Muna, Jose C -pg 393
Muna, Jose D -pg 169
Muna, Jose P -pg 169
Muna, Josefa D -pg 169
Muna, Josefa S -pg 430
Muna, Juan D -pg 17
Muna, Juan F -pg 18
Muna, Juan -pg 281
Muna, Juana -pg 309
Muna, Magdalena C -pg 393
Muna, Manuel C -pg 197

Muna, Manuel C -pg 393
Muna, Maria C -pg 393
Muna, Maria M -pg 49
Muna, Maria S -pg 431
Muna, Mariano D -pg 449
Muna, Mother C -pg 332
Muna, Pedro S -pg 430
Muna, Roque S -pg 431
Muna, Rosa F -pg 17
Muna, Rufina C -pg 393
Muna, Saturnina G -pg 332
Muna, Sibera S -pg 431
Muna, Tomasa G -pg 332
Muna, Vicenta C -pg 332
Muna, Vicenta -pg 281
Muna, Vicente F -pg 17
Munoz, Adela F -pg 312
Munoz, Alejandro Sta R -pg 359
Munoz, Ana B -pg 344
Munoz, Antonio I -pg 344
Munoz, Dolores S -pg 408
Munoz, Enrique C -pg 315
Munoz, Francisco C -pg 408
Munoz, Isabel I -pg 345
Munoz, Isabel S -pg 408
Munoz, Jesus F -pg 258
Munoz, Jesus I -pg 344
Munoz, Jesusa F -pg 312
Munoz, Joaquin I -pg 258
Munoz, Joaquina I -pg 344
Munoz, Jose C -pg 344
Munoz, Jose C -pg 344
Munoz, Jose F -pg 312
Munoz, Jose I -pg 344
Munoz, Josefa F -pg 258
Munoz, Juan C -pg 312
Munoz, Juan I -pg 345
Munoz, Juan S -pg 408
Munoz, Manuel C -pg 315
Munoz, Manuela C -pg 359
Munoz, Ramon I -pg 345
Munoz, Regina F -pg 312
Munoz, Rosa I -pg 344
Munoz, Rosa I -pg 344
Munoz, Vicente F -pg 312
Myers, Guadalupe S -pg 407
Myers, Robert S -pg 407
Namauleg, Ana P -pg 360
Namauleg, Catalina P -pg 360
Namauleg, Eufracia Q -pg 207
Namauleg, Jesus E -pg 64
Namauleg, Joaquin N -pg 64

Namauleg, Joaquin N -pg 360
Namauleg, Jose E -pg 64
Namauleg, Lorenza P -pg 360
Namauleg, Magdalena P -pg 360
Namauleg, Maria E -pg 64
Namauleg, Maria P -pg 360
Namauleg, Maria T -pg 207
Namauleg, Rosa E -pg 64
Namauleg, Ursia P -pg 360
Nangauta, Conception T -pg 492
Nangauta, Emiliana N -pg 476
Nangauta, Gertrudes T -pg 492
Nangauta, Isabel N -pg 476
Nangauta, Joaquin T -pg 492
Nangauta, Josefina T -pg 492
Nangauta, Juan T -pg 492
Nangauta, Julian C -pg 492
Nangauta, Lucia C -pg 488
Nangauta, Luis C -pg 488
Nangauta, Ramon T -pg 492
Nangauta, Soledad C -pg 488
Nangauta, Vicente C -pg 488
Nangauta, Vicente T -pg 492
Nanguata, Antonia C -pg 488
Nanguata, Candalarea C -pg 487
Nanguata, Isabel Q -pg 487
Nanguata, Jose C -pg 488
Nanguata, Juan B -pg 487
Nanguata, Maria C -pg 488
Nanguata, Mariano C -pg 488
Nanguata, Patricio C -pg 487
Nankawa, Catalina D -pg 178
Nankawa, H 0 -pg 178
Nankawa, Pedro D -pg 178
Nankawa, Rufina D -pg 178
Naputi, Albert M -pg 517
Naputi, Ana B -pg 170
Naputi, Ana C -pg 506
Naputi, Ana D -pg 505
Naputi, Ana F -pg 508
Naputi, Ana L -pg 506
Naputi, Ana SN -pg 523
Naputi, Antonia D -pg 505
Naputi, Antonia T -pg 511
Naputi, Antonio C -pg 522
Naputi, Carmen D -pg 505
Naputi, Carmen M -pg 517
Naputi, Concepcion M -pg 515
Naputi, Cristobal F -pg 508
Naputi, Dolores M -pg 513
Naputi, Dolores M -pg 516
Naputi, Dolores SN -pg 523

Naputi, Elena C -pg 522
Naputi, Elerio F -pg 22
Naputi, Enrique P -pg 506
Naputi, Enriqueta C -pg 522
Naputi, Especiosa C -pg 506
Naputi, Eufemira C -pg 456
Naputi, Ignacia P -pg 527
Naputi, Jesus B -pg 170
Naputi, Jesus C -pg 506
Naputi, Jesus N -pg 170
Naputi, Jesus T -pg 516
Naputi, Joaquin F -pg 22
Naputi, Jose B -pg 170
Naputi, Jose C -pg 522
Naputi, Jose M -pg 515
Naputi, Jose SN -pg 523
Naputi, Jose T -pg 506
Naputi, Josefa R -pg 378
Naputi, Juan D -pg 522
Naputi, Juan F -pg 508
Naputi, Juan M -pg 515
Naputi, Juan T -pg 515
Naputi, Lucas D -pg 523
Naputi, Lucas T -pg 527
Naputi, Manuel P -pg 527
Naputi, Marcela SN -pg 523
Naputi, Maria B -pg 170
Naputi, Maria C -pg 506
Naputi, Maria C -pg 522
Naputi, Maria F -pg 508
Naputl, Marla F -pg 510
Naputi, Maria M -pg 515
Naputi, Maria M -pg 517
Naputi, Maria N F -pg 508
Naputi, Nicolasa D -pg 505
Naputi, Pio C -pg 506
Naputi, Ramon F -pg 508
Naputi, Remedios M -pg 515
Naputi, Rita C -pg 522
Naputi, Rita D -pg 515
Naputi, Rosa B -pg 170
Naputi, Rosa P -pg 527
Naputi, Rosalia C -pg 522
Naputi, Sebastian M -pg 515
Naputi, Soledad C -pg 522
Naputi, Teresa D -pg 505
Naputi, Venancio -pg 378
Naputi, Vicente D -pg 505
Naputi, Vicente P -pg 508
Naputi, Vicente T -pg 505
Naputy, Antonina C -pg 493
Naputy, Carmela -pg 495

Naputy, Enrique C -pg 493
Naputy, Jesus A -pg 478
Naputy, Joaquin C -pg 493
Naputy, Jose A -pg 478
Naputy, Jose C -pg 493
Naputy, Juan C -pg 493
Naputy, Lorenzo E -pg 493
Naputy, Narcisa C -pg 493
Naputy, Pedro N -pg 496
Naputy, Simona C -pg 493
Nauta, Antonia S -pg 266
Nauta, Antonio T -pg 202
Nauta, Carmen T -pg 208
Nauta, Emelia S -pg 266
Nauta, Eugenia T -pg 202
Nauta, Felicita T -pg 372
Nauta, Francisca T -pg 208
Nauta, Ignacio Q -pg 372
Nauta, Jesus N -pg 208
Nauta, Jesus Q -pg 372
Nauta, Joaquin S -pg 266
Nauta, Joaquin -pg 266
Nauta, Joaquina Q -pg 371
Nauta, Jose N -pg 372
Nauta, Jose S -pg 266
Nauta, Juan S -pg 266
Nauta, Juan T -pg 202
Nauta, Lucia Q -pg 371
Nauta, Magdalena N -pg 208
Nauta, Manuel Q -pg 371
Nauta, Maria N -pg 208
Nauta, Maria Q -pg 371
Nauta, Maria S -pg 266
Nauta, Mariano N -pg 371
Nauta, Martina Q -pg 371
Nauta, Paulina T -pg 208
Nauta, Pedro Q -pg 371
Nauta, Pedro T -pg 208
Nauta, Rosa T -pg 202
Nauta, Vicente Q -pg 371
Navaro, Crispina M -pg 99
Navaro, Donisio M -pg 99
Navaro, Juan M -pg 99
Navaro, Maria M -pg 99
Navaro, Mariano M -pg 99
Nededoc, Ana C -pg 454
Nededoc, Andre -pg 444
Nededoc, Antonia P -pg 448
Nededoc, Beronica P -pg 448
Nededoc, Candilara C -pg 444
Nededoc, Carmen C -pg 432
Nededoc, Carmen C -pg 454

Nededoc, Dolores R -pg 455
Nededoc, Emelio C -pg 454
Nededoc, Enrique C -pg 454
Nededoc, Enrique P -pg 448
Nededoc, Felicisa C -pg 432
Nededoc, Felix P -pg 448
Nededoc, Francisco C -pg 454
Nededoc, Ignacio P -pg 448
Nededoc, Jesus C -pg 432
Nededoc, Joaquin C -pg 432
Nededoc, Joaquin C -pg 444
Nededoc, Joaquin P -pg 448
Nededoc, Jose C -pg 432
Nededoc, Jose N -pg 454
Nededoc, Jose P -pg 448
Nededoc, Juan C -pg 432
Nededoc, Juan N -pg 447
Nededoc, Juan P -pg 448
Nededoc, Juan S -pg 455
Nededoc, Magdalena P -pg 448
Nededoc, Matea R -pg 455
Nededoc, Nicolasa C -pg 444
Nededoc, Nicolasa N -pg 433
Nededoc, Pedro P -pg 448
Nededoc, Roque R -pg 455
Nededoc, Rosa N -pg 434
Nededoc, Tedora C -pg 454
Nededoc, Vicente C -pg 444
Nededoc, Vicente P -pg 448
Nededoc, Vicente S -pg 432
Nededog, Beatris A -pg 195
Nededog, Concepcion A -pg 195
Nego, Isabel P -pg 121
Nego, Jose D -pg 68
Nego, Rosa D -pg 68
Nego, Trudes D -pg 68
Nego, Vicente D -pg 68
Nelson, Catherine C -pg 212
Nelson, Florence -pg 212
Nelson, Henry -pg 212
Nelson, Margaret -pg 212
Nelson, Peter M -pg 212
Nelson, Peter -pg 212
Nenete, Grillerma M -pg 125
Nenete, Ignacio M -pg 125
Nenete, Jesus M -pg 126
Nenete, Jose C -pg 125
Nenete, Maria M -pg 126
Nenete, Rosario M -pg 126
Ninaisan, Ana 0 -pg 165
Ninaisan, Francisca 0 -pg 165
Ninaisan, Ignacio 0 -pg 165

Ninaisan, Jose 0 -pg 165
Ninaisan, Juan 0 -pg 165
Ninaisan, Maria 0 -pg 165
Ninaisan, Rosa 0 -pg 165
Ninete, Joaquin C -pg 351
Ninete, Pedro P -pg 351
Ninete, Rosalia P -pg 351
Ninete, Vicente P -pg 351
Noda, N -pg 245
Ocampo, Eliseo -pg 311
Ocampo, Jorge -pg 311
Ocampo, Maria E -pg 311
Ocampo, Pacifica -pg 311
Ocampo, Pemental -pg 311
Ochia, Alfredo B -pg 245
Ochia, Artemio B -pg 245
Ochia, B -pg 245
Ochia, Gonzalo B -pg 245
Ochia, Herman B -pg 245
Ochia, Jose B -pg 245
Ochia, Maria B -pg 245
Ochia, Soledad B -pg 245
Oconner, Patrick J -pg 426
O'Connor, Antonia U -pg 318
O'Connor, Isabel U -pg 318
Ogo, Ana C -pg 558
Ogo, Ana D -pg 536
Ogo, Ana M -pg 555
Ogo, Ana 0 -pg 161
Ogo, Andrea D -pg 536
Ogo, Antonia D -pg 536
Ogo, Antonia 0 -pg 558
Ogo, Dolores S -pg 553
Ogo, Dominga 0 -pg 125
Ogo, Esperanza 0 -pg 17
Ogo, Francisco 0 -pg 161
Ogo, Francisco A -pg 196
Ogo, Francisco M -pg 553
Ogo, Isabel M -pg 555
Ogo, Jesus 0 -pg 553
Ogo, Joaquina 0 -pg 558
Ogo, Jose C -pg 555
Ogo, Jose D -pg 536
Ogo, Jose 0 -pg 536
Ogo, Jose T -pg 351
Ogo, Juan 0 -pg 161
Ogo, Juan 0 -pg 161
Ogo, Magdalena 0 -pg 553
Ogo, Manuel G -pg 196
Ogo, Manuel L -pg 553
Ogo, Maria 0 -pg 144
Ogo, Maria 0 -pg 553

Ogo, Maria T -pg 351
Ogo, Pedro A -pg 351
Ogo, Ramon O -pg 553
Ogo, Ramona O -pg 125
Ogo, Rufina T -pg 351
Ogo, Vicente J -pg 558
Ojeda, Amalia T -pg 350
Ojeda, Ana P -pg 158
Ojeda, Ana T -pg 350
Ojeda, Antonia G -pg 325
Ojeda, Carmen G -pg 325
Ojeda, Carmen P -pg 158
Ojeda, Consolacion P -pg 158
Ojeda, Eliso G -pg 325
Ojeda, Eugenia G -pg 325
Ojeda, Felisidad G -pg 325
Ojeda, Francisco M -pg 175
Ojeda, Jose M -pg 350
Ojeda, Juan A -pg 175
Ojeda, Juan M -pg 176
Ojeda, Maria G -pg 325
Ojeda, Maria P -pg 158
Ojeda, Pedro C -pg 325
Ojeda, Rosa M -pg 175
Ojeda, Rosalia G -pg 325
Okada, Carlos S -pg 228
Okada, Edward S -pg 228
Okada, Joaquina S -pg 228
Okada, Juan S -pg 228
Okada, Shintoro J -pg 228
Okazaki, Carmen B -pg 378
Okazaki, Jesus B -pg 378
Okazaki, Joaquin Q -pg 378
Okazaki, Joaquina B -pg 378
Okazaki, Rita B -pg 378
Okiyama, Ana C -pg 309
Okiyama, Ana C -pg 435
Okiyama, Carmen C -pg 309
Okiyama, Francisco K -pg 435
Okiyama, Ginusuki F -pg 308
Okiyama, Jacoba C -pg 309
Okiyama, Jesus C -pg 435
Okiyama, Maria C -pg 309
Olano, Angel U -pg 410
Oliaz, Joaquin 0 -pg 59
Onedera, Ana S -pg 440
Onedera, Carmen S -pg 440
Onedera, Juan S -pg 440
Onedera, Juan Jito -pg 440
Onedera, Maria S -pg 440
Onedera, Maria S -pg 440
Ooka, Antolin C -pg 405

Ooka, Antonio C -pg 405
Ooka, Jesus C -pg 405
Ooka, Mateo C -pg 405
Ooka, Rita C -pg 405
Ooka, Takichi O -pg 405
Ooka, Tomas C -pg 405
Oracion, Maria C -pg 205
Oroso, Ana C -pg 216
Oroso, Emeliana C -pg 216
Oroso, Enrique C -pg 216
Oroso, Maria C -pg 217
Ozone, Fudesaburo -pg 191
Pablo, Alfonso G -pg 307
Pablo, Amable B -pg 538
Pablo, Ana B -pg 538
Pablo, Ana V -pg 108
Pablo, Antonia C -pg 128
Pablo, Antonia D -pg 536
Pablo, Antonia V -pg 108
Pablo, Antonio A -pg 541
Pablo, Antonio D -pg 536
Pablo, Antonio P -pg 115
Pablo, Benjamin A -pg 534
Pablo, Bernadita A -pg 536
Pablo, Concepcion B -pg 115
Pablo, Concepcion V -pg 108
Pablo, Concepcion V -pg 217
Pablo, Dolores A -pg 541
Pablo, Dolores A -pg 541
Pablo, Dolores B -pg 297
Pablo, Dolores B -pg 538
Pablo, Dolores V -pg 108
Pablo, Elena A -pg 534
Pablo, Elena G -pg 307
Pablo, Engracia D -pg 536
Pablo, Esperanza A -pg 540
Pablo, Felicidad A -pg 541
Pablo, Felix A -pg 541
Pablo, Gertrudes B -pg 115
Pablo, Gregorio B -pg 538
Pablo, Ignacio -pg 307
Pablo, Jacinto A -pg 200
Pablo, Jesus B -pg 115
Pablo, Jesus D -pg 536
Pablo, Joaquin A -pg 541
Pablo, Joaquin B -pg 538
Pablo, Joaquin P -pg 128
Pablo, Joaquin V -pg 108
Pablo, Joaquina D -pg 536
Pablo, Jose A -pg 200
Pablo, Jose A -pg 307
Pablo, Jose B -pg 115

Pablo, Jose C -pg 90
Pablo, Jose D -pg 536
Pablo, Jose G -pg 307
Pablo, Jose P -pg 89
Pablo, Jose P -pg 200
Pablo, Josefa B -pg 200
Pablo, Juan B -pg 200
Pablo, Juan C -pg 128
Pablo, Juan P -pg 16
Pablo, Juan P -pg 90
Pablo, Juan SN -pg 536
Pablo, Juan V -pg 108
Pablo, Juan -pg 253
Pablo, Juana -pg 214
Pablo, Magdalena B -pg 115
Pablo, Manuel C -pg 16
Pablo, Maria 0 -pg 115
Pablo, Maria 0 -pg 115
Pablo, Maria A -pg 200
Pablo, Maria A -pg 534
Pablo, Maria B -pg 200
Pablo, Maria C -pg 128
Pablo, Maria D -pg 536
Pablo, Maria P -pg 90
Pablo, Maria V -pg 108
Pablo, Mariano A -pg 538
Pablo, Natividad V -pg 108
Pablo, Nicolasa G -pg 307
Pablo, Ramon A -pg 534
Pablo, Regina A -pg 541
Pablo, Remedios 0 -pg 115
Pablo, Rosa A -pg 534
Pablo, Rosa B -pg 200
Pablo, Rosa G -pg 307
Pablo, Serafin A -pg 534
Pablo, Tomas B -pg 538
Pablo, Trinidad A -pg 534
Pablo, Vicente B -pg 538
Paget, Alfred G -pg 425
Palacios, Francisca C -pg 47
Palacios, Francisco C -pg 47
Palacios, Francisco M -pg 47
Palacios, Jose C -pg 47
Palacios, Jose T -pg 47
Palacios, Josefina C -pg 47
Palacios, Juan T -pg 47
Palacios, Maria C -pg 47
Palacios, Maria C -pg 47
Palacios, Maria T -pg 47
Palomo, Ana C -pg 157
Palomo, Ana R -pg 88
Palomo, Ana A G -pg 433

Palomo, Antonio R -pg 151
Palomo, Asuncion A -pg 135
Palomo, Carmen G -pg 433
Palomo, Carmen T -pg 210
Palomo, Dominga T -pg 210
Palomo, Francisca G -pg 433
Palomo, Francisco D -pg 88
Palomo, Francisco P -pg 211
Palomo, Gabina A -pg 135
Palomo, Getrudes T -pg 210
Palomo, Gregorio P -pg 169
Palomo, Ignacio C -pg 111
Palomo, Ignacio D -pg 433
Palomo, Ignacio T -pg 211
Palomo, Jesus LG -pg 148
Palomo, Jesus N -pg 158
Palomo, Jesus R -pg 88
Palomo, Joaquin B -pg 142
Palomo, Joaquin LG -pg 149
Palomo, Jose C -pg 157
Palomo, Jose C -pg 157
Palomo, Jose G -pg 433
Palomo, Jose N -pg 158
Palomo, Jose T -pg 210
Palomo, Juan D -pg 88
Palomo, Juan G -pg 433
Palomo, Juan P -pg 88
Palomo, Juan P -pg 211
Palomo, Manuel A -pg 135
Palomo, Maria C -pg 158
Palomo, Maria C -pg 455
Palomo, Maria G -pg 433
Palomo, Maria R -pg 88
Palomo, Maria SM -pg 111
Palomo, Patricia C -pg 455
Palomo, Pedro G -pg 455
Palomo, Ramon C -pg 158
Palomo, Rita 0 -pg 151
Palomo, Rita D -pg 88
Palomo, Rosa P -pg 156
Palomo, Rufina P -pg 211
Palomo, Silvestre G -pg 433
Palomo, Teresa N -pg 158
Palomo, Tita LG -pg 148
Palomo, Vicente A -pg 88
Palomo, Vicente C -pg 158
Palomo, Vicente D -pg 88
Palomo, Vicente G -pg 433
Palomo, Vicente R -pg 88
Palting, Florencia D -pg 246
Palting, Margarito D -pg 246
Palting, Pacracio R -pg 246

Pangelinan, Alfonso C -pg 280
Pangelinan, Ana C -pg 280
Pangelinan, Ana F -pg 551
Pangelinan, Ana G -pg 48
Pangelinan, Ana G -pg 285
Pangelinan, Ana P -pg 258
Pangelinan, Ana P -pg 342
Pangelinan, Ana R -pg 31
Pangelinan, Ana R -pg 246
Pangelinan, Ana T -pg 413
Pangelinan, Andrea S -pg 400
Pangelinan, Aniceto -pg 305
Pangelinan, Antonia B -pg 13
Pangelinan, Antonia G -pg 285
Pangelinan, Antonia Q -pg 546
Pangelinan, Antonia -pg 225
Pangelinan, Antonio C -pg 280
Pangelinan, Antonio M -pg 195
Pangelinan, Antonio T -pg 294
Pangelinan, Antonio U -pg 140
Pangelinan, Artemio -pg 220
Pangelinan, Barsalisa B -pg 213
Pangelinan, Bartola A -pg 332
Pangelinan, Benedicto S -pg 400
Pangelinan, Candaleria C -pg 280
Pangelinan, Carmelo P -pg 164
Pangelinan, Carmen M -pg 195
Pangelinan, Carmen Q -pg 546
Pangelinan, Concepcion L -pg 346
Pangelinan, Concepcion M -pg 175
Pangelinan, Concepcion M -pg 333
Pangelinan, Concepcion -pg 220
Pangelinan, Cristina S -pg 400
Pangelinan, Dolores G -pg 106
Pangelinan, Dolores M -pg 175
Pangelinan, Dolores Q -pg 114
Pangelinan, Dominga P -pg 139
Pangelinan, Eliza C -pg 277
Pangelinan, Emelio -pg 332
Pangelinan, Emilia S -pg 400
Pangelinan, Emliana Q -pg 546
Pangelinan, Enrique 0 -pg 139
Pangelinan, Enrique G -pg 45
Pangelinan, Felix T jr -pg 413
Pangelinan, Felix U -pg 140
Pangelinan, Francisco 0 -pg 139
Pangelinan, Francisco B -pg 276
Pangelinan, Francisco B -pg 429
Pangelinan, Francisco C -pg 338
Pangelinan, Francisco F -pg 551
Pangelinan, Francisco G -pg 44
Pangelinan, Francisco M -pg 333

Pangelinan, Francisco P -pg 246
Pangelinan, Francisco P -pg 343
Pangelinan, Francisco R -pg 164
Pangelinan, Francisco S -pg 400
Pangelinan, Francisco -pg 214
Pangelinan, Genoveva G -pg 45
Pangelinan, Genoveva -pg 238
Pangelinan, Gloria T -pg 413
Pangelinan, Guido B -pg 179
Pangelinan, Herminichilda M -pg 551
Pangelinan, Hilaria L -pg 346
Pangelinan, Ignacia G -pg 44
Pangelinan, Ignacia M -pg 195
Pangelinan, Ignacio D -pg 285
Pangelinan, Ignacio P -pg 246
Pangelinan, Ignacio R -pg 164
Pangelinan, Jesus 0 -pg 139
Pangelinan, Jesus C -pg 277
Pangelinan, Jesus G -pg 44
Pangelinan, Jesus G -pg 265
Pangelinan, Jesus M -pg 551
Pangelinan, Jesus Q -pg 546
Pangelinan, Jesus R -pg 546
Pangelinan, Joaquin B -pg 179
Pangelinan, Joaquin C -pg 293
Pangelinan, Joaquin G -pg 285
Pangelinan, Joaquin M -pg 188
Pangelinan, Joaquin P -pg 188
Pangelinan, Joaquin T -pg 140
Pangelinan, Joaquin -pg 220
Pangelinan, Joaquina C -pg 277
Pangelinan, Joaquina R -pg 31
Pangelinan, Joaquina T -pg 294
Pangelinan, Jose B -pg 179
Pangelinan, Jose C -pg 13
Pangelinan, Jose C -pg 195
Pangelinan, Jose C -pg 346
Pangelinan, Jose C -pg 421
Pangelinan, Jose C -pg 546
Pangelinan, Jose C -pg 551
Pangelinan, Jose G -pg 44
Pangelinan, Jose G -pg 114
Pangelinan, Jose G -pg 285
Pangelinan, Jose M -pg 175
Pangelinan, Jose M -pg 195
Pangelinan, Jose M -pg 551
Pangelinan, Jose P -pg 246
Pangelinan, Jose Q -pg 546
Pangelinan, Jose R -pg 31
Pangelinan, Jose T -pg 45
Pangelinan, Jose -pg 225

Pangelinan, Jose -pg 337
Pangelinan, Josefa B -pg 179
Pangelinan, Josefa C -pg 276
Pangelinan, Josefa C -pg 337
Pangelinan, Josefina T -pg 413
Pangelinan, Juan A -pg 332
Pangelinan, Juan B -pg 554
Pangelinan, Juan M -pg 195
Pangelinan, Juan M -pg 333
Pangelinan, Juan P -pg 246
Pangelinan, Juan Q -pg 114
Pangelinan, Juan S -pg 111
Pangelinan, Juan SN -pg 333
Pangelinan, Juan -pg 351
Pangelinan, Juana B -pg 213
Pangelinan, Juana L -pg 346
Pangelinan, Juana R -pg 31
Pangelinan, Juana -pg 231
Pangelinan, Juana -pg 281
Pangelinan, Julia C -pg 277
Pangelinan, Laura S -pg 400
Pangelinan, Lino T -pg 294
Pangelinan, Lorenzo L -pg 346
Pangelinan, Luis -pg 421
Pangelinan, Luisa L -pg 346
Pangelinan, Luisa -pg 225
Pangelinan, Magdalena B -pg 179
Pangelinan, Magdalena F -pg 551
Pangelinan, Magdalena G -pg 285
Pangelinan, Manuel B -pg 179
Pangelinan, Manuel C -pg 280
Pangelinan, Manuel C -pg 550
Pangelinan, Manuel P -pg 246
Pangelinan, Manuel P -pg 265
Pangelinan, Manuel Q -pg 114
Pangelinan, Manuela C -pg 280
Pangelinan, Margarita M -pg 195
Pangelinan, Maria A -pg 332
Pangelinan, Maria A -pg 332
Pangelinan, Maria B -pg 213
Pangelinan, Maria B -pg 429
Pangelinan, Maria B -pg 554
Pangelinan, Maria C -pg 280
Pangelinan, Maria C -pg 280
Pangelinan, Maria C -pg 343
Pangelinan, Maria C -pg 343
Pangelinan, Maria D -pg 338
Pangelinan, Maria G -pg 106
Pangelinan, Maria G -pg 285
Pangelinan, Maria G -pg 285
Pangelinan, Maria L -pg 346
Pangelinan, Maria M -pg 188

Pangelinan, Maria M -pg 333
Pangelinan, Maria M -pg 551
Pangelinan, Maria P -pg 246
Pangelinan, Maria P -pg 265
Pangelinan, Maria P -pg 294
Pangelinan, Maria P -pg 342
Pangelinan, Maria Q -pg 546
Pangelinan, Maria Q -pg 546
Pangelinan, Maria R -pg 164
Pangelinan, Maria S -pg 33
Pangelinan, Maria T -pg 293
Pangelinan, Maria U -pg 140
Pangelinan, Matias M -pg 175
Pangelinan, Matilde M -pg 188
Pangelinan, Natividad L -pg 429
Pangelinan, Nicolasa P -pg 265
Pangelinan, Nieves -pg 238
Pangelinan, Nives C -pg 558
Pangelinan, Pedro B -pg 400
Pangelinan, Pedro C -pg 343
Pangelinan, Pedro M -pg 333
Pangelinan, Pedro P -pg 185
Pangelinan, Pedro P -pg 265
Pangelinan, Pedro R -pg 558
Pangelinan, Pedro -pg 223
Pangelinan, Ramon Q -pg 546
Pangelinan, Ramona M -pg 188
Pangelinan, Ramona R -pg 164
Pangelinan, Regina G -pg 44
Pangelinan, Rita G -pg 285
Pangelinan, Rita L -pg 346
Pangelinan, Rita Q -pg 114
Pangelinan, Rosa C -pg 277
Pangelinan, Rosa LG -pg 45
Pangelinan, Rosa M -pg 195
Pangelinan, Rosa M -pg 551
Pangelinan, Rosalia L -pg 346
Pangelinan, Rosalia M -pg 188
Pangelinan, Rosario C -pg 280
Pangelinan, Rosario L -pg 346
Pangelinan, Rufina C -pg 421
Pangelinan, Silvino D -pg 294
Pangelinan, Tomas M -pg 188
Pangelinan, Tomas P -pg 343
Pangelinan, Tomas -pg 220
Pangelinan, Trinidad P -pg 343
Pangelinan, Venancio U -pg 140
Pangelinan, Vicente C -pg 90
Pangelinan, Vicente C -pg 277
Pangelinan, Vicente C -pg 280
Pangelinan, Vicente G -pg 285
Pangelinan, Vicente M -pg 195

Pangelinan, Vicente P -pg 106
Pangelinan, Vicente P -pg 314
Pangelinan, Vicente R -pg 164
Pangelinan, Vicente S -pg 111
Pangelinan, Vicente T -pg 44
Pangelinan, Vicente U -pg 140
Pangelinan, Vicente -pg 220
Pangelinan, Virginia S -pg 400
Pascual, Jesus R -pg 351
Paulino, Ana C -pg 503
Paulino, Ana N -pg 529
Paulino, Angela L -pg 507
Paulino, Carmen D -pg 503
Paulino, Carmen N -pg 529
Paulino, Cleto C -pg 503
Paulino, Concepcion L -pg 507
Paulino, Concepcion T -pg 502
Paulino, Fabiana C -pg 503
Paulino, Felomena F -pg 502
Paulino, Ignacia F -pg 502
Paulino, Jesus D -pg 518
Paulino, Joaquina T -pg 502
Paulino, Jose A -pg 502
Paulino, Jose C -pg 72
Paulino, Juan C -pg 503
Paulino, Juan L -pg 507
Paulino, Juan N -pg 507
Paulino, Juan T -pg 508
Paulino, Leocadio C -pg 503
Paulino, Luis C -pg 502
Paulino, Manuel A -pg 502
Paulino, Manuel F -pg 502
Paulino, Margarita L -pg 507
Paulino, Maria Q -pg 529
Paulino, Maria SN -pg 508
Paulino, Mariano F -pg 502
Paulino, Nicolas C -pg 503
Paulino, Ramon F -pg 502
Paulino, Rosalia SN -pg 508
Paulino, Santiago N -pg 518
Paulino, Vicente D -pg 503
Paulino, Vicente F -pg 502
Paulino, Vicente M -pg 527
Paulino, Ynes L -pg 507
Payne, Ana A -pg 129
Payne, Patrick A -pg 129
Payne, Thomas SN -pg 169
Peraira, Ana A -pg 329
Peraira, Francisco C -pg 285
Peraira, Herman C -pg 286
Peraira, Ignacio C -pg 285
Peraira, Josefa C -pg 285

Peraira, Juan A -pg 329
Peraira, Juan C -pg 285
Peraira, Manuel D -pg 285
Peraira, Maria B C -pg 285
Peraira, Milagro A -pg 329
Peraira, Pilar C -pg 285
Peraira, Rita C -pg 285
Pereda, Ana C -pg 266
Pereda, Ana M -pg 522
Pereda, Antonio P -pg 259
Pereda, Anunsacion M -pg 522
Pereda, Ascension C -pg 255
Pereda, Asencion P -pg 258
Pereda, Catalina C -pg 266
Pereda, Concepcion P -pg 259
Pereda, Fidela C -pg 255
Pereda, Francisco C -pg 255
Pereda, Gabriel P -pg 266
Pereda, Gabriel S -pg 255
Pereda, Ignacio P -pg 258
Pereda, Isabel C -pg 255
Pereda, Jesus P -pg 259
Pereda, Jesus S -pg 259
Pereda, Jose B -pg 90
Pereda, Josefa B -pg 90
Pereda, Josefa B jr -pg 90
Pereda, Juan C -pg 266
Pereda, Juan P -pg 259
Pereda, Juan S -pg 90
Pereda, Margarita C -pg 255
Pereda, Maria C -pg 255
Pereda, Maria C -pg 266
Pereda, Maria P -pg 259
Pereda, Maria P -pg 259
Pereda, Natividad C -pg 255
Pereda, Nicomedes C -pg 522
Pereda, Pedro C -pg 266
Pereda, Rosa C -pg 255
Pereda, Rosa C -pg 255
Pereda, Rosa C -pg 266
Pereda, Susana B -pg 90
Pereda, Vicente S -pg 258
Peredo, Ana B -pg 545
Peredo, Ana C -pg 315
Peredo, Antonio M -pg 315
Peredo, Antonio S -pg 25
Peredo, Baldemero T -pg 112
Peredo, Camilo J -pg 545
Peredo, Carmen M -pg 315
Peredo, Concepcion LG -pg 26
Peredo, Dominga T -pg 112
Peredo, Fernando G -pg 315

Peredo, Francisco B -pg 545
Peredo, Francisco P -pg 56
Peredo, Ignacio B -pg 545
Peredo, Jesus B -pg 20
Peredo, Joaquin B -pg 545
Peredo, Joaquin LG -pg 26
Peredo, Joaquina C -pg 315
Peredo, Jose B -pg 112
Peredo, Jose B -pg 545
Peredo, Jose C -pg 315
Peredo, Jose T -pg 112
Peredo, Juan B -pg 545
Peredo, Juan LG -pg 25
Peredo, Juana T -pg 112
Peredo, Maria B -pg 545
Peredo, Maria M -pg 315
Peredo, Mercedes M -pg 315
Peredo, Pedro B -pg 545
Peredo, Pedro M -pg 315
Peredo, Ramona LG -pg 25
Peredo, Remedios M -pg 315
Perez, Albert E -pg 310
Perez, Alfreda C -pg 237
Perez, Amanda L -pg 259
Perez, Amelia D -pg 36
Perez, Ana A -pg 141
Perez, Ana A -pg 271
Perez, Ana B -pg 181
Perez, Ana B -pg 213
Perez, Ana C -pg 90
Perez, Ana C -pg 237
Perez, Ana C -pg 274
Perez, Ana C -pg 397
Perez, Ana C jr -pg 91
Perez, Ana G -pg 265
Perez, Ana LG -pg 233
Perez, Ana M -pg 414
Perez, Ana N -pg 386
Perez, Ana S -pg 374
Perez, Ana T -pg 159
Perez, Ana T -pg 410
Perez, Ana T jr -pg 410
Perez, Angel R -pg 263
Perez, Angelica C -pg 275
Perez, Antonia M -pg 234
Perez, Antonio O -pg 171
Perez, Antonio B -pg 214
Perez, Antonio B -pg 408
Perez, Antonio C -pg 91
Perez, Antonio C -pg 233
Perez, Antonio C -pg 234
Perez, Antonio C -pg 386

Perez, Antonio C -pg 397
Perez, Antonio D -pg 36
Perez, Antonio F -pg 294
Perez, Antonio LG -pg 233
Perez, Antonio M -pg 237
Perez, Antonio N -pg 386
Perez, Artemio C -pg 275
Perez, Asuncion C -pg 91
Perez, Atanacio T -pg 23
Perez, Aurelia P -pg 327
Perez, Basilia C -pg 382
Perez, Beatris S -pg 374
Perez, Beatris T -pg 410
Perez, Benancio C -pg 237
Perez, Biatris T -pg 23
Perez, Brigida T -pg 23
Perez, Caesario B -pg 259
Perez, Candaleria S -pg 229
Perez, Carmelo C -pg 405
Perez, Carmen C -pg 86
Perez, Carmen C -pg 409
Perez, Carmen D -pg 23
Perez, Carmen L -pg 179
Perez, Carmen P -pg 276
Perez, Cecilia P -pg 233
Perez, Clotilde P -pg 233
Perez, Clotilde T -pg 159
Perez, Concepcion C -pg 231
Perez, Concepcion C -pg 423
Perez, Concepcion M -pg 237
Perez, Concepcion S -pg 230
Perez, Concepcion -pg 299
Perez, Consolacion G -pg 265
Perez, Consuelo D -pg 55
Perez, Daniel L -pg 436
Perez, Degadina B -pg 213
Perez, Dinna S -pg 374
Perez, Dolores A -pg 249
Perez, Dolores A -pg 271
Perez, Dolores C -pg 210
Perez, Dolores C -pg 257
Perez, Dolores C -pg 397
Perez, Dolores D -pg 36
Perez, Dolores F -pg 41
Perez, Dolores M -pg 47
Perez, Dolores R -pg 263
Perez, Doroteo C -pg 436
Perez, Dortotea P -pg 233
Perez, Edward E -pg 309
Perez, Elisa C -pg 231
Perez, Eliza T -pg 23
Perez, Emelia C -pg 274

Perez, Emelia F -pg 234
Perez, Emeliana R -pg 292
Perez, Emilia T -pg 159
Perez, Emiliana F -pg 41
Perez, Encarnacion -pg 382
Perez, Engracia B -pg 213
Perez, Engracia B -pg 274
Perez, Engracia C -pg 402
Perez, Enrique D -pg 55
Perez, Ernesto P -pg 233
Perez, Felipe C -pg 91
Perez, Felipe C -pg 263
Perez, Felisa M -pg 237
Perez, Felisa S -pg 314
Perez, Felix F -pg 36
Perez, Francisca D -pg 36
Perez, Francisca M -pg 168
Perez, Francisco A -pg 141
Perez, Francisco B -pg 213
Perez, Francisco D -pg 54
Perez, Francisco G -pg 265
Perez, Francisco L -pg 223
Perez, Francisco M -pg 170
Perez, Francisco M -pg 237
Perez, Francisco T -pg 23
Perez, Francisco T -pg 159
Perez, Francisco -pg 299
Perez, Gerardo C -pg 436
Perez, Gregorio C -pg 231
Perez, Gregorio C -pg 234
Perez, Gregorlo D -pg 36
Perez, Gregorio F -pg 309
Perez, Gregorio G -pg 153
Perez, Gregorio S -pg 177
Perez, Gregorio T -pg 159
Perez, Henry L -pg 223
Perez, Honoria C -pg 170
Perez, Ignacia C -pg 403
Perez, Ignacio B -pg 213
Perez, Ignacio L -pg 179
Perez, Ignacio T -pg 168
Perez, Ignacio V -pg 265
Perez, Inara C -pg 403
Perez, Isabel G -pg 265
Perez, Isabel T -pg 23
Perez, Isabel T -pg 159
Perez, Jesus B -pg 274
Perez, Jesus C -pg 170
Perez, Jesus C -pg 397
Perez, Jesus F -pg 41
Perez, Jesus F -pg 54
Perez, Jesus LG -pg 237

Perez, Jesus M -pg 168
Perez, Jesus M -pg 237
Perez, Jesus P -pg 149
Perez, Jesus S -pg 229
Perez, Joaquin A -pg 141
Perez, Joaquin C -pg 170
Perez, Joaquin C -pg 213
Perez, Joaquin C -pg 237
Perez, Joaquin C -pg 275
Perez, Joaquin C -pg 314
Perez, Joaquin D -pg 36
Perez, Joaquin F -pg 234
Perez, Joaquin S -pg 274
Perez, Joaquin S -pg 382
Perez, Joaquin T -pg 223
Perez, Joaquina F -pg 234
Perez, Joaquina G -pg 104
Perez, Jose A -pg 249
Perez, Jose B -pg 174
Perez, Jose C -pg 90
Perez, Jose C -pg 231
Perez, Jose C -pg 275
Perez, Jose C -pg 423
Perez, Jose D -pg 36
Perez, Jose F -pg 41
Perez, Jose F -pg 234
Perez, Jose F -pg 259
Perez, Jose G -pg 105
Perez, Jose LG -pg 234
Perez, Jose M -pg 168
Perez, Jose M -pg 237
Perez, Jose M -pg 414
Perez, Jose P -pg 90
Perez, Jose P -pg 148
Perez, Jose P -pg 174
Perez, Jose R -pg 263
Perez, Jose R -pg 292
Perez, Jose S -pg 229
Perez, Jose S -pg 231
Perez, Jose S -pg 314
Perez, Jose S -pg 374
Perez, Jose T -pg 159
Perez, Jose M -pg 41
Perez, Josefa A -pg 224
Perez, Josefa D -pg 36
Perez, Josefa G -pg 104
Perez, Josefa M -pg 237
Perez, Josefa P -pg 151
Perez, Josefa S -pg 130
Perez, Josefa S -pg 177
Perez, Josefina B -pg 174
Perez, Josefina C -pg 231

Perez, Josefina C -pg 237
Perez, Josefina D -pg 36
Perez, Juan 0 -pg 88
Perez, Juan C -pg 179
Perez, Juan C -pg 231
Perez, Juan D -pg 36
Perez, Juan F -pg 41
Perez, Juan L -pg 179
Perez, Juan L -pg 223
Perez, Juan LG -pg 236
Perez, Juan M -pg 414
Perez, Juan N -pg 386
Perez, Juan P -pg 149
Perez, Juan P -pg 327
Perez, Juan S -pg 271
Perez, Juan S -pg 374
Perez, Juan T -pg 159
Perez, Juan T -pg 224
Perez, Juan -pg 382
Perez, Juana B -pg 174
Perez, Juana B -pg 274
Perez, Juana C -pg 345
Perez, Juana R -pg 456
Perez, Laurion C -pg 423
Perez, Leonisa P -pg 327
Perez, Locario C -pg 275
Perez, Luis A -pg 271
Perez, Luis C -pg 148
Perez, Luis P -pg 148
Perez, Luis S -pg 177
Perez, Magdalena C -pg 90
Perez, Manuel B -pg 174
Perez, Manuel C -pg 231
Perez, Manuel D -pg 36
Perez, Manuel F -pg 159
Perez, Manuel R -pg 263
Perez, Manuel T -pg 86
Perez, Manuela C -pg 274
Perez, Margarita D -pg 54
Perez, Maria A -pg 105
Perez, Maria A -pg 141
Perez, Maria A -pg 271
Perez, Maria B -pg 181
Perez, Maria B -pg 185
Perez, Maria C -pg 170
Perez, Maria C -pg 210
Perez, Maria C -pg 231
Perez, Maria C -pg 411
Perez, Maria C -pg 436
Perez, Maria D -pg 36
Perez, Maria D -pg 54
Perez, Maria L -pg 179

Perez, Maria L -pg 223
Perez, Maria L -pg 223
Perez, Maria L -pg 259
Perez, Maria M -pg 168
Perez, Maria M -pg 237
Perez, Maria N -pg 386
Perez, Maria P -pg 148
Perez, Maria P -pg 210
Perez, Maria P -pg 402
Perez, Maria P jr -pg 148
Perez, Maria S -pg 129
Perez, Maria S -pg 321
Perez, Maria S -pg 374
Perez, Maria T -pg 23
Perez, Mariano C -pg 283
Perez, Mariano C -pg 397
Perez, Mariano T -pg 129
Perez, Matias LG -pg 151
Perez, Merfida M -pg 168
Perez, Monica M -pg 244
Perez, Nicolasa P -pg 233
Perez, Nieves B -pg 130
Perez, Nieves L -pg 264
Perez, Oliva B -pg 274
Perez, Pedro C -pg 90
Perez, Pedro D -pg 36
Perez, Pedro G -pg 141
Perez, Pedro I -pg 215
Perez, Pilar S -pg 229
Perez, Pilar T -pg 294
Perez, Rafaela C -pg 423
Perez, Ramon A -pg 249
Perez, Ramona T -pg 294
Perez, Rita B -pg 174
Perez, Rita B -pg 181
Perez, Rita S -pg 374
Perez, Rosa A -pg 141
Perez, Rosa C -pg 170
Perez, Rosa C -pg 403
Perez, Rosa C -pg 436
Perez, Rosa E -pg 310
Perez, Rosa F -pg 234
Perez, Rosa M -pg 168
Perez, Rosa M -pg 237
Perez, Rosa R -pg 292
Perez, Rosalia B -pg 259
Perez, Rosalia M -pg 237
Perez, Rosario C -pg 91
Perez, Rosario C -pg 423
Perez, Rosario E -pg 309
Perez, Rosario L -pg 259
Perez, Santiago C -pg 397

Perez, Santiago T -pg 397
Perez, Segundo B -pg 274
Perez, Soledad P -pg 148
Perez, Soledad R -pg 292
Perez, Tomas E -pg 309
Perez, Tomasa B -pg 259
Perez, Tomasa E -pg 84
Perez, Ursula T -pg 23
Perez, Vicente B -pg 130
Perez, Vicente B -pg 181
Perez, Vicente B -pg 185
Perez, Vicente B -pg 274
Perez, Vicente F -pg 177
Perez, Vicente L -pg 223
Perez, Vicente M -pg 292
Perez, Vicente P -pg 148
Perez, Vicente P -pg 168
Perez, Vicente Q -pg 382
Perez, Vicente S -pg 374
Perez, Vicente T -pg 159
Perez, Vicente T -pg 402
Peterson, Annie W -pg 239
Peterson, Elmer W -pg 239
Peterson, Fred W -pg 239
Peterson, Mabel W -pg 239
Peterson, Rufina W -pg 239
Petros, Ana L -pg 378
Petros, Joaquin L -pg 378
Petros, Jose L -pg 378
Petros, Lorenzo M -pg 378
Petros, Magdalena L -pg 378
Petros, Pedro L -pg 378
Petros, Vicente L -pg 378
Pimley, William -pg 425
Pinaula, Antonio C -pg 112
Pinaula, Feliciana 0 -pg 138
Pinaula, Feliciana C -pg 112
Pinaula, Jose P -pg 112
Pinaula, Jose -pg 348
Pinaula, Juan G -pg 440
Pinaula, Juliana A -pg 452
Pinaula, Leon B -pg 452
Pinaula, Soledad G -pg 452
Pinaula, Vicente A -pg 530
Pineda, Dolores C -pg 448
Pineda, Dolores G -pg 448
Pineda, Francisco G -pg 448
Pineda, Jose A -pg 448
Pineda, Manuel C -pg 448
Pineda, Maxima G -pg 448
Pineda, Victoria G -pg 448
Pitko, Rudolp C -pg 426

Pocahigui, Dolores O -pg 551
Pocahigui, Domingo P -pg 551
Pocahigui, Felix O -pg 551
Pocahigui, Francisco P -pg 548
Pocahigui, Isabel P -pg 548
Pocahigui, Jesus O -pg 551
Pocahigui, Jose O -pg 551
Pocahigui, Maria O -pg 551
Pocahigui, Maria P -pg 548
Pocahigui, Pedro -pg 548
Pocahigui, Rafael O -pg 551
Portusach, Antonia M -pg 278
Portusach, Beatrice M -pg 278
Portusach, Emelia M -pg 278
Portusach, Magdalena M -pg 278
Portusach, Maria M -pg 278
Qiudachay, Jesus A -pg 102
Quenga, Ana M -pg 306
Quenga, Ana S -pg 386
Quenga, Ana SN -pg 368
Quenga, Angelina SN -pg 369
Quenga, Angustia SN -pg 368
Quenga, Antonia C -pg 368
Quenga, Antonia M -pg 306
Quenga, Antonia SN -pg 369
Quenga, Antonio C -pg 368
Quenga, Barbara T -pg 369
Quenga, Carlos SN -pg 369
Quenga, Carolina SN -pg 368
Quenga, Cristina SN -pg 368
Quenga, Dolores C -pg 368
Quenga, Dolores C -pg 372
Quenga, Dolores T -pg 369
Quenga, Enrique C -pg 372
Quenga, Feix C -pg 369
Quenga, Felix C -pg 372
Quenga, Francisco T -pg 306
Quenga, Gabina C -pg 368
Quenga, Jesus S -pg 368
Quenga, Joaquin SN -pg 368
Quenga, Joaquin SN -pg 368
Quenga, Jose C -pg 368
Quenga, Jose S -pg 386
Quenga, Jose SN -pg 368
Quenga, Jose T -pg 369
Quenga, Josefina C -pg 368
Quenga, Juan B -pg 386
Quenga, Juan SN -pg 368
Quenga, Juana B -pg 369
Quenga, Lorenzo T -pg 369
Quenga, Lourdes SN -pg 369
Quenga, Magdalena B -pg 369

Quenga, Magdalena S -pg 386
Quenga, Manuel Q -pg 374
Quenga, Manuel SN -pg 368
Quenga, Manuel SN -pg 368
Quenga, Manuel T -pg 369
Quenga, Marcela Q -pg 374
Quenga, Maria B -pg 369
Quenga, Maria B jr -pg 369
Quenga, Maria S -pg 386
Quenga, Maria S jr -pg 386
Quenga, Maria SN -pg 369
Quenga, Maria T -pg 369
Quenga, Maria T -pg 369
Quenga, Matilde M -pg 306
Quenga, Milagro SN -pg 368
Quenga, Natividad SN -pg 368
Quenga, Pedro B -pg 369
Quenga, Rosalia C -pg 368
Quenga, Rufina C -pg 372
Quenga, Sebastian C -pg 368
Quenga, Servino T -pg 369
Quenga, Severa C -pg 368
Quenga, Teodoro SN -pg 369
Quenga, Vicenta B -pg 369
Quenga, Vicenta Q -pg 374
Quenga, Vicenta T -pg 369
Quenga, Vicente C -pg 368
Quenga, Vicente SN -pg 368
Quenga, Vicente SN -pg 369
Quichocho, Agatomia P -pg 345
Quichocho, Ana B -pg 96
Quichocho, Ana D -pg 551
Quichocho, Ana P -pg 345
Quichocho, Ana P -pg 547
Quichocho, Ana Q -pg 558
Quichocho, Ana T -pg 94
Quichocho, Antonia P -pg 322
Quichocho, Antonio C -pg 62
Quichocho, Biatris Q -pg 556
Quichocho, Carmela N -pg 63
Quichocho, Catalina Q -pg 96
Quichocho, Concepcion A -pg 106
Quichocho, Consolacion -pg 377
Quichocho, Dolores C -pg 233
Quichocho, Dolores I -pg 556
Quichocho, Eufasia P -pg 345
Quichocho, Felipe A -pg 106
Quichocho, Francisca N -pg 63
Quichocho, Francisca Q -pg 556
Quichocho, Francisco Q -pg 556
Quichocho, Ignacio 0 -pg 182
Quichocho, Ignacio C -pg 552

Quichocho, Ignacio -pg 377
Quichocho, Jesus C -pg 63
Quichocho, Jesus C -pg 233
Quichocho, Jesus C -pg 552
Quichocho, Jesus L -pg 157
Quichocho, Jesus P -pg 322
Quichocho, Jesus P -pg 345
Quichocho, Jesus Q -pg 62
Quichocho, Jesus Q -pg 93
Quichocho, Jesus Q -pg 94
Quichocho, Jesus T -pg 93
Quichocho, Joaquin A -pg 106
Quichocho, Joaquin D -pg 552
Quichocho, Joaquin M -pg 108
Quichocho, Joaquina C -pg 62
Quichocho, Joaquina Q -pg 555
Quichocho, Joaquina T -pg 93
Quichocho, Jose 0 -pg 166
Quichocho, Jose 0 -pg 174
Quichocho, Jose C -pg 552
Quichocho, Jose N -pg 63
Quichocho, Jose P -pg 322
Quichocho, Jose P -pg 345
Quichocho, Jose P -pg 546
Quichocho, Jose Q -pg 93
Quichocho, Jose Q -pg 94
Quichocho, Jose Q -pg 121
Quichocho, Jose Q -pg 132
Quichocho, Jose Q -pg 543
Quichocho, Jose R -pg 157
Quichocho, Jose R -pg 329
Quichocho, Jose SA -pg 107
Quichocho, Jose SN -pg 132
Quichocho, Josefa 0 -pg 175
Quichocho, Josefa C -pg 552
Quichocho, Josefa P -pg 546
Quichocho, Josefa Q -pg 181
Quichocho, Josefa SN -pg 132
Quichocho, Juan 0 -pg 146
Quichocho, Juan B -pg 157
Quichocho, Juan P -pg 556
Quichocho, Juan Q -pg 558
Quichocho, Juan SA -pg 107
Quichocho, Juan T -pg 94
Quichocho, Julia C -pg 62
Quichocho, Lourdes SN -pg 132
Quichocho, Luisa SA -pg 107
Quichocho, Manuel I -pg 556
Quichocho, Manuel P -pg 322
Quichocho, Manuel Q -pg 96
Quichocho, Manuel SA -pg 107
Quichocho, Manuel T -pg 174

Quichocho, Maria I -pg 556
Quichocho, Maria L -pg 157
Quichocho, Maria N -pg 556
Quichocho, Maria P -pg 121
Quichocho, Maria P -pg 345
Quichocho, Maria P -pg 546
Quichocho, Maria Q -pg 93
Quichocho, Maria Q -pg 94
Quichocho, Maria Q -pg 233
Quichocho, Maria Q -pg 558
Quichocho, Maria R -pg 157
Quichocho, Maria T -pg 93
Quichocho, Maria T -pg 94
Quichocho, Maria T -pg 174
Quichocho, Mariana -pg 369
Quichocho, Mercedes C -pg 552
Quichocho, Nicolas LG -pg 93
Quichocho, Nicolas Q -pg 94
Quichocho, Nicolasa Q -pg 63
Quichocho, Nicolasa Q -pg 94
Quichocho, Nicolasa S -pg 345
Quichocho, Patrosino P -pg 345
Quichocho, Paula C -pg 94
Quichocho, Pedro N -pg 63
Quichocho, Preciosa A -pg 106
Quichocho, Prodencio 0 -pg 101
Quichocho, Rafael 0 -pg 174
Quichocho, Rita G -pg 101
Quichocho, Rita Q -pg 558
Quichocho, Rosa G -pg 153
Quichocho, Rosa LG -pg 174
Quichocho, Rosa N -pg 556
Quichocho, Rosa P -pg 121
Quichocho, Rosa Q -pg 93
Quichocho, Rosa Q -pg 94
Quichocho, Rosa T -pg 93
Quichocho, Rosa T -pg 94
Quichocho, Rosario P -pg 547
Quichocho, Rosario T -pg 93
Quichocho, Rufina L -pg 157
Quichocho, Soledad A -pg 106
Quichocho, Soledad P -pg 547
Quichocho, Teodoro 0 -pg 174
Quichocho, Teresa Q -pg 555
Quichocho, Tomas Q -pg 63
Quichocho, Tomasa 0 -pg 153
Quichocho, Tomasa Q -pg 555
Quichocho, Trinidad I -pg 556
Quichocho, Trinidad Q -pg 165
Quichocho, Vicenta LG -pg 174
Quichocho, Vicente Q -pg 63
Quichocho, Vicente Q -pg 93

Quichocho, Vicente Q -pg 345
Quichocho, Vicente SA -pg 107
Quidachay, Adela T -pg 468
Quidachay, Amanda T -pg 529
Quidachay, Ana A -pg 103
Quidachay, Ana A -pg 117
Quidachay, Ana B -pg 532
Quidachay, Ana D -pg 463
Quidachay, Ana P -pg 548
Quidachay, Ana R -pg 539
Quidachay, Ana T -pg 468
Quidachay, Ana T -pg 546
Quidachay, Ana V -pg 104
Quidachay, Andrea R -pg 539
Quidachay, Angela T -pg 472
Quidachay, Antonia B -pg 544
Quidachay, Antonia S -pg 129
Quidachay, Antonio B -pg 217
Quidachay, Antonio G -pg 104
Quidachay, Antonio Q -pg 532
Quidachay, Ascemcion T -pg 468
Quidachay, Baldovino A -pg 104
Quidachay, Candelaria R -pg 539
Quidachay, Caridad B -pg 532
Quidachay, Caridad V -pg 104
Quidachay, Concepcion B -pg 544
Quidachay, Consolacion B -pg 217
Quidachay, Cornelio P -pg 548
Quidachay, Delgadina S -pg 546
Quidachay, Dolores T -pg 478
Quidachay, Elisa D -pg 463
Quidachay, Enrique -pg 188
Quidachay, Enriqueta T -pg 468
Quidachay, Felix T -pg 478
Quidachay, Francisco Q -pg 532
Quidachay, Francisco R -pg 539
Quidachay, Francisco T -pg 468
Quidachay, Francisco T -pg 478
Quidachay, Jesus A -pg 104
Quidachay, Jesus A -pg 117
Quidachay, Jesus B -pg 217
Quidachay, Jesus B -pg 544
Quidachay, Jesus G -pg 532
Quidachay, Jesus T -pg 478
Quidachay, Jesus V -pg 104
Quidachay, Joaquin A -pg 117
Quidachay, Joaquin D -pg 463
Quidachay, Joaquin P -pg 548
Quidachay, Joaquina 0 -pg 83
Quidachay, Jose D -pg 532
Quidachay, Jose M -pg 289
Quidachay, Jose P -pg 548

Quidachay, Jose T -pg 463
Quidachay, Jose T -pg 472
Quidachay, Jose T -pg 532
Quidachay, Jose V -pg 104
Quidachay, Juan B -pg 532
Quidachay, Juan M -pg 546
Quidachay, Juan Q -pg 544
Quidachay, Juan R -pg 539
Quidachay, Juan T -pg 468
Quidachay, Juan -pg 217
Quidachay, Manuela V -pg 104
Quidachay, Maria A -pg 104
Quidachay, Maria B -pg 532
Quidachay, Maria D -pg 463
Quidachay, Maria G -pg 532
Quidachay, Maria T -pg 472
Quidachay, Maria T -pg 478
Quidachay, Maria V -pg 104
Quidachay, Mariano G -pg 532
Quidachay, Mariano P -pg 546
Quidachay, Pedro T -pg 478
Quidachay, Prodencio T -pg 468
Quidachay, Ramon 0 -pg 121
Quidachay, Ramon D -pg 463
Quidachay, Remedio B -pg 217
Quidachay, Remedios B -pg 544
Quidachay, Rita S -pg 546
Quidachay, Teresa B -pg 532
Quidachay, Veronica 0 -pg 121
Quidachay, Vicente A -pg 117
Quidachay, Vicente B -pg 217
Quidachay, Vicente B -pg 544
Quidachay, Vicente P -pg 548
Quidachay, Vicente Q -pg 539
Quidachay, Vicente T -pg 468
Quidagua, Ana C -pg 66
Quidagua, Antonia T -pg 483
Quidagua, Ignacia C -pg 66
Quidagua, Ignacio T -pg 483
Quidagua, Juan S -pg 66
Quidagua, Maria C -pg 66
Quidagua, Maria T -pg 483
Quiduagua, Jose B -pg 488
Quiduagua, Maria T -pg 488
Quifunas, Felicitas F -pg 544
Quifunas, Jose C -pg 544
Quifunas, Jose F -pg 544
Quifunas, Manuel A -pg 544
Quifunas, Maria F -pg 544
Quinata, Ana A -pg 471
Quinata, Ana LG -pg 504
Quinata, Ana M -pg 471

Quinata, Ana Q -pg 463
Quinata, Ana S -pg 464
Quinata, Ana T -pg 466
Quinata, Anastacio T -pg 469
Quinata, Angelina M -pg 471
Quinata, Antonia T -pg 462
Quinata, Antonina S -pg 464
Quinata, Antonio A -pg 462
Quinata, Antonio A -pg 463
Quinata, Antonio A -pg 465
Quinata, Antonio A -pg 469
Quinata, Antonio I -pg 460
Quinata, Antonio I -pg 470
Quinata, Augustin M -pg 465
Quinata, Baldivino M -pg 460
Quinata, Beatris A -pg 472
Quinata, Carlota T -pg 469
Quinata, Cayetano A -pg 504
Quinata, Dionisio M -pg 471
Quinata, Dolores A -pg 465
Quinata, Dolores C -pg 271
Quinata, Dolores Q -pg 463
Quinata, Edwardo Q -pg 469
Quinata, Elogracia D -pg 472
Quinata, Emelia M -pg 460
Quinata, Engracia M -pg 471
Quinata, Enrique C -pg 271
Quinata, Eugenio A -pg 420
Quinata, Faustina -pg 421
Quinata, Faustino C -pg 461
Quinata, Faustino M -pg 461
Quinata, Felicitas A -pg 465
Quinata, Felisa A -pg 471
Quinata, Francisca C -pg 463
Quinata, Francisco D -pg 472
Quinata, Francisco I -pg 470
Quinata, Gregorio C -pg 463
Quinata, Guardalupe D -pg 472
Quinata, Guillerma M -pg 460
Quinata, Hermenijildo Q -pg 466
Quinata, Hilarion A -pg 472
Quinata, Ignacio A -pg 471
Quinata, Isabel A -pg 465
Quinata, Jacinto Q -pg 469
Quinata, Jesus C -pg 461
Quinata, Jesus S -pg 460
Quinata, Jesus S -pg 472
Quinata, Joaquin A -pg 465
Quinata, Joaquin M -pg 471
Quinata, Joaquina C -pg 271
Quinata, Joaquina M -pg 460
Quinata, Joaquina T -pg 462

Quinata, Jose A -pg 472
Quinata, Jose C -pg 271
Quinata, Jose C -pg 461
Quinata, Jose G -pg 463
Quinata, Jose M -pg 460
Quinata, Jose S -pg 460
Quinata, Jose S -pg 471
Quinata, Jose V -pg 270
Quinata, Josefina A -pg 472
Quinata, Josepha A -pg 472
Quinata, Josepha T -pg 466
Quinata, Juan A -pg 472
Quinata, Juan A -pg 472
Quinata, Juan Q -pg 460
Quinata, Lidia S -pg 464
Quinata, Lucia T -pg 463
Quinata, Lucio M -pg 460
Quinata, Magdalena T -pg 466
Quinata, Margarita S -pg 464
Quinata, Maria A -pg 465
Quinata, Maria A -pg 471
Quinata, Maria C -pg 271
Quinata, Maria C -pg 461
Quinata, Maria Q -pg 469
Quinata, Maria Q -pg 469
Quinata, Maria S -pg 472
Quinata, Mariano A -pg 465
Quinata, Miguel A -pg 470
Quinata, Milagro A -pg 472
Quinata, Nieves A -pg 469
Quinata, Pedro I -pg 460
Quinata, Ramon C -pg 461
Quinata, Remedio M -pg 471
Quinata, Rita A -pg 469
Quinata, Rita C -pg 271
Quinata, Rosa A -pg 465
Quinata, Rosa C -pg 270
Quinata, Sibera T -pg 462
Quinata, Teresa I -pg 470
Quinata, Tomasa S -pg 460
Quinata, Trinidad C -pg 271
Quinata, Trinidad M -pg 471
Quinata, Veronica D -pg 472
Quinata, Vicenta M -pg 460
Quinata, Vicente A -pg 464
Quinata, Vicente A -pg 465
Quinata, Vicente A -pg 469
Quinata, Vicente A -pg 472
Quinata, Vicente Q -pg 469
Quinata, Vicente T -pg 469
Quinene, Ana C -pg 475
Quinene, Ana F -pg 477

Quinene, Ana M -pg 485
Quinene, Ana T -pg 481
Quinene, Ana -pg 225
Quinene, Ascemcion F -pg 477
Quinene, Cerilo T -pg 481
Quinene, Felicita Q -pg 476
Quinene, Ignacia F -pg 507
Quinene, Jesus M -pg 485
Quinene, Jose F -pg 477
Quinene, Jose Q -pg 476
Quinene, Juan T -pg 474
Quinene, Librada C -pg 475
Quinene, Magdalena F -pg 477
Quinene, Maria F -pg 477
Quinene, Mariano M -pg 485
Quinene, Pedro F -pg 485
Quinene, Santiago F -pg 477
Quinene, Silvestre M -pg 485
Quinene, Vicente M -pg 485
Quinene, Vicente T -pg 475
Quintanilla, Ana D -pg 167
Quintanilla, Ana L -pg 415
Quintanilla, Ana V -pg 415
Quintanilla, Ana -pg 419
Quintanilla, Andres L -pg 445
Quintanilla, Andresina -pg 419
Quintanilla, Aniceto SN -pg 519
Quintanilla, Antonia C -pg 110
Quintanilla, Antonia P -pg 410
Quintanilla, Antonia P -pg 416
Quintanilla, Antonio SN -pg 415
Quintanilla, Bernabe SN -pg 445
Quintanilla, Carlos C -pg 110
Quintanilla, Carmen C -pg 110
Quintanilla, Carmen L -pg 415
Quintanilla, Carmen R -pg 422
Quintanilla, Carmen SN -pg 415
Quintanilla, Carmen V -pg 415
Quintanilla, Emilia C -pg 110
Quintanilla, Emiterio R -pg 519
Quintanilla, Felix C -pg 416
Quintanilla, Felix V -pg 415
Quintanilla, Francisca C -pg 420
Quintanilla, Francisca -pg 420
Quintanilla, Francisco C -pg 420
Quintanilla, Francisco R -pg 422
Quintanilla, Francisco T -pg 111
Quintanilla, Getrudes R -pg 422
Quintanilla, Guillermo V -pg 415
Quintanilla, Ignacio M -pg 59
Quintanilla, Ignacio P -pg 416
Quintanilla, Ignacio R -pg 422

Quintanilla, Jesus D -pg 167
Quintanilla, Jesus L -pg 454
Quintanilla, Jesus SN -pg 519
Quintanilla, Joaquin R -pg 410
Quintanilla, Joaquin SN -pg 519
Quintanilla, Jose C -pg 110
Quintanilla, Jose C -pg 415
Quintanilla, Jose C -pg 417
Quintanilla, Jose C -pg 420
Quintanilla, Jose L -pg 415
Quintanilla, Jose R -pg 422
Quintanilla, Jose SN -pg 519
Quintanilla, Jose V -pg 415
Quintanilla, Jose -pg 234
Quintanilla, Jose -pg 419
Quintanilla, Josefa D -pg 167
Quintanilla, Juan C -pg 110
Quintanilla, Juan L -pg 455
Quintanilla, Juan P -pg 167
Quintanilla, Juan R -pg 422
Quintanilla, Juan -pg 419
Quintanilla, Juana D -pg 167
Quintanilla, Lucio SN -pg 415
Quintanilla, Lucy P -pg 410
Quintanilla, Luisa T -pg 454
Quintanilla, Manuel 0 -pg 166
Quintanilla, Manuel P -pg 416
Quintanilla, Manuel -pg 419
Quintanilla, Manuela SN -pg 519
Quintanilla, Manuela V -pg 415
Quintanilla, Maria C -pg 110
Quintanilla, Maria C -pg 110
Quintanilla, Maria C -pg 417
Quintanilla, Maria C -pg 420
Quintanilla, Maria L -pg 445
Quintanilla, Maria M -pg 111
Quintanilla, Maria P -pg 416
Quintanilla, Maria SN -pg 519
Quintanilla, Matias SN -pg 415
Quintanilla, Milagros P -pg 416
Quintanilla, Natividad D -pg 167
Quintanilla, Nicolas 0 -pg 167
Quintanilla, Pedro Q -pg 415
Quintanilla, Ramon T -pg 110
Quintanilla, Regina D -pg 167
Quintanilla, Rita R -pg 422
Quintanilla, Rosa C -pg 110
Quintanilla, Rosalia R -pg 422
Quintanilla, Soledad L -pg 415
Quintanilla, Soledad -pg 419
Quintanilla, Vicente C -pg 110
Quintanilla, Vicente C -pg 422

Quintanilla, Vicente SN -pg 513
Quintanilla, Vicente -pg 419
Quitanoc, Bartola G -pg 436
Quitanoc, Emelia S -pg 437
Quitanoc, Ramon S -pg 437
Quitanoc, Remedio S -pg 437
Quitanoc, Rita G -pg 436
Quitanoc, Rodevico S -pg 436
Quitanoc, Vicente G -pg 436
Quitaro, Agustin P -pg 543
Quitaro, Jesus B -pg 543
Quitaro, Jose B -pg 544
Quitaro, Juan B -pg 544
Quitaro, Soledad B -pg 543
Quitonguico, Amparo T -pg 123
Quitonguico, Antonio O -pg 123
Quitonguico, Concepcion O -pg 123
Quitonguico, Engracia O -pg 123
Quitonguico, Joaquin O -pg 123
Quitonguico, Pedro Q -pg 207
Quitonguico, Simona F -pg 207
Quitugua, Adela C -pg 201
Quitugua, Ana B -pg 14
Quitugua, Ana C -pg 159
Quitugua, Ana F -pg 355
Quitugua, Ana L -pg 39
Quitugua, Ana M -pg 376
Quitugua, Ana P -pg 14
Quitugua, Ana Q -pg 420
Quitugua, Ana T -pg 163
Quitugua, Antonia A -pg 392
Quitugua, Antonia C -pg 394
Quitugua, Antonia -pg 420
Quitugua, Antonio M -pg 376
Quitugua, Carmen A -pg 125
Quitugua, Consuelo C -pg 201
Quitugua, Demetrio T -pg 357
Quitugua, Dolores C -pg 394
Quitugua, Dolores G -pg 192
Quitugua, Dolores Q -pg 376
Quitugua, Eliza F -pg 355
Quitugua, Enrique T -pg 357
Quitugua, Enrique -pg 351
Quitugua, Felipe M -pg 306
Quitugua, Fermina R -pg 193
Quitugua, Francisco B -pg 39
Quitugua, Francisco C -pg 202
Quitugua, Francisco Q -pg 392
Quitugua, Ignacio P -pg 14
Quitugua, Ines S -pg 376
Quitugua, Jesus T -pg 357
Quitugua, Joaquin G -pg 192

Quitugua, Joaquin P -pg 14
Quitugua, Joaquin Q -pg 161
Quitugua, Joaquin R -pg 39
Quitugua, Joaquin T -pg 357
Quitugua, Joaquina C -pg 161
Quitugua, Jose A -pg 14
Quitugua, Jose C -pg 192
Quitugua, Jose C -pg 393
Quitugua, Jose D -pg 161
Quitugua, Jose L -pg 39
Quitugua, Jose P -pg 14
Quitugua, Jose Q -pg 125
Quitugua, Jose Q -pg 357
Quitugua, Josefa C -pg 192
Quitugua, Juan C -pg 201
Quitugua, Juan C -pg 394
Quitugua, Juan G -pg 192
Quitugua, Juan Q -pg 355
Quitugua, Juana S -pg 192
Quitugua, Juliana M -pg 306
Quitugua, Magdalena I -pg 125
Quitugua, Magdalena P -pg 185
Quitugua, Manuel C -pg 159
Quitugua, Maria A -pg 392
Quitugua, Maria C -pg 159
Quitugua, Maria D -pg 144
Quitugua, Maria D -pg 161
Quitugua, Maria F -pg 355
Quitugua, Maria I -pg 125
Quitugua, Maria P -pg 14
Quitugua, Maria -pg 376
Quitugua, Miguel T -pg 357
Quitugua, Milagro A -pg 392
Quitugua, Milagros P -pg 14
Quitugua, Natividad C -pg 201
Quitugua, Pedro R -pg 356
Quitugua, Ramon Q -pg 159
Quitugua, Ramon Q -pg 377
Quitugua, Rita R -pg 355
Quitugua, Rosa A -pg 360
Quitugua, Rosa S -pg 376
Quitugua, Rosa T -pg 357
Quitugua, Rosalia A -pg 392
Quitugua, Soledad G -pg 192
Quitugua, Teburcio R -pg 355
Quitugua, Vicenta C -pg 161
Quitugua, Vicenta C -pg 192
Quitugua, Vicente O -pg 163
Quitugua, Vicente A -pg 144
Quitugua, Vicente C -pg 192
Quitugua, Vicente C -pg 394
Quitugua, Vicente D -pg 161

Quitugua, Vicente P -pg 14
Quitugua, Vicente Q -pg 201
Quitugua, Vicente Q -pg 355
Quituguac, Conception A -pg 455
Quituguac, Jose A -pg 455
Quituguac, Maria A -pg 455
Quituguac, Vicente G -pg 455
Rabago, Ana C -pg 449
Rabago, Carmen C -pg 449
Rabago, Enrique C -pg 449
Rabago, Jose C -pg 449
Rabago, Josefa C -pg 449
Rabago, Juan C -pg 449
Rabago, Vicente C -pg 449
Rabon, Joaquin C -pg 91
Rabon, Luisa LG -pg 91
Rabon, Mariano C -pg 96
Rabon, Nicolasa C -pg 91
Ramirez, Concepcion T -pg 274
Ramirez, Florencio T -pg 274
Ramirez, Jesus B -pg 274
Ramirez, Jose T -pg 274
Ramirez, Josefina T -pg 274
Ramirez, Juliana T -pg 274
Ramirez, Maria T -pg 274
Rapolla, Antonio C -pg 362
Rapolla, Carmela R -pg 362
Rapolla, Carmen T -pg 363
Rapolla, Enrique C -pg 362
Rapolla, Francisca C -pg 362
Rapolla, Francisco T -pg 362
Rapolla, Juan C -pg 362
Rapolla, Lorenzo C -pg 362
Rapolla, Maria T -pg 363
Rapolla, Natividad R -pg 362
Rapolla, Vicenta T -pg 362
Respecio, Ana M -pg 230
Respecio, Antonio P -pg 230
Respecio, Brigida M -pg 230
Respecio, Roman M -pg 230
Respicio, Carmen P -pg 264
Respicio, Luisa P -pg 264
Respicio, Maria P -pg 264
Reyes, Ana A -pg 486
Reyes, Ana D -pg 259
Reyes, Ana LG -pg 31
Reyes, Ana P -pg 424
Reyes, Ana Q -pg 193
Reyes, Ana R -pg 424
Reyes, Ana S -pg 348
Reyes, Ana S -pg 488
Reyes, Ana SA -pg 138

Reyes, Andres B -pg 435
Reyes, Antonia B -pg 213
Reyes, Antonio C -pg 474
Reyes, Antonio P -pg 425
Reyes, Anunciacion Q -pg 193
Reyes, Apolonia 0 -pg 138
Reyes, Atilana S -pg 489
Reyes, Benita G -pg 70
Reyes, Carmen M -pg 229
Reyes, Cecilia M -pg 488
Reyes, Cerilo B -pg 442
Reyes, Concepcion S -pg 396
Reyes, Consolacion C -pg 433
Reyes, Dolores A -pg 486
Reyes, Dolores M -pg 229
Reyes, Dolores P -pg 424
Reyes, Dolores Q -pg 193
Reyes, Dolores R -pg 300
Reyes, Elisa G -pg 70
Reyes, Enrique C -pg 435
Reyes, Felicita C -pg 435
Reyes, Fermin A -pg 70
Reyes, Fermin R -pg 70
Reyes, Francisca A -pg 487
Reyes, Francisco C -pg 305
Reyes, Francisco G -pg 70
Reyes, Francisco L -pg 187
Reyes, Francisco SA -pg 209
Reyes, Henry M -pg 229
Reyes, Ignacia C -pg 445
Reycs, Ignacia -pg 214
Reyes, Ignacio A -pg 488
Reyes, Ignacio C -pg 305
Reyes, Ignacio C -pg 435
Reyes, Ignacio C -pg 474
Reyes, Ignacio G -pg 69
Reyes, Ignacio M -pg 187
Reyes, Jesus A -pg 486
Reyes, Jesus G -pg 70
Reyes, Jesus LG -pg 31
Reyes, Jesus Q -pg 193
Reyes, Jesus R -pg 209
Reyes, Jesus S -pg 396
Reyes, Jesus T -pg 229
Reyes, Joaquin A -pg 488
Reyes, Joaquin C -pg 474
Reyes, Joaquin P -pg 424
Reyes, Joaquin SA -pg 138
Reyes, Joaquina G -pg 553
Reyes, Jose A -pg 442
Reyes, Jose A -pg 486
Reyes, Jose B -pg 433

Reyes, Jose C -pg 445
Reyes, Jose G -pg 70
Reyes, Jose G -pg 427
Reyes, Jose M -pg 187
Reyes, Jose M -pg 488
Reyes, Jose P -pg 424
Reyes, Jose P -pg 536
Reyes, Jose Q -pg 193
Reyes, Jose R -pg 28
Reyes, Jose R -pg 536
Reyes, Jose S -pg 349
Reyes, Jose S -pg 396
Reyes, Jose SA -pg 138
Reyes, Jose T -pg 348
Reyes, Josefa C -pg 213
Reyes, Josefa M -pg 187
Reyes, Josefina S -pg 488
Reyes, Juan B -pg 213
Reyes, Juan B -pg 396
Reyes, Juan C -pg 445
Reyes, Juan G -pg 70
Reyes, Juan P -pg 424
Reyes, Juan Q -pg 194
Reyes, Juan R -pg 70
Reyes, Juan R -pg 488
Reyes, Juan R -pg 489
Reyes, Juana M -pg 187
Reyes, Laurion R -pg 424
Reyes, Lorenzo M -pg 474
Reyes, Lourdes P -pg 536
Reyes, Luis SA -pg 209
Reyes, Luis T -pg 424
Reyes, Macario B -pg 213
Reyes, Manuel M -pg 187
Reyes, Maria B -pg 442
Reyes, Maria C -pg 433
Reyes, Maria C -pg 435
Reyes, Maria C -pg 445
Reyes, Maria C -pg 474
Reyes, Maria L -pg 497
Reyes, Maria P -pg 424
Reyes, Maria P -pg 536
Reyes, Maria Q -pg 193
Reyes, Maria Q -pg 306
Reyes, Maria R -pg 70
Reyes, Maria S -pg 348
Reyes, Maria S -pg 396
Reyes, Maria SA -pg 209
Reyes, Mariano G -pg 70
Reyes, Mariano R -pg 138
Reyes, Natividad B -pg 442
Reyes, Natividad R -pg 138

Reyes, Nicolas S -pg 488
Reyes, Nicolasa M -pg 187
Reyes, Nicolasa SA -pg 138
Reyes, Oliva SA -pg 138
Reyes, Ramon A -pg 486
Reyes, Ramon A -pg 487
Reyes, Ramon R -pg 209
Reyes, Regina B -pg 213
Reyes, Rita Q -pg 28
Reyes, Rosa P -pg 424
Reyes, Rosa R -pg 424
Reyes, Rosa S -pg 488
Reyes, Salome P -pg 424
Reyes, Segundo M -pg 229
Reyes, Teresa C -pg 474
Reyes, Teresa R -pg 424
Reyes, Trinidad L -pg 497
Reyes, Trinidad P -pg 424
Reyes, Venancio B -pg 445
Reyes, Vicenta M -pg 225
Reyes, Vicente A -pg 487
Reyes, Vicente C -pg 258
Reyes, Vicente G -pg 70
Reyes, Vicente G -pg 553
Reyes, Vicente L -pg 497
Reyes, Vicente Q -pg 193
Reyes, Vicente Q -pg 306
Rice, Ana M -pg 402
Rice, Ana M jr -pg 402
Rice, James H -pg 402
Rice, John T -pg 402
Rice, John -pg 402
Rios, Ana S -pg 373
Rios, Antonia S -pg 373
Rios, Brigido A -pg 243
Rios, Enrique LG -pg 243
Rios, Felipe R -pg 373
Rios, Gregorio -pg 228
Rios, Jesus S -pg 373
Rios, Jose LG -pg 243
Rios, Jose S -pg 373
Rios, Josefa LG -pg 243
Rios, Josefa -pg 304
Rios, Lagrimas S -pg 373
Rios, Manuel R -pg 228
Rios, Maria LG -pg 243
Rios, Maria S -pg 373
Rios, Rita S -pg 373
Rios, Rosa R -pg 228
Rios, Rosa S -pg 373
Rios, Trinidad G -pg 228
Rios, Vicente LG -pg 243

Rivera, Adelia S -pg 447
Rivera, Ana B -pg 429
Rivera, Ana LG -pg 50
Rivera, Ana S -pg 447
Rivera, Andrea G -pg 50
Rivera, Antonia G -pg 440
Rivera, Antonio D -pg 429
Rivera, Asuncion A -pg 126
Rivera, Asuncion U -pg 20
Rivera, Benigno LG -pg 147
Rivera, Biatris D -pg 17
Rivera, Camilo -pg 341
Rivera, Carmen A -pg 126
Rivera, Dolores D -pg 17
Rivera, Dolores G -pg 440
Rivera, Dolores S -pg 443
Rivera, Felix T -pg 447
Rivera, Filomena B -pg 429
Rivera, Francisco A -pg 519
Rivera, Francisco R -pg 59
Rivera, Francisco U -pg 20
Rivera, Gonzalo SN -pg 131
Rivera, Gregorio R -pg 24
Rivera, Ignacio SN -pg 131
Rivera, Ignacio U -pg 131
Rivera, Isabel R -pg 24
Rivera, Jesus G -pg 440
Rivera, Jesus R -pg 24
Rivera, Jesus S -pg 141
Rivera, Jesus -pg 303
Rivera, Jesusa S -pg 141
Rivera, Joaquin D -pg 15
Rivera, Joaquin D -pg 440
Rivera, Joaquin SN -pg 131
Rivera, Joaquin U -pg 303
Rivera, Jose A -pg 519
Rivera, Jose C -pg 141
Rivera, Jose LG -pg 519
Rivera, Jose S -pg 447
Rivera, Jose U -pg 126
Rivera, Josefa A -pg 126
Rivera, Juan D -pg 443
Rivera, Juan G -pg 50
Rivera, Juan LG -pg 146
Rivera, Juan SN -pg 131
Rivera, Juan U -pg 146
Rivera, Juana A -pg 126
Rivera, Leocardo U -pg 147
Rivera, Luisa A -pg 126
Rivera, Magdalena B -pg 125
Rivera, Manuel SN -pg 131
Rivera, Manuel U -pg 125

Rivera, Manuel U -pg 146
Rivera, Maria A -pg 126
Rivera, Maria D -pg 17
Rivera, Maria D -pg 17
Rivera, Maria G -pg 243
Rivera, Maria S -pg 443
Rivera, Maria SN -pg 131
Rivera, Maria SN -pg 131
Rivera, Maria Raquel A -pg 519
Rivera, Mariano G -pg 50
Rivera, Martin B -pg 429
Rivera, Miguel SN -pg 131
Rivera, Natividad S -pg 447
Rivera, Pedro A -pg 519
Rivera, Rosa S -pg 447
Rivera, Seledonia A -pg 519
Rivera, Soledad S -pg 447
Rivera, Vicente 0 -pg 141
Rivera, Vicente B -pg 429
Rivera, Vicente S -pg 447
Rivera, Vicente U -pg 20
Roberto, Ana B -pg 267
Roberto, Andres A -pg 321
Roberto, Antonia B -pg 267
Roberto, Concepcion A -pg 245
Roberto, Cristina B -pg 267
Roberto, Dolores A -pg 245
Roberto, Dolores T -pg 321
Roberto, Emma -pg 255
Roberto, Enrique B -pg 267
Roberto, Felix -pg 267
Roberto, Hessel -pg 255
Roberto, Ignacio T -pg 321
Roberto, Isabel B -pg 267
Roberto, Jose -pg 321
Roberto, Juan A -pg 245
Roberto, Juan -pg 267
Roberto, Lorenza A -pg 321
Roberto, Luisa B -pg 267
Roberto, Manuel B -pg 267
Roberto, Margarita P -pg 321
Roberto, Maria A -pg 321
Roberto, Maria B -pg 267
Roberto, Mercedes B -pg 255
Roberto, Vicente -pg 267
Roberto, Wallace -pg 255
Roberto, William A -pg 321
Rodriges, Ana R -pg 557
Rodriges, Antonia B -pg 557
Rodriges, Carmen D -pg 555
Rodriges, Dolores B -pg 557
Rodriges, Fermina S -pg 557

Rodriges, Jesus B -pg 557
Rodriges, Jose B -pg 557
Rodriges, Jose S -pg 557
Rodriges, Lucas S -pg 557
Rodriges, Maria B -pg 557
Rodriges, Maria R -pg 554
Rodriges, Mariano L -pg 557
Rodriges, Vicente M -pg 555
Rojas, Ana A -pg 58
Rojas, Ana M -pg 271
Rojas, Ana S -pg 367
Rojas, Ana -pg 337
Rojas, Antonia LG -pg 91
Rojas, Antonia S -pg 367
Rojas, Antonio D -pg 58
Rojas, Benita R -pg 227
Rojas, Cecilio -pg 280
Rojas, Concepcion C -pg 55
Rojas, Concepcion C -pg 228
Rojas, Francisca C -pg 106
Rojas, Francisco A -pg 91
Rojas, Francisco S -pg 227
Rojas, Ignacio -pg 337
Rojas, Joaquin C -pg 227
Rojas, Joaquin R -pg 242
Rojas, Jose S -pg 227
Rojas, Jose -pg 337
Rojas, Juan C -pg 227
Rojas, Juan R -pg 367
Rojas, Juan S -pg 367
Rojas, Juana C -pg 227
Rojas, Juana D -pg 337
Rojas, Magdalena S -pg 367
Rojas, Manuel C -pg 230
Rojas, Manuel S -pg 367
Rojas, Margarita S -pg 227
Rojas, Maria C -pg 55
Rojas, Maria M -pg 242
Rojas, Maria R -pg 18
Rojas, Maria R -pg 227
Rojas, Maria S -pg 227
Rojas, Mariano M -pg 227
Rojas, Mariano -pg 338
Rojas, Natividad C -pg 228
Rojas, Nieves C -pg 55
Rojas, Pedro A -pg 55
Rojas, Pedro R -pg 271
Rojas, Pedro S -pg 227
Rojas, Pedro S -pg 367
Rojas, Ramon S -pg 367
Rojas, Rosa C -pg 55
Rojas, Tomas C -pg 228

Rojas, Vicente T -pg 106
Ronaquillo, Micaila M -pg 376
Rosa, Ana de la 0 -pg 38
Rosa, Carmen Q -pg 423
Rosa, Emilio 0 -pg 105
Rosa, Felix La Rosa -pg 105
Rosa, Josefa G -pg 105
Rosa, Lucas La Rosa -pg 105
Rosa, Maria G -pg 105
Rosa, Mariano M -pg 382
Rosa, Teresa G -pg 105
Rosa, Trinidad -pg 234
Rosario, Amanda 0 -pg 164
Rosario, Ana A -pg 118
Rosario, Ana LG -pg 22
Rosario, Ana P -pg 76
Rosario, Ana T -pg 116
Rosario, Ana T -pg 117
Rosario, Angelina L -pg 71
Rosario, Antonia T -pg 116
Rosario, Antonio C -pg 77
Rosario, Antonio T -pg 111
Rosario, Antonio T -pg 531
Rosario, Beatris 0 -pg 164
Rosario, Bruno M -pg 88
Rosario, Carlos R -pg 243
Rosario, Carmen S -pg 24
Rosario, Catalina T -pg 531
Rosario, Concepcion C -pg 37
Rosario, Concepcion LG -pg 22
Rosario, Consuelo A -pg 125
Rosario, Crisy SA -pg 111
Rosario, Dolores A -pg 125
Rosario, Dolores A -pg 164
Rosario, Dolores M -pg 125
Rosario, Dolores T -pg 531
Rosario, Domingo C -pg 37
Rosario, Domingo M -pg 229
Rosario, Domingo Q -pg 531
Rosario, Domingo R -pg 145
Rosario, Domingo R -pg 243
Rosario, Enrique L -pg 72
Rosario, Francisca LG -pg 22
Rosario, Francisco C -pg 32
Rosario, Francisco F -pg 26
Rosario, Francisco R -pg 243
Rosario, Francisco T -pg 531
Rosario, Gertrudes C -pg 32
Rosario, Gregorio P -pg 76
Rosario, Ignacia B -pg 128
Rosario, Ignacio L -pg 71
Rosario, Ignacio P -pg 71

Rosario, Jesus C -pg 37
Rosario, Jesus C -pg 304
Rosario, Jesus P -pg 76
Rosario, Jesus -pg 217
Rosario, Joaquin C -pg 71
Rosario, Joaquin C -pg 90
Rosario, Joaquin F -pg 18
Rosario, Joaquina B -pg 162
Rosario, Jose A -pg 90
Rosario, Jose B -pg 76
Rosario, Jose B -pg 243
Rosario, Jose L -pg 53
Rosario, Jose L -pg 72
Rosario, Jose L -pg 252
Rosario, Jose P -pg 76
Rosario, Jose R -pg 243
Rosario, Jose S -pg 125
Rosario, Jose T -pg 531
Rosario, Josefa C -pg 36
Rosario, Josefina 0 -pg 125
Rosario, Juan A -pg 133
Rosario, Juan B -pg 77
Rosario, Juan C -pg 304
Rosario, Juan F -pg 22
Rosario, Juan R -pg 118
Rosario, Juan R -pg 243
Rosario, Juan T -pg 531
Rosario, Juan -pg 217
Rosario, Juliana B -pg 128
Rosario, Lorenzo C -pg 557
Rosario, Lourdes P -pg 76
Rosario, Luisa LG -pg 22
Rosario, Luisa M -pg 228
Rosario, Magdalena A -pg 90
Rosario, Magdalena C -pg 37
Rosario, Manuel B -pg 266
Rosario, Manuel L -pg 71
Rosario, Manuel L -pg 252
Rosario, Manuel T -pg 116
Rosario, Maria 0 -pg 114
Rosario, Maria C -pg 37
Rosario, Maria C -pg 77
Rosario, Maria C jr -pg 77
Rosario, Maria L -pg 252
Rosario, Maria R -pg 243
Rosario, Maria S -pg 24
Rosario, Maria T -pg 116
Rosario, Miguel R -pg 243
Rosario, Milagros L -pg 71
Rosario, Nicolasa L -pg 71
Rosario, Pedro A -pg 116
Rosario, Pedro C -pg 37

Rosario, Pedro L -pg 252
Rosario, Remedios C -pg 37
Rosario, Rosa L -pg 72
Rosario, Rosa M -pg 125
Rosario, Rosa R -pg 243
Rosario, Rosalia L -pg 252
Rosario, Rufina T -pg 117
Rosario, Silvestre C -pg 70
Rosario, Silvestre C -pg 71
Rosario, Soledad SA -pg 111
Rosario, Teresa C -pg 36
Rosario, Tomas R -pg 243
Rosario, Trinidad T -pg 531
Rosario, Vicenta C -pg 37
Rosario, Vicenta C -pg 122
Rosario, Vicenta R -pg 243
Rosario, Vicente A -pg 90
Rosario, Vicente B -pg 128
Rosario, Vicente C -pg 77
Rosario, Vicente F -pg 32
Rosario, Vicente G -pg 122
Rosario, Vicente LG -pg 22
Rosendo, Manuel H -pg 61
Rupley, Juan I -pg 303
Rupley, Magdalena I -pg 303
S Nicolas, Dolores C -pg 199
S Nicolas, Geronimo C -pg 198
S Nicolas, Jose T -pg 199
S Nicolas, Josefa -pg 209
S Nicolas, Juan C -pg 199
S Nicolas, Maria C -pg 199
S Nicolas, Pedro C -pg 199
S Nicolas, Vicente C -pg 199
Sablan, Agueda A -pg 193
Sablan, Alfredo C -pg 442
Sablan, Amalia B -pg 172
Sablan, Amalia R -pg 171
Sablan, Ana A -pg 218
Sablan, Ana A -pg 343
Sablan, Ana B -pg 172
Sablan, Ana C -pg 155
Sablan, Ana C -pg 190
Sablan, Ana G -pg 33
Sablan, Ana P -pg 190
Sablan, Ana P -pg 433
Sablan, Ana S -pg 57
Sablan, Ana S -pg 57
Sablan, Ana S -pg 401
Sablan, Ana S -pg 409
Sablan, Ana T -pg 450
Sablan, Angel A -pg 193
Sablan, Antonia LG -pg 147

Sablan, Antonia P -pg 44
Sablan, Antonia Q -pg 432
Sablan, Antonio C -pg 66
Sablan, Antonio C -pg 190
Sablan, Antonio C -pg 427
Sablan, Antonio D -pg 172
Sablan, Antonio G -pg 433
Sablan, Antonio LG -pg 147
Sablan, Antonio Q -pg 432
Sablan, Antonio R -pg 172
Sablan, Asencion A -pg 292
Sablan, Asuncion S -pg 418
Sablan, Augusto F -pg 57
Sablan, Candelaria C -pg 190
Sablan, Carlos T -pg 195
Sablan, Carmen A -pg 218
Sablan, Carmen C -pg 65
Sablan, Carmen C -pg 190
Sablan, Carmen S -pg 401
Sablan, Cecilio S -pg 432
Sablan, Concepcion M -pg 37
Sablan, Cristina B -pg 172
Sablan, Cristobal LG -pg 147
Sablan, Cristobal Q -pg 432
Sablan, Diego S -pg 433
Sablan, Dolores A -pg 218
Sablan, Dolores B -pg 172
Sablan, Dolores B -pg 401
Sablan, Dolores D -pg 128
Sablan, Dolores LG -pg 147
Sablan, Dolores Q -pg 432
Sablan, Ejinio T -pg 37
Sablan, Elena S -pg 408
Sablan, Emerenciana A -pg 193
Sablan, Emilia C -pg 190
Sablan, Enrique B -pg 172
Sablan, Enrique C -pg 190
Sablan, Enrique P -pg 416
Sablan, Enrique -pg 388
Sablan, Estfania C -pg 442
Sablan, Felix S -pg 57
Sablan, Feliza D -pg 128
Sablan, Fidel T -pg 37
Sablan, Francisco A -pg 218
Sablan, Francisco B -pg 172
Sablan, Francisco C -pg 442
Sablan, Francisco F -pg 57
Sablan, Francisco S -pg 408
Sablan, Francisco S -pg 409
Sablan, Francisco S -pg 411
Sablan, Francisco S -pg 433
Sablan, Gregorio S -pg 57

Sablan, Guadalupe B -pg 433
Sablan, Guadalupe P -pg 416
Sablan, Guadalupe T -pg 37
Sablan, Guillermo D -pg 189
Sablan, Honorato A -pg 193
Sablan, Ignacia P -pg 433
Sablan, Ignacio C -pg 150
Sablan, Iluminada A -pg 193
Sablan, Isabel C -pg 349
Sablan, Isabel R -pg 172
Sablan, Jesus C -pg 442
Sablan, Jesus D -pg 172
Sablan, Jesus L -pg 336
Sablan, Jesus P -pg 44
Sablan, Jesusa P -pg 416
Sablan, Joaquin A -pg 401
Sablan, Joaquin B -pg 401
Sablan, Joaquin C -pg 415
Sablan, Joaquin D -pg 171
Sablan, Joaquin P -pg 406
Sablan, Joaquin R -pg 155
Sablan, Joaquina A -pg 292
Sablan, Jose A -pg 218
Sablan, Jose A -pg 292
Sablan, Jose A -pg 343
Sablan, Jose B -pg 172
Sablan, Jose B -pg 172
Sablan, Jose C -pg 65
Sablan, Jose C -pg 155
Sablan, Jose C -pg 349
Sablan, Jose C -pg 450
Sablan, Jose L -pg 195
Sablan, Jose M -pg 37
Sablan, Jose P -pg 44
Sablan, Jose P -pg 190
Sablan, Jose P -pg 416
Sablan, Jose S -pg 401
Sablan, Jose T -pg 37
Sablan, Jose -pg 409
Sablan, Josefa B -pg 172
Sablan, Josefa D -pg 128
Sablan, Josefa S -pg 409
Sablan, Juan A -pg 349
Sablan, Juan C -pg 416
Sablan, Juan D -pg 408
Sablan, Juan R -pg 433
Sablan, Juan S -pg 57
Sablan, Juan S -pg 401
Sablan, Juan S -pg 401
Sablan, Juan T -pg 450
Sablan, Juan J P -pg 433
Sablan, Lino A -pg 147

Sablan, Lino R -pg 336
Sablan, Lorenzo A -pg 292
Sablan, Lourdes A -pg 193
Sablan, Lourdes S -pg 409
Sablan, Luis C -pg 418
Sablan, Macaila S -pg 409
Sablan, Magdalena L -pg 336
Sablan, Manuel C -pg 44
Sablan, Manuel C -pg 320
Sablan, Manuel E -pg 37
Sablan, Manuel L -pg 336
Sablan, Manuel S -pg 409
Sablan, Manuel T -pg 37
Sablan, Manuela B -pg 172
Sablan, Marcial A -pg 193
Sablan, Margarita R -pg 171
Sablan, Maria A -pg 193
Sablan, Maria B -pg 172
Sablan, Maria B -pg 172
Sablan, Maria B -pg 401
Sablan, Maria B -pg 442
Sablan, Maria C -pg 65
Sablan, Maria C -pg 155
Sablan, Maria C -pg 190
Sablan, Maria C jr -pg 155
Sablan, Maria F -pg 57
Sablan, Maria G -pg 433
Sablan, Maria M -pg 37
Sablan, Maria S -pg 388
Sablan, Maria S -pg 412
Sablan, Maria T -pg 37
Sablan, Maria T -pg 195
Sablan, Maria T -pg 450
Sablan, Maria D P -pg 433
Sablan, Mariano C -pg 155
Sablan, Martina S -pg 388
Sablan, Natividad C -pg 155
Sablan, Natividad C -pg 349
Sablan, Nicolas B -pg 172
Sablan, Nicolasa S -pg 388
Sablan, Nieves L -pg 336
Sablan, Pedro B -pg 172
Sablan, Pedro C -pg 349
Sablan, Pedro D -pg 422
Sablan, Pedro P -pg 57
Sablan, Pedro R -pg 37
Sablan, Pedro F P -pg 433
Sablan, Rafael C -pg 349
Sablan, Ramon M -pg 37
Sablan, Ramon R -pg 171
Sablan, Ramon T -pg 37
Sablan, Regina C -pg 349

Sablan, Rita T -pg 37
Sablan, Rosa A -pg 401
Sablan, Rosa F -pg 57
Sablan, Rosa L -pg 416
Sablan, Rosa P -pg 433
Sablan, Rosa S -pg 409
Sablan, Rosalia R -pg 171
Sablan, Rosalia S -pg 418
Sablan, Rosalia T -pg 195
Sablan, Rosario C -pg 190
Sablan, Rosario T -pg 37
Sablan, Segundo F -pg 57
Sablan, Silvestre A -pg 401
Sablan, Soledad T -pg 195
Sablan, Teresa P -pg 44
Sablan, Tomas P -pg 400
Sablan, Tomasa P -pg 416
Sablan, Vicenta B -pg 172
Sablan, Vicenta C -pg 150
Sablan, Vicenta D -pg 127
Sablan, Vicenta S -pg 57
Sablan, Vicente A -pg 401
Sablan, Vicente B -pg 172
Sablan, Vicente C -pg 349
Sablan, Vicente G -pg 127
Sablan, Vicente LG -pg 147
Sablan, Vicente P -pg 218
Sablan, Vicente P -pg 416
Sablan, Vicente R -pg 33
Sablan, Vicente S -pg 388
Sablan, Vicente S -pg 401
Sablan, Vicente T -pg 450
Sablan, Vicente U -pg 400
Sablan, Vicente -pg 409
Sablan, Virginia T -pg 37
Saccomani, Amelia 0 -pg 33
Saccomani, Elbira 0 -pg 33
Saccomani, Erculi 0 -pg 33
Saccomani, Ida 0 -pg 33
Saccomani, Remedio 0 -pg 33
Saccomani, Seserina 0 -pg 33
Sahagon, Ana R -pg 536
Sahagon, Enrique Q -pg 79
Sahagon, Felicitas R -pg 535
Sahagon, Francisco Q -pg 79
Sahagon, Ignacia Q -pg 79
Sahagon, Ignacio R -pg 535
Sahagon, Joaquina R -pg 536
Sahagon, Jose Q -pg 79
Sahagon, Jose R -pg 535
Sahagon, Magdalena Q -pg 79
Sahagon, Manuel C -pg 535

Sahagon, Maria Q -pg 79
Sahagon, Rebelato C -pg 79
Sahagon, Trinidad Q -pg 79
Sahagon, Vicenta R -pg 535
Sakai, Ana F -pg 297
Sakai, Juan -pg 297
Sakai, Rita F -pg 297
Sakakibara, Concepcion P -pg 244
Sakakibara, Florence P -pg 244
Sakakibara, Hana P -pg 244
Sakakibara, Nogi P -pg 244
Sakakibara, S -pg 244
Sakuras, Luis C -pg 536
Salas, Agapito N -pg 206
Salas, Albina L -pg 326
Salas, Ana A -pg 379
Salas, Ana B -pg 117
Salas, Ana C -pg 226
Salas, Ana C -pg 258
Salas, Ana C -pg 326
Salas, Ana C -pg 375
Salas, Ana D -pg 133
Salas, Ana I -pg 375
Salas, Ana LG -pg 329
Salas, Ana M -pg 374
Salas, Ana S -pg 287
Salas, Ana SN -pg 27
Salas, Andres Q -pg 345
Salas, Antonia D -pg 133
Salas, Antonia F -pg 374
Salas, Antonio C -pg 375
Salas, Antonio D -pg 258
Salas, Antonio LG -pg 96
Salas, Antonio Q -pg 326
Salas, Antonio SN -pg 27
Salas, Atanasio LG -pg 329
Salas, Aurea G -pg 255
Salas, Avelina T -pg 463
Salas, Bartola SN -pg 27
Salas, Benigno D -pg 230
Salas, Caridad B -pg 436
Salas, Carlos L -pg 325
Salas, Carmen A -pg 379
Salas, Carmen M -pg 457
Salas, Carmen T -pg 185
Salas, Catalina J -pg 358
Salas, Catalina -pg 287
Salas, Cecelia G -pg 452
Salas, Cecilio L -pg 255
Salas, Cecilio M -pg 374
Salas, Clotilde E -pg 324
Salas, Clotilde S -pg 113

Salas, Concepcion C -pg 113
Salas, Concepcion I -pg 219
Salas, Consolacion F -pg 117
Salas, Dionisio LG -pg 329
Salas, Dolores A -pg 206
Salas, Dolores I -pg 374
Salas, Dolores S -pg 276
Salas, Domingo C -pg 265
Salas, Elestina S -pg 442
Salas, Elisa C -pg 265
Salas, Elpidia S -pg 113
Salas, Emeterio G -pg 255
Salas, Emeterio S -pg 228
Salas, Engracia C -pg 326
Salas, Engracia S -pg 287
Salas, Enrique A -pg 206
Salas, Enrique S -pg 287
Salas, Esperanza S -pg 287
Salas, Felisa J -pg 358
Salas, Felix B -pg 117
Salas, Felix G -pg 325
Salas, Felix I -pg 219
Salas, Felix S -pg 287
Salas, Francisco B -pg 431
Salas, Francisco C -pg 265
Salas, Francisco LG -pg 329
Salas, Francisco P -pg 225
Salas, Francisco S -pg 276
Salas, Francisco S -pg 323
Salas, Francisco S -pg 452
Salas, Galo G -pg 325
Salas, Genoveva I -pg 314
Salas, Ignacia B -pg 431
Salas, Ignacia M -pg 228
Salas, Ignacio C -pg 375
Salas, Ignacio N -pg 206
Salas, Ignacio Q -pg 323
Salas, Isabel S -pg 442
Salas, Javier D -pg 117
Salas, Jesus A -pg 206
Salas, Jesus I -pg 314
Salas, Jesus J -pg 358
Salas, Jesus L -pg 325
Salas, Jesus LG -pg 329
Salas, Jesus S -pg 119
Salas, Jesus S -pg 375
Salas, Jesus SN -pg 27
Salas, Joaquin C -pg 226
Salas, Joaquin C -pg 326
Salas, Joaquin F -pg 374
Salas, Joaquin G -pg 452
Salas, Joaquin J -pg 358

Salas, Joaquin LG -pg 329
Salas, Joaquin Q -pg 345
Salas, Joaquina T -pg 186
Salas, Jose 0 -pg 113
Salas, Jose A -pg 198
Salas, Jose C -pg 27
Salas, Jose C -pg 226
Salas, Jose C -pg 258
Salas, Jose C -pg 375
Salas, Jose C -pg 442
Salas, Jose D -pg 133
Salas, Jose G -pg 255
Salas, Jose I -pg 375
Salas, Jose J -pg 358
Salas, Jose L -pg 325
Salas, Jose LG -pg 329
Salas, Jose M -pg 228
Salas, Jose M -pg 374
Salas, Jose N -pg 408
Salas, Jose Q -pg 329
Salas, Jose S -pg 194
Salas, Jose S -pg 432
Salas, Jose SN -pg 27
Salas, Jose T -pg 463
Salas, Jose T -pg 552
Salas, Josefa B -pg 117
Salas, Josefa C -pg 375
Salas, Josefa F -pg 133
Salas, Josefa I -pg 219
Salas, Josefa M -pg 228
Salas, Juan A -pg 206
Salas, Juan B -pg 431
Salas, Juan C -pg 375
Salas, Juan I -pg 314
Salas, Juan J -pg 552
Salas, Juan M -pg 457
Salas, Juan Q -pg 345
Salas, Juan S -pg 119
Salas, Juan S -pg 185
Salas, Juan S -pg 276
Salas, Juan S -pg 287
Salas, Juan S -pg 345
Salas, Juan S -pg 456
Salas, Juana D -pg 44
Salas, Locia M -pg 457
Salas, Lucas S -pg 44
Salas, Luisa S -pg 323
Salas, Magdalena C -pg 375
Salas, Magdalena S -pg 287
Salas, Manuel B -pg 431
Salas, Manuel F -pg 436
Salas, Manuel J -pg 358

Salas, Manuel -pg 427
Salas, Manuela C -pg 326
Salas, Manuela SN -pg 27
Salas, Marcela C -pg 375
Salas, Maria B -pg 117
Salas, Maria B -pg 436
Salas, Maria C -pg 226
Salas, Maria C -pg 226
Salas, Maria C -pg 326
Salas, Maria C -pg 375
Salas, Maria C -pg 431
Salas, Maria D -pg 133
Salas, Maria E -pg 324
Salas, Maria F -pg 327
Salas, Maria I -pg 219
Salas, Maria I -pg 219
Salas, Maria I -pg 314
Salas, Maria I -pg 375
Salas, Maria J -pg 358
Salas, Maria L -pg 325
Salas, Maria LG -pg 329
Salas, Maria M -pg 206
Salas, Maria M -pg 228
Salas, Maria S -pg 323
Salas, Maria S -pg 409
Salas, Maria S -pg 442
Salas, Maria S -pg 456
Salas, Mariano SN -pg 27
Salas, Martina C -pg 375
Salas, Matilde L -pg 325
Salas, Mercedes I -pg 219
Salas, Mercedes LG -pg 96
Salas, Miguel LG -pg 329
Salas, Miguel S -pg 276
Salas, Nicolas Q -pg 327
Salas, Nicolasa J -pg 358
Salas, Nicolasa L -pg 255
Salas, Patricio S -pg 287
Salas, Pedro C -pg 264
Salas, Pedro C -pg 265
Salas, Pedro E -pg 358
Salas, Pilar L -pg 325
Salas, Providencia L -pg 326
Salas, Rafael 0 -pg 133
Salas, Rafaela L -pg 326
Salas, Ramon C -pg 96
Salas, Ramon S -pg 287
Salas, Ramona LG -pg 329
Salas, Ramunda F -pg 113
Salas, Regina 0 -pg 133
Salas, Regina C -pg 326
Salas, Remedios C -pg 326

Salas, Remigio C -pg 457
Salas, Ricardo E -pg 324
Salas, Rita C -pg 258
Salas, Rita LG -pg 329
Salas, Rosa C -pg 226
Salas, Rosa C -pg 264
Salas, Rosa F -pg 374
Salas, Rosa LG -pg 329
Salas, Rosa S -pg 287
Salas, Rosalia I -pg 219
Salas, Rosalia S -pg 456
Salas, Rosario C -pg 326
Salas, Rosario Q -pg 345
Salas, Salvador L -pg 326
Salas, Selestina T -pg 552
Salas, Simplicia L -pg 325
Salas, Soledad A -pg 206
Salas, Soledad I -pg 374
Salas, Soledad M -pg 457
Salas, Susana Q -pg 345
Salas, Susperanca C -pg 326
Salas, Teresa J -pg 358
Salas, Teresa SN -pg 27
Salas, Tomasa B -pg 117
Salas, Tomasa LG -pg 329
Salas, Tomasa S -pg 96
Salas, Trinidad G -pg 255
Salas, Trinidad G -pg 452
Salas, Venancio A -pg 206
Salas, Veronica -pg 227
Salas, Vicente A -pg 206
Salas, Vicente C -pg 226
Salas, Vicente C -pg 452
Salas, Vicente D -pg 431
Salas, Vicente E -pg 206
Salas, Vicente I -pg 219
Salas, Vicente M -pg 374
Salas, Vicente M -pg 457
Salas, Vicente S -pg 219
Salas, Vicente S -pg 379
Salas, Vicente S -pg 452
Salas, Victoria S -pg 230
Salas, Virginia -pg 227
Salles, Jose I -pg 264
Salles, Jose T -pg 264
Salles, Nieves T -pg 264
Saluago, Cristina C -pg 382
Saluznamnam, Ana B -pg 455
Saluznamnam, Antonia S -pg 489
Saluznamnam, Consolacion B -pg 455
Saluznamnam, Faustina T -pg 441

Saluznamnam, Ignacia T -pg 441
Saluznamnam, Juan T -pg 453
Saluznamnam, Maria B -pg 454
Saluznamnam, Maria S -pg 489
Saluznamnam, Maria S -pg 489
Saluznamnam, Olimpia S -pg 489
Saluznamnam, Vicente T -pg 454
San Agustin, Agueda O -pg 119
San Agustin, Alejandra C -pg 170
San Agustin, Amalia L -pg 162
San Agustin, Ana B -pg 338
San Agustin, Ana C -pg 84
San Agustin, Ana C -pg 84
San Agustin, Antonia O -pg 170
San Agustin, Antonia C -pg 84
San Agustin, Asencion G -pg 338
San Agustin, Asuncion D -pg 120
San Agustin, Candido S -pg 122
San Agustin, Caridad R -pg 75
San Agustin, Concepcion G -pg 84
San Agustin, Dolores B -pg 338
San Agustin, Dolores D -pg 120
San Agustin, Dolores E -pg 160
San Agustin, Dolores L -pg 162
San Agustin, Doroteo G -pg 84
San Agustin, Faustino C -pg 170
San Agustin, Francisco C -pg 79
San Agustin, Francisco E -pg 84
San Agustin, Francisco G -pg 84
San Agustin, Francisco R -pg 75
San Agustin, Francisco S -pg 113
San Agustin, George S -pg 122
San Agustin, Gonzalo C -pg 79
San Agustin, Ignacio C -pg 119
San Agustin, Isabel R -pg 75
San Agustin, Isabel S -pg 113
San Agustin, Jesus O -pg 107
San Agustin, Jesus D -pg 120
San Agustin, Joaquin C -pg 86
San Agustin, Joaquin C -pg 119
San Agustin, Joaquina D -pg 120
San Agustin, Jose O -pg 119
San Agustin, Jose O -pg 160
San Agustin, Jose C -pg 79
San Agustin, Jose C -pg 79
San Agustin, Jose C -pg 84
San Agustin, Jose C -pg 180
San Agustin, Jose D -pg 120
San Agustin, Jose E -pg 75
San Agustin, Josefa B -pg 338
San Agustin, Josefa M -pg 170
San Agustin, Josefa P -pg 82

San Agustin, Juan C -pg 84
San Agustin, Juan C -pg 122
San Agustin, Juan C -pg 180
San Agustin, Juan E -pg 162
San Agustin, Juan R -pg 75
San Agustin, Juana O -pg 107
San Agustin, Juana C -pg 119
San Agustin, Juana C -pg 180
San Agustin, Manuel C -pg 79
San Agustin, Manuel R -pg 75
San Agustin, Maria C -pg 79
San Agustin, Maria C -pg 84
San Agustin, Maria C -pg 180
San Agustin, Maria D -pg 120
San Agustin, Maria L -pg 162
San Agustin, Maria S -pg 113
San Agustin, Maria S -pg 113
San Agustin, Maria S -pg 122
San Agustin, Mariano O -pg 160
San Agustin, Mariano C -pg 84
San Agustin, Mariano T -pg 160
San Agustin, Miguel E -pg 113
San Agustin, Miguel S -pg 113
San Agustin, Nicolasa C -pg 119
San Agustin, Nita S -pg 113
San Agustin, Pedro M -pg 171
San Agustin, Pedro -pg 338
San Agustin, Ramon S -pg 122
San Agustin, Ramunda S -pg 113
San Agustin, Remedios B -pg 338
San Agustin, Rosa C -pg 119
San Agustin, Rosa L -pg 162
San Agustin, Rosa S -pg 113
San Agustin, Rosalia D -pg 120
San Agustin, Rosario D -pg 120
San Agustin, Veronica S -pg 122
San Agustin, Vicenta S -pg 122
San Agustin, Vicente B -pg 338
San Agustin, Vicente D -pg 82
San Agustin, Vicente G -pg 84
San Agustin, Vicente T -pg 119
San Agustin, Victor M -pg 170
San Miguel, Ana Q -pg 111
San Miguel, Jose E -pg 106
San Miguel, Jose M -pg 20
San Miguel, Juan Q -pg 111
San Miguel, Manuel Q -pg 111
San Miguel, Trinidad Q -pg 111
San Miguel, Vicenta R -pg 20
San Nicolas, Adela F -pg 129
San Nicolas, Agapito T -pg 522
San Nicolas, Agustin M -pg 512

San Nicolas, Alfonsina M -pg 506
San Nicolas, Amparo D -pg 166
San Nicolas, Amparo M -pg 452
San Nicolas, Ana A -pg 160
San Nicolas, Ana A -pg 313
San Nicolas, Ana A -pg 557
San Nicolas, Ana C -pg 64
San Nicolas, Ana C -pg 92
San Nicolas, Ana C -pg 447
San Nicolas, Ana C -pg 499
San Nicolas, Ana C -pg 499
San Nicolas, Ana C -pg 508
San Nicolas, Ana D -pg 166
San Nicolas, Ana M -pg 311
San Nicolas, Ana M -pg 351
San Nicolas, Ana P -pg 47
San Nicolas, Ana S -pg 363
San Nicolas, Ana S -pg 535
San Nicolas, Ana T -pg 523
San Nicolas, Andrea C -pg 499
San Nicolas, Andrea C -pg 508
San Nicolas, Angelina M -pg 520
San Nicolas, Antonia C -pg 447
San Nicolas, Antonia LG -pg 508
San Nicolas, Antonia S -pg 363
San Nicolas, Antonio O -pg 132
San Nicolas, Antonio B -pg 441
San Nicolas, Antonio C -pg 499
San Nicolas, Antonio C -pg 508
San Nicolas, Antonio D -pg 166
San Nicolas, Antonio E -pg 476
San Nicolas, Antonio F -pg 384
San Nicolas, Antonio SN -pg 92
San Nicolas, Antonio SN -pg 535
San Nicolas, Asuncion -pg 398
San Nicolas, Augustin T -pg 73
San Nicolas, Aurelia M -pg 520
San Nicolas, Beatrice M -pg 311
San Nicolas, Beatrice M -pg 351
San Nicolas, Beatris C -pg 92
San Nicolas, Benita B -pg 131
San Nicolas, Carlina F -pg 384
San Nicolas, Carlina S -pg 363
San Nicolas, Carlos M -pg 520
San Nicolas, Carmen L -pg 512
San Nicolas, Carmen R -pg 316
San Nicolas, Carmen S -pg 535
San Nicolas, Carmen -pg 215
San Nicolas, Catalina C -pg 63
San Nicolas, Concepcion Q -pg 132
San Nicolas, Concepcion S -pg 535
San Nicolas, Conception C -pg 499

San Nicolas, Conception M -pg 457
San Nicolas, Consolacion C -pg 222
San Nicolas, Consolacion C -pg 378
San Nicolas, Consolacion S -pg 363
San Nicolas, Consuelo C -pg 366
San Nicolas, Consuelo C -pg 499
San Nicolas, Dolores 0 -pg 132
San Nicolas, Dolores A -pg 313
San Nicolas, Dolores C -pg 21
San Nicolas, Dolores N -pg 513
San Nicolas, Dolores N -pg 556
San Nicolas, Dolores -pg 232
San Nicolas, Dominarja C -pg 63
San Nicolas, Dominga A -pg 313
San Nicolas, Elario B -pg 132
San Nicolas, Elias N -pg 519
San Nicolas, Elizabeth M -pg 520
San Nicolas, Engracia T -pg 221
San Nicolas, Enrique R -pg 316
San Nicolas, Enrique S -pg 535
San Nicolas, Eugenio T -pg 222
San Nicolas, Eugenio V -pg 221
San Nicolas, Faustino -pg 256
San Nicolas, Felicitas L -pg 26
San Nicolas, Felipe A -pg 317
San Nicolas, Felipe T -pg 515
San Nicolas, Felipe U -pg 318
San Nicolas, Felix C -pg 447
San Nicolas, Felix L -pg 499
San Nicolas, Filomeno -pg 366
San Nicolas, Florencio A -pg 365
San Nicolas, Frailon S -pg 478
San Nicolas, Francisca C -pg 80
San Nicolas, Francisca S -pg 535
San Nicolas, Francisco A -pg 365
San Nicolas, Francisco A -pg 448
San Nicolas, Francisco C -pg 64
San Nicolas, Francisco C -pg 499
San Nicolas, Francisco C -pg 506
San Nicolas, Francisco D -pg 391
San Nicolas, Francisco P -pg 256
San Nicolas, Francisco R -pg 316
San Nicolas, Francisco S -pg 114
San Nicolas, Francisco T -pg 221
San Nicolas, Francisco T -pg 522
San Nicolas, Geronimo S -pg 444
San Nicolas, Geronimo T -pg 522
San Nicolas, Grabiela C -pg 366
San Nicolas, Gregorio A -pg 365
San Nicolas, Gregorio C -pg 43
San Nicolas, Guadalupe T -pg 28
San Nicolas, Guillermo F -pg 384

San Nicolas, Ignacia A -pg 317
San Nicolas, Ignacia R -pg 424
San Nicolas, Ignacia S -pg 363
San Nicolas, Ignacio A -pg 556
San Nicolas, Ignacio C -pg 51
San Nicolas, Ignacio G -pg 100
San Nicolas, Ignacio LG -pg 508
San Nicolas, Ignacio P -pg 256
San Nicolas, Isabel C -pg 515
San Nicolas, Isabel P -pg 48
San Nicolas, Isidora C -pg 515
San Nicolas, Jesus A -pg 313
San Nicolas, Jesus A -pg 557
San Nicolas, Jesus C -pg 379
San Nicolas, Jesus C -pg 508
San Nicolas, Jesus P -pg 216
San Nicolas, Jesus S -pg 43
San Nicolas, Jesus S -pg 334
San Nicolas, Jesus S -pg 391
San Nicolas, Jesus SN -pg 451
San Nicolas, Jesus T -pg 522
San Nicolas, Joaquin 0 -pg 132
San Nicolas, Joaquin A -pg 313
San Nicolas, Joaquin C -pg 447
San Nicolas, Joaquin G -pg 50
San Nicolas, Joaquin L -pg 512
San Nicolas, Joaquin P -pg 26
San Nicolas, Joaquin P -pg 47
San Nicolas, Joaquin S -pg 62
San Nicolas, Joaquin S -pg 363
San Nicolas, Joaquin T -pg 334
San Nicolas, Joaquina C -pg 44
San Nicolas, Joaquina C -pg 508
San Nicolas, Joaquina M -pg 476
San Nicolas, Joaquina R -pg 316
San Nicolas, Jose A -pg 279
San Nicolas, Jose A -pg 392
San Nicolas, Jose B -pg 441
San Nicolas, Jose C -pg 47
San Nicolas, Jose C -pg 64
San Nicolas, Jose C -pg 279
San Nicolas, Jose C -pg 316
San Nicolas, Jose C -pg 366
San Nicolas, Jose C -pg 379
San Nicolas, Jose C -pg 447
San Nicolas, Jose C -pg 499
San Nicolas, Jose C -pg 527
San Nicolas, Jose D -pg 166
San Nicolas, Jose F -pg 384
San Nicolas, Jose G -pg 80
San Nicolas, Jose G -pg 100
San Nicolas, Jose L -pg 512

San Nicolas, Jose M -pg 457
San Nicolas, Jose M -pg 476
San Nicolas, Jose N -pg 556
San Nicolas, Jose Q -pg 132
San Nicolas, Jose S -pg 62
San Nicolas, Jose S -pg 216
San Nicolas, Jose S -pg 363
San Nicolas, Jose S -pg 391
San Nicolas, Jose T -pg 62
San Nicolas, Jose T -pg 221
San Nicolas, Jose T -pg 522
San Nicolas, Jose -pg 215
San Nicolas, Josefa A -pg 444
San Nicolas, Josefa B -pg 441
San Nicolas, Josefina C -pg 379
San Nicolas, Josefina W -pg 384
San Nicolas, Juan 0 -pg 132
San Nicolas, Juan 0 -pg 132
San Nicolas, Juan A -pg 313
San Nicolas, Juan A -pg 317
San Nicolas, Juan A -pg 546
San Nicolas, Juan C -pg 499
San Nicolas, Juan C -pg 527
San Nicolas, Juan M -pg 452
San Nicolas, Juan M -pg 476
San Nicolas, Juan M -pg 519
San Nicolas, Juan P -pg 47
San Nicolas, Juan P -pg 384
San Nicolas, Juan S -pg 363
San Nicolas, Juan S -pg 409
San Nicolas, Juan T -pg 496
San Nicolas, Juan V -pg 309
San Nicolas, Juana R -pg 316
San Nicolas, Lorenzo A -pg 317
San Nicolas, Lucas L -pg 512
San Nicolas, Lucia T -pg 522
San Nicolas, Luis A -pg 317
San Nicolas, Luis D -pg 166
San Nicolas, Luis S -pg 222
San Nicolas, Luis S -pg 363
San Nicolas, Lusiano C -pg 131
San Nicolas, Magdalena A -pg 317
San Nicolas, Magdalena G -pg 100
San Nicolas, Magdalena L -pg 384
San Nicolas, Magdalena R -pg 316
San Nicolas, Manuel LG -pg 508
San Nicolas, Manuel -pg 378
San Nicolas, Manuela S -pg 334
San Nicolas, Manuela S -pg 391
San Nicolas, Manuela T -pg 28
San Nicolas, Marcela C -pg 63
San Nicolas, Margarita C -pg 50

San Nicolas, Maria A -pg 365
San Nicolas, Maria A -pg 392
San Nicolas, Maria A -pg 557
San Nicolas, Maria A jr -pg 365
San Nicolas, Maria C -pg 44
San Nicolas, Maria C -pg 51
San Nicolas, Maria C -pg 63
San Nicolas, Maria C -pg 92
San Nicolas, Maria C -pg 366
San Nicolas, Maria C -pg 402
San Nicolas, Maria C -pg 441
San Nicolas, Maria C -pg 498
San Nicolas, Maria C -pg 499
San Nicolas, Maria C -pg 508
San Nicolas, Maria C -pg 527
San Nicolas, Maria D -pg 166
San Nicolas, Maria G -pg 100
San Nicolas, Maria G -pg 132
San Nicolas, Maria L -pg 512
San Nicolas, Maria M -pg 452
San Nicolas, Maria M -pg 476
San Nicolas, Maria M -pg 519
San Nicolas, Maria P -pg 47
San Nicolas, Maria P -pg 47
San Nicolas, Maria R -pg 317
San Nicolas, Maria S -pg 62
San Nicolas, Maria S -pg 113
San Nicolas, Maria S -pg 363
San Nicolas, Maria S -pg 363
San Nicolas, Maria S -pg 441
San Nicolas, Maria S -pg 535
San Nicolas, Maria SN -pg 28
San Nicolas, Maria T -pg 28
San Nicolas, Maria T -pg 221
San Nicolas, Maria T -pg 478
San Nicolas, Maria T -pg 496
San Nicolas, Maria T -pg 515
San Nicolas, Maria T -pg 522
San Nicolas, Mariano C -pg 63
San Nicolas, Mariano C -pg 508
San Nicolas, Mariano P -pg 48
San Nicolas, Mariano R -pg 424
San Nicolas, Marina S -pg 384
San Nicolas, Martina C -pg 21
San Nicolas, Martina L -pg 512
San Nicolas, Miguel C -pg 50
San Nicolas, Nicolas T -pg 495
San Nicolas, Nicolasa C -pg 92
San Nicolas, Nicolasa T -pg 522
San Nicolas, Nicolasa -pg 348
San Nicolas, Nieves D -pg 166
San Nicolas, Nieves M -pg 452

San Nicolas, Olimpia R -pg 316
San Nicolas, Olimpia T -pg 221
San Nicolas, Panta L -pg 498
San Nicolas, Paula SN -pg 18
San Nicolas, Pedro C -pg 499
San Nicolas, Pedro D -pg 392
San Nicolas, Pedro R -pg 316
San Nicolas, Pedro S -pg 313
San Nicolas, Pedro SN -pg 52
San Nicolas, Quintin M -pg 506
San Nicolas, Ramon T -pg 522
San Nicolas, Ramona C -pg 499
San Nicolas, Ramona T -pg 221
San Nicolas, Ramona U -pg 318
San Nicolas, Regina C -pg 402
San Nicolas, Regina D -pg 166
San Nicolas, Remedios Q -pg 80
San Nicolas, Remedios T -pg 28
San Nicolas, Rita A -pg 313
San Nicolas, Rita A -pg 313
San Nicolas, Rita A -pg 365
San Nicolas, Rita P -pg 256
San Nicolas, Rita T -pg 495
San Nicolas, Rosa A -pg 160
San Nicolas, Rosa A -pg 392
San Nicolas, Rosa C -pg 92
San Nicolas, Rosa C -pg 527
San Nicolas, Rosa N -pg 513
San Nicolas, Rosa P -pg 48
San Nicolas, Rosa R -pg 316
San Nicolas, Rosalia C -pg 366
San Nicolas, Rosalia P -pg 216
San Nicolas, Rosario M -pg 476
San Nicolas, Rosario S -pg 43
San Nicolas, Rufina T -pg 496
San Nicolas, Seferina C -pg 527
San Nicolas, Severa C -pg 366
San Nicolas, Soledad D -pg 166
San Nicolas, Soledad G -pg 100
San Nicolas, Soledad M -pg 546
San Nicolas, Soledad A M -pg 520
San Nicolas, Susana C -pg 92
San Nicolas, Teresa C -pg 64
San Nicolas, Tomasa M -pg 506
San Nicolas, Tomasa S -pg 535
San Nicolas, Trinidad C -pg 508
San Nicolas, Trinidad I -pg 309
San Nicolas, Trinidad M -pg 311
San Nicolas, Trinidad M -pg 351
San Nicolas, Trinidad P -pg 48
San Nicolas, Trinidad S -pg 334
San Nicolas, Trinidad S -pg 535

San Nicolas, Venancio S -pg 535
San Nicolas, Vicenta C -pg 51
San Nicolas, Vicenta C -pg 279
San Nicolas, Vicenta C -pg 366
San Nicolas, Vicenta C -pg 508
San Nicolas, Vicenta D -pg 166
San Nicolas, Vicenta T -pg 221
San Nicolas, Vicente 0 -pg 132
San Nicolas, Vicente A -pg 100
San Nicolas, Vicente B -pg 441
San Nicolas, Vicente C -pg 442
San Nicolas, Vicente C -pg 499
San Nicolas, Vicente C -pg 508
San Nicolas, Vicente C -pg 522
San Nicolas, Vicente E -pg 495
San Nicolas, Vicente F -pg 384
San Nicolas, Vicente F -pg 457
San Nicolas, Vicente G -pg 100
San Nicolas, Vicente I -pg 311
San Nicolas, Vicente I -pg 351
San Nicolas, Vicente LG -pg 21
San Nicolas, Vicente N -pg 557
San Nicolas, Vicente S -pg 28
San Nicolas, Vicente S -pg 391
San Nicolas, Vicente SN -pg 447
San Nicolas, Vicente T -pg 222
San Nicolas, Vicente T -pg 365
San Nicolas, Vicente U -pg 318
Sanchez, Adriano C -pg 122
Sanchez, Amparo G -pg 421
Sanchez, Amparo Q -pg 472
Sanchez, Ana C -pg 122
Sanchez, Ana S -pg 468
Sanchez, Angelina Q -pg 472
Sanchez, Antonia C -pg 122
Sanchez, Antonio A -pg 467
Sanchez, Antonio S -pg 460
Sanchez, Caradad S -pg 464
Sanchez, Carmela S -pg 464
Sanchez, Carmen S -pg 464
Sanchez, Ceriaco A -pg 407
Sanchez, Crispin S -pg 468
Sanchez, Elena Q -pg 464
Sanchez, Eleuteria A -pg 122
Sanchez, Eliza D -pg 424
Sanchez, Emelia Q -pg 460
Sanchez, Engracia C -pg 122
Sanchez, Enoveva C -pg 449
Sanchez, Enrique Q -pg 463
Sanchez, Enriqueta S -pg 407
Sanchez, Estaquia S -pg 464
Sanchez, Estefania Q -pg 464

Sanchez, Felica T -pg 463
Sanchez, Feliciana T -pg 469
Sanchez, Francisco Q -pg 465
Sanchez, Francisco Q -pg 472
Sanchez, Ignacio Q -pg 460
Sanchez, Isabel C -pg 122
Sanchez, Jesus A -pg 464
Sanchez, Joaquin Q -pg 460
Sanchez, Joaquin Q -pg 464
Sanchez, Joaquin Q -pg 465
Sanchez, Joaquina Q -pg 464
Sanchez, Jose Q -pg 464
Sanchez, Jose S -pg 464
Sanchez, Jose S -pg 468
Sanchez, Josefa A -pg 122
Sanchez, Josefa S -pg 409
Sanchez, Juan C -pg 449
Sanchez, Juana S -pg 409
Sanchez, Julia C -pg 122
Sanchez, Lorenzo Q -pg 420
Sanchez, Lucas A -pg 467
Sanchez, Manuel S -pg 463
Sanchez, Manuela Q -pg 464
Sanchez, Manuela S -pg 468
Sanchez, Maria A -pg 464
Sanchez, Maria C -pg 449
Sanchez, Maria Q -pg 460
Sanchez, Maria S -pg 468
Sanchez, Mariano T -pg 469
Sanchez, Micerecordia C -pg 122
Sanchez, Moises C -pg 464
Sanchez, Nicolas S -pg 464
Sanchez, Pablo A -pg 121
Sanchez, Petronila Q -pg 464
Sanchez, Polonia A -pg 467
Sanchez, Regina A -pg 467
Sanchez, Rosario C -pg 122
Sanchez, Segundo C -pg 122
Sanchez, Simon A -pg 122
Sanchez, Susana A -pg 464
Sanchez, Teodora Q -pg 464
Sanchez, Teodoro S -pg 424
Sanchez, Trudes T -pg 463
Sanchez, Ursula Q -pg 464
Sanchez, Vicenta T -pg 469
Sanchez, Vicente Q -pg 464
Santiago, Ana C -pg 462
Santiago, Ana Q -pg 465
Santiago, Ana S -pg 487
Santiago, Antonia S -pg 487
Santiago, Carmen C -pg 462
Santiago, Consolacion M -pg 490

Santiago, Dolores C -pg 462
Santiago, Domingo Q -pg 465
Santiago, Felicidad S -pg 487
Santiago, Filipe M -pg 487
Santiago, Francisca Q -pg 167
Santiago, Graviela Q -pg 465
Santiago, Gregorio S -pg 490
Santiago, Isabel G -pg 167
Santiago, Jose C -pg 462
Santiago, Jose Q -pg 167
Santiago, Jose Q -pg 466
Santiago, Juan Q -pg 466
Santiago, Juana S -pg 487
Santiago, Justo Q -pg 465
Santiago, Marcela Q -pg 465
Santiago, Mariano M -pg 465
Santiago, Rita M -pg 487
Santiago, Simon Q -pg 462
Santiago, Teresa Q -pg 466
Santiago, Vicente M -pg 490
Santiago, Vicente Q -pg 465
Santos, Abraham S -pg 420
Santos, Adela M -pg 535
Santos, Agustin S -pg 422
Santos, Alejandra S -pg 419
Santos, Alvasio I -pg 348
Santos, Amalia S -pg 407
Santos, Ampara D -pg 145
Santos, Amparo C -pg 387
Santos, Amparo S -pg 51
Santos, Ana B -pg 364
Santos, Ana B -pg 396
Santos, Ana B -pg 402
Santos, Ana C -pg 108
Santos, Ana C -pg 348
Santos, Ana C -pg 352
Santos, Ana C -pg 388
Santos, Ana C -pg 391
Santos, Ana I -pg 387
Santos, Ana L -pg 421
Santos, Ana LG -pg 214
Santos, Ana M -pg 49
Santos, Ana P -pg 135
Santos, Ana P -pg 330
Santos, Ana Q -pg 390
Santos, Ana R -pg 51
Santos, Ana R -pg 226
Santos, Ana S -pg 74
Santos, Ana S -pg 78
Santos, Ana SN -pg 114
Santos, Ana SN -pg 379
Santos, Ana T -pg 145

Santos, Ana V -pg 78
Santos, Ana -pg 226
Santos, Angela Q -pg 390
Santos, Angela S -pg 74
Santos, Angelina C -pg 389
Santos, Angelina G -pg 324
Santos, Antonia C -pg 388
Santos, Antonia I -pg 535
Santos, Antonia M -pg 326
Santos, Antonia R -pg 51
Santos, Antonia S -pg 51
Santos, Antonia S -pg 388
Santos, Antonia -pg 226
Santos, Antonina Q -pg 390
Santos, Antonio A -pg 290
Santos, Antonio B -pg 223
Santos, Antonio B -pg 397
Santos, Antonio C -pg 69
Santos, Antonio C -pg 87
Santos, Antonio C -pg 330
Santos, Antonio L -pg 57
Santos, Antonio M -pg 425
Santos, Antonio Q -pg 390
Santos, Antonio S -pg 401
Santos, Antonio U -pg 535
Santos, Antonio -pg 380
Santos, Apolenar P -pg 51
Santos, Ascemcion C -pg 445
Santos, Aurelia H -pg 398
Santos, Barbara S -pg 380
Santos, Beatris B -pg 364
Santos, Blas A -pg 362
Santos, Carlos M -pg 326
Santos, Carmelo A -pg 290
Santos, Carmelo SN -pg 198
Santos, Carmen C -pg 445
Santos, Carmen F -pg 366
Santos, Carmen S -pg 401
Santos, Catalina A -pg 365
Santos, Catalina C -pg 389
Santos, Catalina G -pg 425
Santos, Cecilia P -pg 330
Santos, Clementina R -pg 215
Santos, Clotide M -pg 43
Santos, Concepcion C -pg 68
Santos, Concepcion G -pg 336
Santos, Concepcion L -pg 421
Santos, Concepcion S -pg 401
Santos, Consolacion T -pg 386
Santos, Cresanta T -pg 134
Santos, Cristobal R -pg 215
Santos, Delfina S -pg 401

Santos, Delgadina Q -pg 389
Santos, Dolores B -pg 363
Santos, Dolores C -pg 55
Santos, Dolores C -pg 348
Santos, Dolores C -pg 388
Santos, Dolores L -pg 421
Santos, Dolores R -pg 215
Santos, Dolores S -pg 80
Santos, Dolores SN -pg 379
Santos, Dolores SN -pg 393
Santos, Dolores T -pg 51
Santos, Dolores T -pg 134
Santos, Dolores T -pg 425
Santos, Emelia C -pg 445
Santos, Emiliana T -pg 424
Santos, Emilio V -pg 80
Santos, Enrique B -pg 364
Santos, Enrique S -pg 145
Santos, Ested S -pg 387
Santos, Faustina C -pg 290
Santos, Feliciana S -pg 407
Santos, Feliciana T -pg 51
Santos, Felicidad D -pg 526
Santos, Felix A -pg 387
Santos, Felix J -pg 112
Santos, Felix T -pg 425
Santos, Felomena Q -pg 43
Santos, Fortoso M -pg 326
Santos, Francisca S -pg 80
Santos, Francisco A -pg 389
Santos, Francisco B -pg 215
Santos, Francisco B -pg 363
Santos, Francisco C -pg 35
Santos, Francisco F -pg 326
Santos, Francisco M -pg 228
Santos, Francisco M -pg 326
Santos, Francisco P -pg 78
Santos, Francisco P -pg 136
Santos, Francisco Q -pg 43
Santos, Francisco Q -pg 390
Santos, Francisco S -pg 51
Santos, Francisco S -pg 393
Santos, Francisco V -pg 78
Santos, Francisco -pg 391
Santos, Froilan T -pg 263
Santos, Geronimo P -pg 51
Santos, Gertrudes T -pg 145
Santos, Getrudes B -pg 364
Santos, Getrudes Q -pg 390
Santos, Gil M -pg 423
Santos, Gregorio C -pg 35
Santos, Gregorio C -pg 387

Santos, Ignacia M -pg 43
Santos, Ignacio 0 -pg 143
Santos, Ignacio A -pg 74
Santos, Ignacio A -pg 290
Santos, Ignacio M -pg 327
Santos, Ignacio Q -pg 43
Santos, Ignacio Q -pg 390
Santos, Ignacio S -pg 388
Santos, Ignacio T -pg 425
Santos, Ignacio -pg 391
Santos, Ines C -pg 389
Santos, Ines P -pg 330
Santos, Isabel 0 -pg 116
Santos, Isabel C -pg 445
Santos, Isabel H -pg 397
Santos, Isabel P -pg 71
Santos, Izequiel -pg 255
Santos, Jesus A -pg 362
Santos, Jesus B -pg 55
Santos, Jesus B -pg 111
Santos, Jesus C -pg 35
Santos, Jesus C -pg 388
Santos, Jesus F -pg 389
Santos, Jesus G -pg 223
Santos, Jesus M -pg 327
Santos, Jesus M -pg 535
Santos, Jesus P -pg 135
Santos, Jesus P -pg 330
Santos, Jesus R -pg 43
Santos, Jesus S -pg 74
Santos, Jesus S -pg 301
Santos, Jesus S -pg 407
Santos, Jesus SN -pg 181
Santos, Jesus T -pg 134
Santos, Jesus T -pg 145
Santos, Jesus V -pg 78
Santos, Jesus V -pg 141
Santos, Jesus -pg 272
Santos, Joaquin B -pg 114
Santos, Joaquin C -pg 68
Santos, Joaquin C -pg 79
Santos, Joaquin D -pg 526
Santos, Joaquin J -pg 174
Santos, Joaquin Q -pg 390
Santos, Joaquin S -pg 80
Santos, Joaquin S -pg 380
Santos, Joaquin S -pg 420
Santos, Joaquin T -pg 134
Santos, Joaquin T -pg 263
Santos, Joaquin U -pg 226
Santos, Joaquina R -pg 51
Santos, Joaquina -pg 226

Santos, Jorge -pg 396
Santos, Jose A -pg 336
Santos, Jose B -pg 215
Santos, Jose B -pg 370
Santos, Jose C -pg 68
Santos, Jose C -pg 370
Santos, Jose C -pg 388
Santos, Jose C -pg 406
Santos, Jose C -pg 538
Santos, Jose D -pg 145
Santos, Jose I -pg 387
Santos, Jose L -pg 419
Santos, Jose L -pg 421
Santos, Jose M -pg 423
Santos, Jose M -pg 535
Santos, Jose P -pg 135
Santos, Jose P -pg 227
Santos, Jose Q -pg 43
Santos, Jose Q -pg 390
Santos, Jose R -pg 51
Santos, Jose R -pg 330
Santos, Jose S -pg 47
Santos, Jose S -pg 78
Santos, Jose S -pg 111
Santos, Jose S -pg 185
Santos, Jose S -pg 380
Santos, Jose SN -pg 379
Santos, Jose T -pg 35
Santos, Jose T -pg 134
Santos, Jose T -pg 145
Santos, Jose V -pg 78
Santos, Jose V -pg 141
Santos, Jose -pg 226
Santos, Jose -pg 380
Santos, Jose -pg 396
Santos, Josefa B -pg 363
Santos, Josefa B -pg 444
Santos, Josefa G -pg 223
Santos, Josefa P -pg 273
Santos, Josefa -pg 227
Santos, Juan A -pg 71
Santos, Juan A -pg 362
Santos, Juan B -pg 444
Santos, Juan C -pg 55
Santos, Juan C -pg 78
Santos, Juan C -pg 330
Santos, Juan C -pg 394
Santos, Juan G -pg 397
Santos, Juan LG -pg 141
Santos, Juan LG -pg 214
Santos, Juan M -pg 49
Santos, Juan M -pg 326

Santos, Juan M -pg 365
Santos, Juan M -pg 535
Santos, Juan N -pg 181
Santos, Juan P -pg 136
Santos, Juan P -pg 227
Santos, Juan P -pg 273
Santos, Juan P -pg 330
Santos, Juan S -pg 51
Santos, Juan S -pg 78
Santos, Juan T -pg 49
Santos, Juan T -pg 386
Santos, Juan V -pg 145
Santos, Juan -pg 324
Santos, Juan -pg 380
Santos, Juan -pg 388
Santos, Juana A -pg 365
Santos, Juana C -pg 445
Santos, Juana M -pg 49
Santos, Juana M -pg 535
Santos, Juana S -pg 423
Santos, Juliana C -pg 78
Santos, Justo N -pg 181
Santos, Lagrimas SN -pg 379
Santos, Leonida M -pg 326
Santos, Leonila D -pg 145
Santos, Lorenzo C -pg 81
Santos, Lorenzo C -pg 388
Santos, Lourdes M -pg 393
Santos, Lourdes -pg 227
Santos, Lucia C -pg 394
Santos, Luis C -pg 408
Santos, Luis T -pg 424
Santos, Luis T jr -pg 425
Santos, Luis -pg 388
Santos, Luisa A -pg 290
Santos, Luisa G -pg 324
Santos, Luisa G -pg 324
Santos, Magdalena A -pg 290
Santos, Magdalena C -pg 388
Santos, Magdalena Q -pg 377
Santos, Manuel A -pg 363
Santos, Manuel C -pg 348
Santos, Manuel C -pg 419
Santos, Manuel F -pg 366
Santos, Manuel L -pg 68
Santos, Manuel M -pg 228
Santos, Manuel S -pg 377
Santos, Manuel U -pg 534
Santos, Manuel -pg 226
Santos, Manuel -pg 380
Santos, Marcos U -pg 254
Santos, Maria A -pg 290

Santos, Maria A -pg 360
Santos, Maria A -pg 362
Santos, Maria A -pg 362
Santos, Maria B -pg 111
Santos, Maria B -pg 364
Santos, Maria B -pg 397
Santos, Maria C -pg 68
Santos, Maria C -pg 330
Santos, Maria C -pg 330
Santos, Maria C -pg 388
Santos, Maria C -pg 389
Santos, Maria C -pg 414
Santos, Maria C -pg 445
Santos, Maria C -pg 445
Santos, Maria G -pg 223
Santos, Maria G -pg 254
Santos, Maria G -pg 336
Santos, Maria G -pg 396
Santos, Maria G jr -pg 396
Santos, Maria H -pg 397
Santos, Maria I -pg 535
Santos, Maria L -pg 421
Santos, Maria LG -pg 141
Santos, Maria M -pg 43
Santos, Maria M -pg 388
Santos, Maria M -pg 423
Santos, Maria N -pg 181
Santos, Maria P -pg 273
Santos, Maria P -pg 286
Santos, Maria P -pg 330
Santos, Maria P -pg 419
Santos, Maria S -pg 57
Santos, Maria S -pg 74
Santos, Maria S -pg 78
Santos, Maria S -pg 184
Santos, Maria S -pg 401
Santos, Maria S -pg 406
Santos, Maria S -pg 420
Santos, Maria S jr -pg 406
Santos, Maria SN -pg 379
Santos, Maria SN -pg 380
Santos, Maria T -pg 134
Santos, Maria T -pg 145
Santos, Maria U -pg 254
Santos, Maria V -pg 78
Santos, Maria -pg 214
Santos, Maria -pg 303
Santos, Mariana M -pg 263
Santos, Mariano B -pg 491
Santos, Mariano C -pg 379
Santos, Mariano C -pg 444
Santos, Martin M -pg 362

Santos, Martina S -pg 388
Santos, Matilde T -pg 134
Santos, Mercedes C -pg 79
Santos, Miguel C -pg 35
Santos, Miguel G -pg 401
Santos, Milagros C -pg 35
Santos, Natividad C -pg 388
Santos, Natividad R -pg 51
Santos, Nicolas C -pg 388
Santos, Nicolas F -pg 327
Santos, Nicolas S -pg 51
Santos, Nicolas S -pg 108
Santos, Nicolas S -pg 365
Santos, Nicolasa Q -pg 390
Santos, Nicolasa S -pg 388
Santos, Nieves S -pg 393
Santos, Nieves T -pg 147
Santos, Paz S -pg 74
Santos, Pedro A -pg 362
Santos, Pedro C -pg 348
Santos, Pedro C -pg 370
Santos, Pedro M -pg 49
Santos, Pedro P -pg 227
Santos, Pedro S -pg 74
Santos, Pedro S -pg 78
Santos, Pedro T -pg 421
Santos, Pedro V -pg 286
Santos, Pilar T -pg 408
Santos, Polonoria F -pg 439
Santos, Ramon C -pg 79
Santos, Ramona M -pg 534
Santos, Regina B -pg 363
Santos, Regina C -pg 388
Santos, Regina S -pg 78
Santos, Remedios C -pg 55
Santos, Requiel R -pg 215
Santos, Rita A -pg 313
Santos, Rita A -pg 362
Santos, Rita B -pg 364
Santos, Rita C -pg 68
Santos, Rita P -pg 227
Santos, Rita T -pg 51
Santos, Rita T -pg 424
Santos, Romaldo G -pg 254
Santos, Roque S -pg 445
Santos, Roque T -pg 51
Santos, Rosa B -pg 364
Santos, Rosa C -pg 41
Santos, Rosa C -pg 255
Santos, Rosa C -pg 348
Santos, Rosa C -pg 370
Santos, Rosa F -pg 365

Santos, Rosa M -pg 43
Santos, Rosa M -pg 49
Santos, Rosa M -pg 423
Santos, Rosa M -pg 534
Santos, Rosa P -pg 135
Santos, Rosa R -pg 51
Santos, Rosa S -pg 185
Santos, Rosa S -pg 401
Santos, Rosa V -pg 78
Santos, Rosalia B -pg 363
Santos, Rosalia S -pg 407
Santos, Rosalia SN -pg 380
Santos, Rosario C -pg 348
Santos, Rosario G -pg 336
Santos, Rosario P -pg 136
Santos, Rosario S -pg 74
Santos, Rosario -pg 226
Santos, Rufina I -pg 387
Santos, Santiago -pg 380
Santos, Saturnina B -pg 363
Santos, Sebastian J -pg 344
Santos, Soledad I -pg 535
Santos, Soledad S -pg 94
Santos, Soledad SN -pg 181
Santos, Teburcio A -pg 388
Santos, Tedora B -pg 444
Santos, Teresa C -pg 370
Santos, Teresa D -pg 526
Santos, Teresa M -pg 423
Santos, Tomas R -pg 215
Santos, Tomas T -pg 425
Santos, Tomasa 0 -pg 143
Santos, Tomasa G -pg 223
Santos, Tomasa S -pg 57
Santos, Toribio B -pg 394
Santos, Ursula B -pg 215
Santos, Vicenta M -pg 228
Santos, Vicenta S -pg 94
Santos, Vicenta S -pg 143
Santos, Vicente A -pg 363
Santos, Vicente A -pg 379
Santos, Vicente C -pg 68
Santos, Vicente C -pg 370
Santos, Vicente G -pg 223
Santos, Vicente M -pg 78
Santos, Vicente M -pg 135
Santos, Vicente S -pg 51
Santos, Vicente S -pg 401
Santos, Vicente S -pg 407
Santos, Vicente SN -pg 163
Santos, Vicente T -pg 145
Santos, Vicente U -pg 535

Santos, Vicente -pg 380
Santos, Virginia S -pg 388
Sarang, Satrunina -pg 311
Sarmiento, Basilisa B -pg 403
Sarmiento, Juan B -pg 403
Sarmiento, Juan P -pg 403
Sarmiento, Maria P -pg 403
Sarmiento, Soledad B -pg 403
Sawada, K -pg 248
Sawada, Nao -pg 248
Sayama, Jesus S -pg 545
Sayama, Joaquina B -pg 545
Sayama, Jose B -pg 545
Scharff, Antonia F -pg 287
Scharff, George -pg 287
Semiya, Antonia A -pg 306
Semiya, Joaquin A -pg 306
Semiya, Jose A -pg 306
Semiya, Juan A -pg 306
Semiya, Takeyoshi -pg 306
Shimizu, Carmen T -pg 308
Shimizu, Ichiryo J -pg 308
Shimizu, Jesus T -pg 308
Shimizu, Joaquin T -pg 308
Shimizu, Jose K -pg 308
Shinazo, Ocha S -pg 459
Shinohara, Takekuma -pg 289
Sholing, Juan P -pg 142
Sholing, Magdalena P -pg 142
Sholing, Rita P -pg 142
Siguenza, Concepcion 0 -pg 114
Siguenza, Consolacion C -pg 278
Siguenza, Dolores C -pg 13
Siguenza, Dolores S -pg 26
Siguenza, Emelia C -pg 278
Siguenza, Felipe T -pg 28
Siguenza, Francisco C -pg 26
Siguenza, Jesus S -pg 26
Siguenza, Joaquin S -pg 26
Siguenza, Joaquin T -pg 28
Siguenza, Jose C -pg 13
Siguenza, Jose P -pg 28
Siguenza, Jose T -pg 28
Siguenza, Jose -pg 278
Siguenza, Juan C -pg 13
Siguenza, Juan C -pg 28
Siguenza, Lorenzo T -pg 330
Siguenza, Maria C -pg 26
Siguenza, Maria C -pg 28
Siguenza, Maria S -pg 26
Siguenza, Maria T -pg 28
Siguenza, Rosalia A -pg 103

Siguenza, Vicente S -pg 13
Simoda, Encarnacion C -pg 233
Simoda, Juana C -pg 233
Simoda, Juana C -pg 233
Simoda, Maria C -pg 233
Singuenza, Ana T -pg 323
Singuenza, Concepcion T -pg 323
Singuenza, Joaquina T -pg 323
Singuenza, Jose T -pg 323
Singuenza, Juana T -pg 323
Singuenza, Rosa T -pg 323
Sococo, Catalina S -pg 373
Sococo, Jose S -pg 373
Sococo, Manuel -pg 367
Soleta, Bernardo M -pg 384
Soleta, Gregorio M -pg 384
Soleta, Maria M -pg 384
Soleta, Mariano S -pg 384
Soriano, Enrique -pg 300
Soriano, Jose G -pg 300
Soriano, Lucia G -pg 300
Soriano, Miguel G -pg 300
Soriano, Rita G -pg 300
Sotomayor, Nicolas -pg 199
Sternberg, Carmen B -pg 325
Sternberg, George B -pg 325
Sternberg, John B -pg 325
Sternberg, Jose B -pg 325
Stone, Charles H -pg 42
Stroup, Lewis H -pg 426
Sturzaeta, Felomeno G -pg 52
Sturzaeta, Melisia F -pg 52
Suarez, Antonio C -pg 18
Suarez, Maria G -pg 18
Suarez, Teresa M -pg 18
Sugiyama, Josefina M -pg 503
Sugiyama, Manuela M -pg 503
Sullivan, Walter T -pg 426
Susuica, Antonio -pg 409
Susuica, Dolores S -pg 409
Susuico, Carpio 0 -pg 178
Susuico, Dominga 0 -pg 178
Susuico, Ignacio 0 -pg 178
Susuico, Jesus 0 -pg 178
Susuico, Jose 0 -pg 178
Susuico, Maria 0 -pg 166
Susuico, Maria S -pg 25
Suzuki, F 0 -pg 160
Suzuki, Shigeno 0 -pg 160
Suzuki, Suckichi -pg 326
Suzuki, Ushimatiu -pg 384
Suzuki, Yoshido 0 -pg 160

Sypingco, Ignacia L -pg 150
Sypingco, Maria L -pg 150
Sypingco, Vicente S -pg 385
Tachira, Dolores C -pg 310
Tachira, Juan D -pg 310
Tachira, Mafada C -pg 310
Tachira, Manuela C -pg 310
Taeantongo, Ana E -pg 477
Taeantongo, Catalina E -pg 477
Taeantongo, Geronimo M -pg 476
Taeantongo, Gregorio E -pg 477
Taeantongo, Ignacio E -pg 477
Taeantongo, Josefa E -pg 477
Taeantongo, Maria E -pg 476
Taeantongo, Pedro E -pg 477
Taeantongo, Ramon M -pg 499
Taenao, Carmelo M -pg 450
Taenao, Carmen M -pg 441
Taenao, Conception M -pg 441
Taenao, Enriquita M -pg 441
Taenao, Ignacia M -pg 441
Taenao, Jesus C -pg 450
Taenao, Joaquina C -pg 450
Taenao, Maria C -pg 450
Taenao, Maria M -pg 441
Tagae, Arayo 0 -pg 50
Taienao, Amparo M -pg 197
Taienao, Carmen M -pg 457
Taienao, Derfina B -pg 453
Taienao, Dolores B -pg 453
Taienao, Guadalupe M -pg 452
Taienao, Joaquin M -pg 452
Taienao, Jose Q -pg 453
Taienao, Maria B -pg 453
Taienao, Vicente M -pg 452
Taigiron, Antonio G -pg 259
Taigiron, Jose G -pg 260
Taigiron, Juliana G -pg 259
Taigiron, Mercedes G -pg 259
Taigiron, Ramona G -pg 259
Taijeron, Ana C -pg 482
Taijeron, Ana T -pg 492
Taijeron, Antonia N -pg 480
Taijeron, Antonio S -pg 482
Taijeron, Barbara J -pg 385
Taijeron, Carmen C -pg 482
Taijeron, Dolores D -pg 482
Taijeron, Dolores J -pg 385
Taijeron, Dolores -pg 369
Taijeron, Elena C -pg 86
Taijeron, Enrique 0 -pg 177
Taijeron, Felisa G -pg 497

Taijeron, Francisca -pg 206
Taijeron, Francisco C -pg 482
Taijeron, Geronimo C -pg 79
Taijeron, Isabel D -pg 482
Taijeron, Isabel E -pg 86
Taijeron, Isidro S -pg 79
Taijeron, Jesus D -pg 482
Taijeron, Jesus J -pg 386
Taijeron, Joaquin J -pg 386
Taijeron, Joaquina C -pg 482
Taijeron, Jose B -pg 478
Taijeron, Jose B -pg 480
Taijeron, Jose D -pg 482
Taijeron, Jose J -pg 385
Taijeron, Jose T -pg 387
Taijeron, Jose T -pg 542
Taijeron, Juan J -pg 385
Taijeron, Juana 0 -pg 177
Taijeron, Margarita C -pg 482
Taijeron, Maria B -pg 477
Taijeron, Maria D -pg 482
Taijeron, Maria E -pg 86
Taijeron, Maria J -pg 385
Taijeron, Maria S -pg 79
Taijeron, Maria T -pg 488
Taijeron, Mariano B -pg 477
Taijeron, Mariano G -pg 497
Taijeron, Pedro T -pg 542
Taijeron, Remedios T -pg 542
Taijeron, Rosario J -pg 385
Taijeron, Silvano -pg 416
Taijeron, Vicenta A -pg 492
Taijeron, Vicente T -pg 385
Taijeron, Vicente T -pg 542
Taijiron, Antonia C -pg 222
Taijiron, Gertrudes C -pg 18
Taijiron, Jesus P -pg 222
Taijiron, Juan C -pg 222
Taijito, Ana B -pg 129
Taijito, Antonio T -pg 458
Taijito, Francisco S -pg 354
Taijito, Francisco T -pg 354
Taijito, Hermina T -pg 354
Taijito, Jose S -pg 354
Taijito, Jose T -pg 354
Taijito, Juan S -pg 354
Taijito, Magdalena S -pg 354
Taijito, Mamerto 0 -pg 129
Taijito, Manuela T -pg 360
Taijito, Maria A -pg 458
Taijito, Maria B -pg 129
Taijito, Maria S -pg 354

Taijito, Mariano T -pg 360
Taijito, Selistina B -pg 129
Taijito, Soledad S -pg 354
Taijito, Vicenta S -pg 354
Taijito, Vicente C -pg 354
Taimanglo, Ana C -pg 517
Taimanglo, Ana M -pg 204
Taimanglo, Ana M -pg 512
Taimanglo, Ana SN -pg 549
Taimanglo, Beatris M -pg 204
Taimanglo, Beatris M -pg 503
Taimanglo, Blas T -pg 512
Taimanglo, Clara M -pg 523
Taimanglo, Dolores M -pg 523
Taimanglo, Dolores T -pg 529
Taimanglo, Engracia Q -pg 104
Taimanglo, Felix Q -pg 104
Taimanglo, Gregorio Q -pg 104
Taimanglo, Guadalupe C -pg 525
Taimanglo, Isabel SN -pg 549
Taimanglo, Isidoro C -pg 525
Taimanglo, Jesus C -pg 517
Taimanglo, Jesus M -pg 523
Taimanglo, Joaquin C -pg 503
Taimanglo, Joaquin Q -pg 104
Taimanglo, Joaquin T -pg 529
Taimanglo, Joaquin -pg 400
Taimanglo, Jose C -pg 517
Taimanglo, Jose M -pg 204
Taimanglo, Jose T -pg 523
Taimanglo, Jose T -pg 529
Taimanglo, Josefa C -pg 503
Taimanglo, Josefa M -pg 523
Taimanglo, Juan C -pg 503
Taimanglo, Juan F -pg 104
Taimanglo, Juan M -pg 204
Taimanglo, Julia M -pg 523
Taimanglo, Maria C -pg 517
Taimanglo, Maria Q -pg 104
Taimanglo, Mariano C -pg 503
Taimanglo, Mariano F -pg 210
Taimanglo, Mariano F -pg 549
Taimanglo, Remedios C -pg 525
Taimanglo, Rita T -pg 210
Taimanglo, Silvano C -pg 517
Taimanglo, Soledad SN -pg 549
Taimanglo, Teresa Q -pg 105
Taimanglo, Trinidad Q -pg 104
Taimanglo, Vicenta M -pg 203
Taimanglo, Vicente M -pg 204
Taimanglo, Victorino T -pg 523
Tainatongo, Juana 0 -pg 114

Tainatongo, Maria D -pg 129
Tainatongo, Vicente 0 -pg 129
Taisague, Ana G -pg 385
Taisague, Antonia S -pg 188
Taisague, Feliza C -pg 552
Taisague, Guadalupe C -pg 104
Taisague, Isabel S -pg 188
Taisague, Joaquin C -pg 188
Taisague, Jose La Rosa -pg 104
Taisague, Juan S -pg 188
Taisague, Maria S -pg 188
Taisague, Rosa S -pg 188
Taisague, Rosalia C -pg 552
Taisague, Vicente G -pg 314
Taisague, Vicente S -pg 188
Taisipig, Ana T -pg 557
Taisipig, Antonia T -pg 557
Taisipig, Carmen M -pg 558
Taisipig, Dolores T -pg 557
Taisipig, Gregorio M -pg 557
Taisipig, Hermina T -pg 557
Taisipig, Jesus T -pg 557
Taisipig, Rosa T -pg 557
Taison, Ana T -pg 303
Taison, Antonio T -pg 303
Taison, Maria T -pg 303
Taison, Romana -pg 303
Taison, Rosa T -pg 303
Taison, Socoro T -pg 303
Taitague, Agueda C -pg 533
Taitague, Aliminda M -pg 516
Taitague, Amalia D -pg 503
Taitague, Ana B -pg 458
Taitague, Ana Cruz -pg 431
Taitague, Angelina D -pg 516
Taitague, Antonia C -pg 458
Taitague, Baldabino B -pg 516
Taitague, Baldabino M -pg 516
Taitague, Candida B -pg 457
Taitague, Catalina C -pg 533
Taitague, Catalina T -pg 516
Taitague, Daniel N -pg 515
Taitague, Domingo C -pg 431
Taitague, Enocencio C -pg 457
Taitague, Felipe B -pg 541
Taitague, Felix B -pg 541
Taitague, Felix C -pg 458
Taitague, Francisco D -pg 542
Taitague, Genoveva B -pg 541
Taitague, Gonzalo M -pg 516
Taitague, Gregorio D -pg 516
Taitague, Henry D -pg 516

Taitague, Jesus D -pg 516
Taitague, Jesus N -pg 515
Taitague, Joaquin N -pg 515
Taitague, Jose C -pg 533
Taitague, Jose D -pg 516
Taitague, Josefa Q -pg 440
Taitague, Josefina B -pg 541
Taitague, Josefina N -pg 515
Taitague, Juan D -pg 516
Taitague, Lorenzo N -pg 515
Taitague, Magdalena B -pg 541
Taitague, Maria B -pg 541
Taitague, Maria N -pg 515
Taitague, Potenciana D -pg 516
Taitague, Ramon D -pg 516
Taitague, Rosario D -pg 516
Taitague, Saturnina M -pg 516
Taitague, Tomas B -pg 458
Taitague, Victoriano L -pg 541
Taitano, Alfredo F -pg 296
Taitano, Ana B -pg 241
Taitano, Ana C -pg 35
Taitano, Ana G -pg 260
Taitano, Ana G -pg 360
Taitano, Ana L -pg 290
Taitano, Ana P -pg 250
Taitano, Ana S -pg 136
Taitano, Ana S -pg 367
Taitano, Andrea G -pg 260
Taitano, Angel R -pg 38
Taitano, Antonia B -pg 241
Taitano, Antonia F -pg 356
Taitano, Antonio C -pg 40
Taitano, Antonio C -pg 72
Taitano, Antonio M -pg 290
Taitano, Antonio R -pg 38
Taitano, Artemio S -pg 235
Taitano, Balbina S -pg 367
Taitano, Baldomero B -pg 72
Taitano, Caridad P -pg 425
Taitano, Carlina M -pg 463
Taitano, Carlos F -pg 89
Taitano, Carlos P -pg 250
Taitano, Carmen G -pg 166
Taitano, Carmen G -pg 354
Taitano, Carmen P -pg 244
Taitano, Carmen T -pg 357
Taitano, Catalina A -pg 463
Taitano, Catalina C -pg 35
Taitano, Catalina F -pg 89
Taitano, Concepcion L -pg 290
Taitano, Concepcion P -pg 244

Taitano, Concepcion R -pg 38
Taitano, Conception C -pg 72
Taitano, Delfina F -pg 297
Taitano, Delfina F -pg 357
Taitano, Dolores F -pg 296
Taitano, Dolores F -pg 357
Taitano, Dolores G -pg 354
Taitano, Dolores P -pg 250
Taitano, Dolores S -pg 235
Taitano, Elminia F -pg 297
Taitano, Emelia G -pg 260
Taitano, Emilia B -pg 357
Taitano, Enrique P -pg 250
Taitano, Esther F -pg 89
Taitano, Faustina C -pg 40
Taitano, Felicita G -pg 354
Taitano, Felicita L -pg 290
Taitano, Felipe B -pg 357
Taitano, Florencio P -pg 244
Taitano, Francisca C -pg 72
Taitano, Francisco C -pg 72
Taitano, Francisco G -pg 260
Taitano, Francisco G -pg 360
Taitano, Francisco M -pg 241
Taitano, Francisco P -pg 250
Taitano, Francisco S -pg 235
Taitano, Francisco S -pg 235
Taitano, Francisco W -pg 299
Taitano, Gregorio P -pg 244
Taitano, Guillermo T -pg 299
Taitano, Isabel C -pg 72
Taitano, Isabel F -pg 89
Taitano, Jesus G -pg 354
Taitano, Jesus R -pg 38
Taitano, Joaquin C -pg 306
Taitano, Joaquin G -pg 341
Taitano, Joaquin L -pg 290
Taitano, Joaquin R -pg 38
Taitano, John 0 -pg 88
Taitano, John F -pg 89
Taitano, Jorge F -pg 297
Taitano, Jorge T -pg 299
Taitano, Jose C -pg 40
Taitano, Jose C -pg 72
Taitano, Jose C -pg 341
Taitano, Jose M -pg 235
Taitano, Jose M -pg 260
Taitano, Jose P -pg 250
Taitano, Jose R -pg 38
Taitano, Jose S -pg 367
Taitano, Jose SN -pg 250
Taitano, Jose W -pg 244

Taitano, Josefina B -pg 241
Taitano, Josefina S -pg 235
Taitano, Juan B -pg 241
Taitano, Juan C -pg 35
Taitano, Juan C -pg 81
Taitano, Juan C -pg 83
Taitano, Juan C -pg 341
Taitano, Juan M -pg 35
Taitano, Juan P -pg 250
Taitano, Juan W -pg 298
Taitano, Juana S -pg 235
Taitano, Julita T -pg 298
Taitano, Justo G -pg 360
Taitano, Leocadio T -pg 354
Taitano, Liberato G -pg 260
Taitano, Loela S -pg 235
Taitano, Magdalena C -pg 311
Taitano, Manuel B -pg 37
Taitano, Manuel B -pg 356
Taitano, Manuel G -pg 260
Taitano, Manuel M -pg 463
Taitano, Manuel T -pg 357
Taitano, Manuela G -pg 354
Taitano, Manuela L -pg 290
Taitano, Marcelina P -pg 244
Taitano, Margarita P -pg 400
Taitano, Maria A -pg 371
Taitano, Maria A -pg 440
Taitano, Maria B -pg 241
Taitano, Maria B -pg 241
Taitano, Maria C -pg 35
Taitano, Maria C -pg 40
Taitano, Maria C -pg 72
Taitano, Maria C -pg 341
Taitano, Maria G -pg 260
Taitano, Maria G -pg 354
Taitano, Maria L -pg 290
Taitano, Maria P -pg 244
Taitano, Maria P -pg 250
Taitano, Maria P -pg 425
Taitano, Maria R -pg 38
Taitano, Maria S -pg 349
Taitano, Maria T -pg 298
Taitano, Mariano B -pg 40
Taitano, Mariano G -pg 260
Taitano, Matias T -pg 359
Taitano, Miguel C -pg 72
Taitano, Miguel C -pg 463
Taitano, Nicolas M -pg 425
Taitano, Pedro G -pg 360
Taitano, Rafael P -pg 250
Taitano, Ramon P -pg 250

Taitano, Ramon R -pg 38
Taitano, Ramon SN -pg 296
Taitano, Remedios -pg 366
Taitano, Rita C -pg 72
Taitano, Rita G -pg 260
Taitano, Rita W -pg 299
Taitano, Roberto F -pg 296
Taitano, Rosa C -pg 306
Taitano, Rosa G -pg 260
Taitano, Rosa L -pg 290
Taitano, Rosa P -pg 425
Taitano, Rosa S -pg 235
Taitano, Rosa S -pg 367
Taitano, Rosalia P -pg 425
Taitano, Rosario A -pg 72
Taitano, Rosario F -pg 89
Taitano, Rosario F -pg 89
Taitano, Rosario G -pg 260
Taitano, Rosario L -pg 290
Taitano, Rosario P -pg 400
Taitano, Rosario T -pg 298
Taitano, Teodoro F -pg 357
Taitano, Trinidad C -pg 40
Taitano, Trinidad F -pg 129
Taitano, Vicente M -pg 463
Taitano, Vicente R -pg 38
Taitano, Vicente S -pg 367
Taitinfong, Ana B -pg 164
Taitinfong, Barbara B -pg 165
Taitinfong, Carmen C -pg 239
Taitinfong, Felix S -pg 117
Taitinfong, Francisca O -pg 132
Taitinfong, Francisco B -pg 165
Taitinfong, Grabela C -pg 239
Taitinfong, Ignacio O -pg 170
Taitinfong, Ignacio B -pg 165
Taitinfong, Ignacio C -pg 239
Taitinfong, Jesus B -pg 164
Taitinfong, Joaquin B -pg 164
Taitinfong, Joaquin S -pg 117
Taitinfong, Joaquina T -pg 28
Taitinfong, Jose B -pg 164
Taitinfong, Jose C -pg 240
Taitinfong, Jose L -pg 165
Taitinfong, Jose S -pg 117
Taitinfong, Juana O -pg 112
Taitinfong, Magdalena C -pg 240
Taitinfong, Maria B -pg 164
Taitinfong, Maria B -pg 165
Taitinfong, Mariano B -pg 165
Taitinfong, Ramon C -pg 240
Taitinfong, Rita C -pg 240

Taitinfong, Vicente B -pg 164
Taitinfong, Vicente L -pg 164
Taitingfong, Ana T -pg 549
Taitingfong, Carmen A -pg 546
Taitingfong, Daniel C -pg 544
Taitingfong, Felipa C -pg 544
Taitingfong, Francisca T -pg 558
Taitingfong, Juan C -pg 544
Taitingfong, Juan C -pg 558
Taitingfong, Juan T -pg 117
Taitingfong, Manuel C -pg 546
Taitingfong, Manuel T -pg 558
Taitingfong, Maria C -pg 558
Taitingfong, Pulfiria T -pg 117
Taitingfong, Remedios C -pg 544
Taitingfong, Rosa C -pg 544
Taitingfong, Teresa T -pg 117
Taitingfong, Vicente S -pg 558
Tajalle, Agapita C -pg 483
Tajalle, Andrea C -pg 359
Tajalle, Antonia C -pg 359
Tajalle, Bartola C -pg 359
Tajalle, Cerilo T -pg 482
Tajalle, Dolores C -pg 484
Tajalle, Dolores M -pg 391
Tajalle, Enrique R -pg 460
Tajalle, Feilx -pg 386
Tajalle, Feliciana S -pg 470
Tajalle, Felix M -pg 392
Tajalle, Francisco M -pg 392
Tajalle, Gertrudes C -pg 484
Tajalle, Gregoria C -pg 484
Tajalle, Joaquina C -pg 387
Tajalle, Jose T -pg 482
Tajalle, Josefa C -pg 352
Tajalle, Juan C -pg 391
Tajalle, Juan S -pg 387
Tajalle, Justo C -pg 387
Tajalle, Manuel C -pg 392
Tajalle, Maria M -pg 391
Tajalle, Maria T -pg 420
Tajalle, Maria T -pg 482
Tajalle, Mariano S -pg 470
Tajalle, Martina C -pg 359
Tajalle, Natividad D -pg 484
Tajalle, Rita T -pg 482
Tajalle, Rosa T -pg 482
Tajalle, Soledad S -pg 387
Tajalle, Tomas C -pg 484
Tajalle, Vicenta S -pg 470
Tajalle, Victorina T -pg 482
Tajamak, Jose -pg 488

Takahashi, Kikuzi -pg 282
Talabera, Antonia Q -pg 174
Talabera, Antonio Q -pg 174
Talabera, Consuelo Q -pg 174
Talabera, Felisitas Q -pg 174
Talabera, Jose Q -pg 174
Talabera, Manuel M -pg 174
Talabera, Maria Q -pg 174
Talabera, Trinidad Q -pg 174
Tanaka, Asuncion S -pg 56
Tanaka, Biatris S -pg 56
Tanaka, Carmen S -pg 56
Tanaka, Emeterio S -pg 56
Tanaka, Jesus S -pg 57
Tanaka, Maria S -pg 56
Tanaka, Remedios S -pg 56
Tanaka, Rosa S -pg 56
Tanaka, Rosario S -pg 56
Tanaka, Tomas S -pg 56
Tanigosh, Manuel C -pg 320
Tass, Juan A -pg 170
Tass, Maria A -pg 170
Tayama, Asuncion M -pg 503
Tayama, Gloria M -pg 503
Tayama, Jose M -pg 503
Tedpahogo, Ana A -pg 490
Tedpahogo, Angelina T -pg 483
Tedpahogo, Aniceto D -pg 483
Tedpahogo, Antonia T -pg 483
Tedpahogo, Ascemcion T -pg 483
Tedpahogo, Carmen T -pg 483
Tedpahogo, Concception A -pg 490
Tedpahogo, Eugenio G -pg 490
Tedpahogo, Felicita P -pg 490
Tedpahogo, Felipe T -pg 483
Tedpahogo, Gabiela M -pg 483
Tedpahogo, Jesus G -pg 490
Tedpahogo, Jose A -pg 490
Tedpahogo, Juan G -pg 490
Tedpahogo, Juana T -pg 483
Tedpahogo, Manuela T -pg 483
Tedpahogo, Maria M -pg 483
Tedpahogo, Maria T -pg 483
Tedpahogo, Nicolasa A -pg 490
Tedpahogo, Pilar T -pg 483
Tedpahogo, Vicente B -pg 490
Tedtaotao, Ana C -pg 505
Tedtaotao, Andres M -pg 504
Tedtaotao, Angela T -pg 504
Tedtaotao, Antonia C -pg 505
Tedtaotao, Casiano M -pg 505
Tedtaotao, Consolacion M -pg 504

Tedtaotao, Dolores C -pg 505
Tedtaotao, Jose C -pg 505
Tedtaotao, Juan T -pg 505
Tedtaotao, Leoncia C -pg 505
Tedtaotao, Magdalena T -pg 505
Tedtaotao, Pedro M -pg 504
Tejada, Dolores G -pg 249
Tejada, Estefania M -pg 249
Tejada, Jose F -pg 248
Tejada, Josefa C -pg 248
Tejada, Maria J -pg 249
Tejada, Pedro C -pg 248
Tejada, Roberto -pg 249
Tejada, Rosa I -pg 249
Tejada, Rosario M -pg 248
Teltras, Andrea A -pg 359
Teltras, Antonia T -pg 357
Teltras, Jose A -pg 359
Teltras, Vicente T -pg 359
Tenorio, Ana M -pg 540
Tenorio, Ana Y -pg 102
Tenorio, Ana B Q -pg 297
Tenorio, Antonia S -pg 74
Tenorio, Antonio R -pg 140
Tenorio, Antonio S -pg 74
Tenorio, Concepcion LT -pg 140
Tenorio, Delfina G -pg 102
Tenorio, Delfina G -pg 344
Tenorio, Dolores LT -pg 140
Tenorio, Dolores S -pg 309
Tenorio, Dolores SN -pg 74
Tenorio, Emiliana A -pg 552
Tenorio, Encarnacion G -pg 203
Tenorio, Enrique Y -pg 102
Tenorio, Francisco I -pg 552
Tenorio, Francisco Q -pg 297
Tenorio, Francisco SN -pg 74
Tenorio, Francisco Y -pg 102
Tenorio, Gonzalo G -pg 344
Tenorio, Gregorio G -pg 102
Tenorio, Gregorio S -pg 74
Tenorio, Ignacio T -pg 47
Tenorio, Jesus B -pg 143
Tenorio, Jesus LT -pg 140
Tenorio, Jesus N -pg 63
Tenorio, Jesus Q -pg 297
Tenorio, Joaquin Q -pg 297
Tenorio, Joaquin S -pg 297
Tenorio, Jose B -pg 74
Tenorio, Jose B -pg 143
Tenorio, Jose G -pg 101
Tenorio, Jose G -pg 203

Tenorio, Jose Q -pg 297
Tenorio, Jose T -pg 344
Tenorio, Juan G -pg 203
Tenorio, Juan Q -pg 297
Tenorio, Juan S -pg 74
Tenorio, Leonardo C -pg 538
Tenorio, Lucia C -pg 538
Tenorio, Luis SN -pg 74
Tenorio, Magdalena D -pg 550
Tenorio, Manuel C -pg 540
Tenorio, Manuel N -pg 63
Tenorio, Manuel T -pg 63
Tenorio, Maria C -pg 540
Tenorio, Maria I -pg 550
Tenorio, Maria LT -pg 140
Tenorio, Maria M -pg 540
Tenorio, Maria Q -pg 297
Tenorio, Maria Q -pg 297
Tenorio, Maria Q -pg 540
Tenorio, Maria Y -pg 102
Tenorio, Mercedes N -pg 63
Tenorio, Natividad N -pg 63
Tenorio, Oliva G -pg 102
Tenorio, Pedro C -pg 540
Tenorio, Ramon Q -pg 297
Tenorio, Remedio N -pg 63
Tenorio, Rita G -pg 60
Tenorio, Rita I -pg 47
Tenorio, Rita N -pg 63
Tenorio, Roberto SN -pg 74
Tenorio, Rosa G -pg 203
Tenorio, Rosa G -pg 344
Tenorio, Teresa N -pg 63
Tenorio, Tomasa SN -pg 74
Tenorio, Vicente B -pg 74
Tenorio, Vicente S -pg 309
Tenorio, Vicente Y -pg 102
Tenorio, Vicente -pg 344
Terlaje, Amalia T -pg 372
Terlaje, Antonia G -pg 194
Terlaje, Baldovino C -pg 434
Terlaje, Carmen F -pg 247
Terlaje, Consolacion B -pg 443
Terlaje, Consuelo F -pg 247
Terlaje, Dolores A -pg 371
Terlaje, Dolores M -pg 434
Terlaje, Dolores S -pg 367
Terlaje, Felix A -pg 367
Terlaje, Filomena B -pg 436
Terlaje, Francisco C -pg 290
Terlaje, Francisco F -pg 314
Terlaje, Francisco T -pg 194

Terlaje, Francisco T -pg 358
Terlaje, Grabiela A -pg 371
Terlaje, Jesus A -pg 371
Terlaje, Jesus F -pg 247
Terlaje, Jesus S -pg 210
Terlaje, Joaquin B -pg 443
Terlaje, Joaquin T -pg 358
Terlaje, Jose C -pg 357
Terlaje, Jose F -pg 247
Terlaje, Jose M -pg 434
Terlaje, Jose S -pg 290
Terlaje, Josefa S -pg 210
Terlaje, Josefa S -pg 357
Terlaje, Juan S -pg 210
Terlaje, Juan T -pg 361
Terlaje, Luis A -pg 247
Terlaje, Luis A -pg 371
Terlaje, Madalena M -pg 434
Terlaje, Magdalena A -pg 358
Terlaje, Manuel T -pg 371
Terlaje, Maria C -pg 290
Terlaje, Maria C -pg 445
Terlaje, Maria F -pg 247
Terlaje, Maria G -pg 194
Terlaje, Maria M -pg 374
Terlaje, Maria M -pg 434
Terlaje, Maria S -pg 210
Terlaje, Maria S -pg 314
Terlaje, Mercedes A -pg 371
Terlaje, Miguel A -pg 371
Terlaje, Pedro F -pg 247
Terlaje, Revostiano B -pg 444
Terlaje, Rosa G -pg 194
Terlaje, Rosalia B -pg 443
Terlaje, Rosalia S -pg 210
Terlaje, Rosario F -pg 247
Terlaje, Saturnina S -pg 194
Terlaje, Teresa S -pg 194
Terlaje, Vicenta S -pg 210
Terlaje, Vicente B -pg 436
Terlaje, Vicente F -pg 247
Terlaje, Vicente S -pg 210
Tertaotao, Antonio G -pg 105
Tertaotao, Gregorio T -pg 102
Tertaotao, Jesus G -pg 105
Tertaotao, Lucas G -pg 105
Tertaotao, Manuel 0 -pg 102
Tertaotao, Marcelina 0 -pg 102
Tertaotao, Rosa G -pg 105
Tertaotao, Salvador T -pg 105
Tichaira, Erminia LG -pg 145
Tichaira, Josefa D -pg 144

Tichaira, Manuel D -pg 144
Tichaira, Maria LG -pg 144
Tichaira, Maria LG -pg 144
Tichaira, Remedios LG -pg 144
Tiquengco, Antonio M -pg 500
Tiquengco, Augustina B -pg 481
Tiquengco, Encarnation C -pg 493
Tiquengco, Enrique B -pg 481
Tiquengco, Francisco B -pg 481
Tiquengco, Gregorio B -pg 493
Tiquengco, Joaquin B -pg 481
Tiquengco, Jose C -pg 494
Tiquengco, Josefina B -pg 481
Tiquengco, Josefina M -pg 500
Tiquengco, Maria C -pg 493
Tiquengco, Maria M -pg 500
Tiquengco, Nicolasa B -pg 474
Tiquengco, Nicolasa M -pg 499
Tiquengco, Petronila P -pg 491
Tiquengco, Rosa P -pg 491
Tiquengco, Rosario B -pg 481
Tiquengco, Vicente B -pg 474
Tiquengco, Vicente B -pg 491
Tokeymiya, Kichiro 0 -pg 42
Tolentino, Carmen L -pg 331
Tolentino, Joaquin T -pg 427
Tolentino, Manuel L -pg 331
Tolentino, Maria L -pg 331
Tolentino, Maximo L -pg 331
Tolentino, Rosalia DG -pg 427
Tolentino, Tomasa DG -pg 427
Tolentino, Tomasa L -pg 331
Tolentino, Vicente L -pg 331
Topasna, Ana LG -pg 187
Topasna, Ana M -pg 470
Topasna, Ascemsion Q -pg 467
Topasna, Candido T -pg 466
Topasna, Eucevio Q -pg 470
Topasna, Felix T -pg 463
Topasna, Francisco Q -pg 470
Topasna, Ignacio T -pg 468
Topasna, Isidoro E -pg 467
Topasna, Jose Q -pg 470
Topasna, Juan E -pg 471
Topasna, Juan Q -pg 467
Topasna, Juan Q -pg 470
Topasna, Natividad Q -pg 467
Topasna, Paterno -pg 187
Topasna, Rafael E -pg 462
Topasna, Soledad Q -pg 470
Torres, Amanda F -pg 22
Torres, Ana C -pg 197

Torres, Ana C -pg 320
Torres, Ana C jr -pg 197
Torres, Ana N -pg 24
Torres, Ana P -pg 142
Torres, Ana P -pg 234
Torres, Ana P -pg 253
Torres, Ana P -pg 318
Torres, Ana P -pg 387
Torres, Ana T -pg 151
Torres, Ana -pg 310
Torres, Ancermo T -pg 151
Torres, Antonia C -pg 282
Torres, Antonio C -pg 302
Torres, Antonio F -pg 22
Torres, Antonio M -pg 253
Torres, Antonio P -pg 39
Torres, Antonio P -pg 446
Torres, Ascemcion D -pg 474
Torres, Ascension P -pg 318
Torres, Carlos P -pg 39
Torres, Carmen C -pg 253
Torres, Carmen LG -pg 237
Torres, Concepcion C -pg 51
Torres, Concepcion C -pg 197
Torres, Concepcion C -pg 253
Torres, Concepcion C -pg 253
Torres, Concepcion C -pg 282
Torres, Concepcion C -pg 282
Torres, Concepcion H -pg 32
Torres, Conception E -pg 60
Torres, Consolacion N -pg 23
Torres, Daniel U -pg 502
Torres, Delfina M -pg 201
Torres, Dolores B -pg 404
Torres, Dolores C -pg 197
Torres, Dolores H -pg 32
Torres, Dolores H -pg 33
Torres, Dolores P -pg 39
Torres, Dolores P -pg 142
Torres, Eduviges E -pg 126
Torres, Felecitas P -pg 142
Torres, Felix C -pg 52
Torres, Felix H -pg 32
Torres, Francisco C -pg 51
Torres, Francisco C -pg 198
Torres, Francisco P -pg 446
Torres, Francisco -pg 253
Torres, Gertrudes D -pg 474
Torres, Gregorio M -pg 244
Torres, Gregorio P -pg 39
Torres, Ignacia C -pg 198
Torres, Ignacia P -pg 446

Torres, Ignacia T -pg 19
Torres, Ignacio R -pg 225
Torres, Jesus F -pg 308
Torres, Jesus H -pg 33
Torres, Jesus N -pg 23
Torres, Jesus P -pg 247
Torres, Jesus P -pg 446
Torres, Jesus T -pg 151
Torres, Jesus T -pg 525
Torres, Joaquin N -pg 24
Torres, Joaquin U -pg 502
Torres, Joaquin -pg 502
Torres, Joaquina M -pg 308
Torres, Joaquina P -pg 39
Torres, Jose A -pg 22
Torres, Jose C -pg 52
Torres, Jose C -pg 91
Torres, Jose C -pg 282
Torres, Jose C -pg 320
Torres, Jose C -pg 331
Torres, Jose D -pg 474
Torres, Jose H -pg 32
Torres, Jose LG -pg 142
Torres, Jose M -pg 51
Torres, Jose M -pg 201
Torres, Jose N -pg 24
Torres, Jose P -pg 39
Torres, Jose P -pg 446
Torres, Jose S -pg 331
Torres, Jose U -pg 502
Torres, Josefa A -pg 244
Torres, Josefa C -pg 303
Torres, Josefa P -pg 318
Torres, Josefa R -pg 237
Torres, Josefa R -pg 329
Torres, Josefa T -pg 151
Torres, Josefina C -pg 198
Torres, Josefina H -pg 33
Torres, Josefina P -pg 387
Torres, Juan C -pg 198
Torres, Juan C -pg 282
Torres, Juan E -pg 39
Torres, Juan LG -pg 124
Torres, Juan M -pg 201
Torres, Juan M -pg 282
Torres, Juan P -pg 446
Torres, Juana M -pg 201
Torres, Juana T -pg 151
Torres, Juliana P -pg 321
Torres, Leon Guerrero Rita -pg 60
Torres, Lope C -pg 282
Torres, Luis E -pg 23

Torres, Luis H -pg 387
Torres, Luis LG -pg 60
Torres, Luis N -pg 24
Torres, Maria A -pg 33
Torres, Maria A -pg 61
Torres, Maria B -pg 198
Torres, Maria C -pg 51
Torres, Maria C -pg 52
Torres, Maria C -pg 197
Torres, Maria C -pg 253
Torres, Maria F -pg 474
Torres, Maria H -pg 32
Torres, Maria N -pg 24
Torres, Maria P -pg 234
Torres, Maria P -pg 318
Torres, Maria P -pg 318
Torres, Maria P -pg 387
Torres, Maria P -pg 446
Torres, Maria R -pg 225
Torres, Maria S -pg 331
Torres, Maria T -pg 151
Torres, Maria U -pg 247
Torres, Maria U -pg 502
Torres, Maria O U -pg 502
Torres, Mariano T -pg 151
Torres, Pedro P -pg 318
Torres, Pilar A -pg 245
Torres, Pilar C -pg 52
Torres, Remedios N -pg 24
Torres, Ricardo C -pg 282
Torres, Rita LG -pg 237
Torres, Rita P -pg 318
Torres, Rosa F -pg 22
Torres, Rosa M -pg 201
Torres, Rosa P -pg 39
Torres, Rosa P -pg 321
Torres, Rosa T -pg 151
Torres, Soledad P -pg 446
Torres, Tomas C -pg 198
Torres, Tomas N -pg 24
Torres, Tomasa C -pg 310
Torres, Trinidad P -pg 91
Torres, Vicente A -pg 32
Torres, Vicente C -pg 198
Torres, Vicente C -pg 201
Torres, Vicente D -pg 474
Torres, Vicente LG -pg 197
Torres, Vicente M -pg 310
Torres, Vicente P -pg 142
Torribio, Iraicoe 0 -pg 59
Toves, Agueda G -pg 194
Toves, Agustin S -pg 147

Toves, Ana A -pg 241
Toves, Ana C -pg 343
Toves, Ana H -pg 161
Toves, Ana I -pg 293
Toves, Ana L -pg 254
Toves, Ana M -pg 537
Toves, Ana M -pg 537
Toves, Ana M -pg 553
Toves, Ana P -pg 344
Toves, Ana Q -pg 179
Toves, Ana Q -pg 179
Toves, Ana S -pg 125
Toves, Antonio LG -pg 179
Toves, Candelaria H -pg 146
Toves, Carmen A -pg 198
Toves, Catlina M -pg 537
Toves, Concepcion A -pg 241
Toves, Concepcion C -pg 344
Toves, Concepcion L -pg 254
Toves, Dolores L -pg 254
Toves, Dolores S -pg 147
Toves, Elena S -pg 147
Toves, Felisidad I -pg 293
Toves, Felix P -pg 348
Toves, Felix U -pg 348
Toves, Francisco A -pg 241
Toves, Francisco Q -pg 179
Toves, Gabriela B -pg 146
Toves, Ines M -pg 193
Toves, Isabel G -pg 555
Toves, Jesus B -pg 146
Toves, Jesus C -pg 52
Toves, Jesus M -pg 554
Toves, Jesus -pg 397
Toves, Joaquin G -pg 554
Toves, Jose A -pg 241
Toves, Jose A -pg 537
Toves, Jose B -pg 146
Toves, Jose C -pg 343
Toves, Jose G -pg 194
Toves, Jose L -pg 254
Toves, Jose Q -pg 146
Toves, Jose Q -pg 179
Toves, Jose S -pg 147
Toves, Jose U -pg 348
Toves, Jose -pg 397
Toves, Josefa H -pg 146
Toves, Josefina -pg 397
Toves, Juan A -pg 241
Toves, Juan B -pg 161
Toves, Juan C -pg 193
Toves, Juan G -pg 241

INDEX
1920 Population Census of Guam: Transcribed

Toves, Juan G -pg 553
Toves, Juan M -pg 348
Toves, Juan Q -pg 179
Toves, Juan -pg 397
Toves, Julia M -pg 193
Toves, Luis S -pg 556
Toves, Magdalena A -pg 241
Toves, Manuela Q -pg 146
Toves, Manuela -pg 397
Toves, Maria A -pg 241
Toves, Maria B -pg 146
Toves, Maria L -pg 254
Toves, Maria M -pg 136
Toves, Maria M -pg 193
Toves, Maria Q -pg 146
Toves, Maria Q -pg 179
Toves, Maria S -pg 28
Toves, Maria S -pg 555
Toves, Maria T -pg 556
Toves, Maria -pg 397
Toves, Nicolas C -pg 134
Toves, Patricio S -pg 147
Toves, Pedro 0 -pg 147
Toves, Pedro I -pg 293
toves, Pedro L -pg 218
Toves, Pedro L -pg 254
Toves, Pedro S -pg 554
Toves, Pedro T -pg 556
Toves, Pedro -pg 397
Toves, Ramon A -pg 537
Toves, Ramon S -pg 555
Toves, Ramon T -pg 537
Toves, Rita B -pg 146
Toves, Rita G -pg 194
Toves, Rita Q -pg 179
Toves, Rosario M -pg 193
Toves, Rosario T -pg 556
Toves, Soledad T -pg 556
Toves, Teodoro M -pg 193
Toves, Vicenta G -pg 554
Toves, Vicente C -pg 343
Toves, Vicente G -pg 194
Toves, Vicente G -pg 555
Toves, Vicente T -pg 556
Tudela, Francisca R -pg 87
Tudela, Ignacia R -pg 87
Tudela, Jose R -pg 87
Tudela, Jose R -pg 87
Tudela, Manuel R -pg 87
Tuncap, Caridad P -pg 204
Tuncap, Clemente N -pg 207
Tuncap, Concepcion N -pg 207

Tuncap, Delfina T -pg 207
Tuncap, Dolores N -pg 207
Tuncap, Escolastica N -pg 207
Tuncap, Felicita D -pg 205
Tuncap, Francisca D -pg 205
Tuncap, Gonzalo P -pg 204
Tuncap, Jesus T -pg 207
Tuncap, Joaquin N -pg 204
Tuncap, Jose P -pg 204
Tuncap, Juan N -pg 207
Tuncap, Juan O -pg 207
Tuncap, Manuel P -pg 204
Tuncap, Maria N -pg 207
Tuncap, Maria P -pg 204
Tuncap, Rita D -pg 205
Tydingco, Ana C -pg 356
Tydingco, Antonia A -pg 446
Tydingco, Antonio C -pg 356
Tydingco, Antonio S -pg 446
Tydingco, Asemcion S -pg 446
Tydingco, Carlos M -pg 446
Tydingco, Carlos P -pg 356
Tydingco, Consolacion C -pg 356
Tydingco, Dolores C -pg 356
Tydingco, Francisca L -pg 356
Tydingco, Francisco S -pg 446
Tydingco, Helen C -pg 356
Tydingco, Jose C -pg 356
Tydingco, Jose S -pg 446
Tydingco, Maria P -pg 356
Tydingco, Maria S -pg 446
Tydingco, Remedio S -pg 446
Tydingco, Rosa S -pg 446
Tydingco, Tomas S -pg 446
Tydingco, Vicente -pg 356
Tyquiengco, Lorenzo B -pg 377
Uchida, Buenaventura S -pg 379
Uchida, Fumi -pg 379
Uchida, Takeo -pg 379
Ulloa, Ana C -pg 146
Ulloa, Ana C -pg 348
Ulloa, Beatris A -pg 138
Ulloa, Engracia S -pg 254
Ulloa, Enoveva J -pg 398
Ulloa, Francisco I -pg 349
Ulloa, Francisco J -pg 398
Ulloa, Gaspar -pg 398
Ulloa, Gregorio S -pg 254
Ulloa, Isabel S -pg 254
Ulloa, Joaquin I -pg 349
Ulloa, Joaquin -pg 349
Ulloa, Joaquina C -pg 114

Ulloa, Joaquina LG -pg 410
Ulloa, Jose SN -pg 254
Ulloa, Josefa S -pg 254
Ulloa, Juan C -pg 146
Ulloa, Juan D -pg 403
Ulloa, Juan I -pg 349
Ulloa, Juan LG -pg 146
Ulloa, Juan LG -pg 410
Ulloa, Juan S -pg 254
Ulloa, Julia A -pg 138
Ulloa, Lucy P A -pg 317
Ulloa, Magdalena S -pg 254
Ulloa, Manuel -pg 317
Ulloa, Marcelo 0 -pg 138
Ulloa, Maria A -pg 138
Ulloa, Maria A -pg 317
Ulloa, Maria C -pg 114
Ulloa, Maria C -pg 146
Ulloa, Maria I -pg 349
Ulloa, Maria LG -pg 410
Ulloa, Maria R -pg 521
Ulloa, Maria S -pg 254
Ulloa, Mariano C -pg 114
Ulloa, Mariano D -pg 409
Ulloa, Nicolasa S -pg 254
Ulloa, Potenciana -pg 348
Ulloa, Preciosa R -pg 538
Ulloa, Regina S -pg 254
Ulloa, Rosa LG -pg 409
Ulloa, Rosa N -pg 134
Ulloa, Rosa R -pg 538
Ulloa, Rosalia A -pg 138
Ulloa, Rosalie I -pg 349
Ulloa, Soledad R -pg 538
Ulloa, Teresa R -pg 538
Ulloa, Vicente D -pg 403
Ulloa, Vicente LG -pg 538
Un Cangco, Maria L -pg 298
Un Cangco, Pedro L -pg 298
Un Cangco, Rosa L -pg 298
Un Cangco, Vicente T -pg 298
Uncanco, Gregorio S -pg 184
Uncanco, Isabel S -pg 184
Uncanco, Jose G -pg 184
Uncanco, Pricila S -pg 184
Uncanco, Vicente G -pg 184
Uncangco, Ana S -pg 330
Uncangco, Bardomero C -pg 330
Uncangco, Concepcion S -pg 330
Uncangco, Eduardo S -pg 330
Uncangco, Jose B -pg 330
Uncangco, Magdalena S -pg 330

Uncangco, Rita S -pg 330
Ungacta, Ana I -pg 211
Ungacta, Antonio I -pg 211
Ungacta, Domingo P -pg 211
Ungacta, Felix -pg 261
Ungacta, Gregorio -pg 261
Ungacta, Juan I -pg 211
Ungacta, Maria I -pg 211
Ungacta, Maria I -pg 211
Ungacta, Nicolasa -pg 262
Ungacta, Rosa -pg 261
Ungacta, Servino I -pg 211
Ungacta, Trinidad I -pg 211
Unpingco, Felipe A -pg 142
Unpingco, Jesus A -pg 142
Unpingco, Jose A -pg 142
Unpingco, Natividad A -pg 502
Unpingco, Rita A -pg 142
Un-Pingco, Ana R -pg 260
Un-Pingco, Consuelo R -pg 260
Un-Pingco, Francisco -pg 261
Un-Pingco, Jesus R -pg 260
Un-Pingco, Jose R -pg 260
Un-Pingco, Josefina R -pg 260
Un-Pingco, Juan R -pg 260
Un-Pingco, Magdalena R -pg 260
Un-Pingco, Maria R -pg 260
Un-Pingco, Maria U -pg 20
Un-Pingco, Pedro -pg 260
Un-Pingco, Rita M -pg 261
Un-Pingco, Rosario R -pg 260
Unsiog, Francisca J -pg 393
Unsiog, Joaquin J -pg 393
Unsiok, Jose N -pg 441
Unsiok, Maria N -pg 441
Unsiok, Venefacio J -pg 441
Untalan, Agustin L -pg 288
Untalan, Ana B -pg 54
Untalan, Ana F -pg 154
Untalan, Ana P -pg 157
Untalan, Antonia B -pg 54
Untalan, Antonia C -pg 198
Untalan, Antonia C -pg 199
Untalan, Antonia L -pg 251
Untalan, Antonia LG -pg 288
Untalan, Antonio L -pg 288
Untalan, Carlota F -pg 155
Untalan, Concepcion B -pg 54
Untalan, Delfina L -pg 251
Untalan, Dolores L -pg 251
Untalan, Eginio C -pg 198
Untalan, Emiliana D -pg 142

Untalan, Enrique LG -pg 288
Untalan, Francisco C -pg 198
Untalan, Guardalupe LG -pg 288
Untalan, Ignacia M -pg 54
Untalan, Jesus B -pg 154
Untalan, Jesus M -pg 54
Untalan, Jesus P -pg 157
Untalan, Joaquin L -pg 288
Untalan, Joaquin P -pg 157
Untalan, Joaquina B -pg 54
Untalan, Joaquina P -pg 157
Untalan, Jose C -pg 56
Untalan, Jose L -pg 251
Untalan, Jose LG -pg 288
Untalan, Jose M -pg 54
Untalan, Jose P -pg 177
Untalan, Josefina F -pg 154
Untalan, Juan M -pg 54
Untalan, Juan R -pg 177
Untalan, Juana C -pg 198
Untalan, Julita R -pg 177
Untalan, Lourdes L -pg 288
Untalan, Luis B -pg 54
Untalan, Luis P -pg 56
Untalan, Manuel L -pg 288
Untalan, Maria B -pg 54
Untalan, Maria F -pg 155
Untalan, Maria M -pg 54
Untalan, Maria P -pg 157
Untalan, Modesta L -pg 288
Untalan, Olimpia L -pg 288
Untalan, Oliva LG -pg 288
Untalan, Oliva R -pg 177
Untalan, Pedro C -pg 288
Untalan, Pedro P -pg 142
Untalan, Rita B -pg 54
Untalan, Rita LG -pg 288
Untalan, Rosa B -pg 54
Untalan, Rosa L -pg 288
Untalan, Rosario L -pg 251
Untalan, Serafina LG -pg 288
Untalan, Teodoro LG -pg 288
Untalan, Tomas F -pg 154
Untalan, Trinidad R -pg 177
Untalan, Vicente P -pg 157
Untalan, Virginia L -pg 288
Usodo, Ana B -pg 558
Usodo, Dolores B -pg 559
Usodo, Gregorio -pg 558
Usodo, Jose B -pg 558
Usodo, Maria B -pg 559
Uson, Jose A -pg 121

Uson, Juan A -pg 121
Uson, Maria A -pg 121
Uson, Ramon O -pg 121
Valenzuela, Antonia S -pg 265
Valenzuela, Francisco S -pg 265
Valenzuela, Ignacio S -pg 265
Valenzuela, Joaquin C -pg 265
Valenzuela, Regina S -pg 265
Vasco, Rita C -pg 18
Velasco, Sebastian -pg 198
Veneziana, Ana G -pg 52
Veneziana, Elizabeth R -pg 52
Veneziana, Enrique G -pg 52
Veneziana, Espiro G -pg 52
Veneziana, George G -pg 52
Veneziana, Patrick G -pg 52
Veneziana, Rosa G -pg 52
Ventura, Maria B? -pg 402
Vera, Ramon O -pg 59
Villagomes, Francisco La T -pg 95
Villagomes, Gregorio La T -pg 95
Villagomes, Josefa La T -pg 94
Villagomes, Juan C -pg 94
Villagomes, Rosabeda La T -pg 94
Villagomez, Ana A -pg 217
Villagomez, Artemio A -pg 217
Villagomez, Carlos C -pg 15
Villagomez, Elena C -pg 15
Villagomez, Francisco P -pg 32
Villagomez, Ignacia C -pg 15
Villagomez, Jesus P -pg 32
Villagomez, Jose C -pg 15
Villagomez, Jose C -pg 32
Villagomez, Jose P -pg 32
Villagomez, Jose -pg 217
Villagomez, Juana C -pg 15
Villagomez, Maria C -pg 15
Villagomez, Maria P -pg 32
Villagomez, Maria P -pg 32
Villagomez, Pedro P -pg 32
Villagomez, Rosa O -pg 139
Villagomez, Rosa C -pg 15
Villagomez, Soledad P -pg 32
Walters, Frank A -pg 170
Walters, Joe A -pg 170
Walters, Rita A -pg 169
Warren, Elenor -pg 333
Warren, Ewart -pg 333
Warren, Frederick -pg 333
Watkin, Dolores -pg 285
Watkin, Rosa -pg 285
White, Ana P -pg 178

White, Antonia C -pg 154
White, Arthur G -pg 426
White, Asuncion A -pg 166
White, Dolores C -pg 154
White, Dolores P -pg 178
White, Jose F -pg 166
White, Juan C -pg 154
White, Juan F -pg 154
White, Magdalena F -pg 154
White, Maria C -pg 154
White, Maria F -pg 154
White, Rafaela P -pg 178
White, Rosa A -pg 166
White, Tomasa F -pg 154
White, William P -pg 154
Wilson, Dolores -pg 239
Wilson, Maria -pg 239
Winsor, Charlotte Mac -pg 426
Winsor, Keiller M -pg 426
Winsor, Sheridan P -pg 426
Winsor, Sheridan P jr -pg 426
Wisle, Dolores T -pg 412
Wisle, Ignacio T -pg 412
Wisle, Jose W -pg 412
Wisle, Juan D -pg 421
Wisle, Maria D -pg 421
Wisle, Supiano T -pg 421
Wisle, Vicente D -pg 421
Wongpat, Antonio B -pg 396
Wongpat, Francisco B -pg 397
Wongpat, Ignacio B -pg 396
Wongpat, Ignacio -pg 396
Wongpat, John B -pg 396
Wongpat, Maria B -pg 396
Wongpat, Vicente B -pg 396
Yamaguchi, Ana A -pg 196
Yamaguchi, Josefina A -pg 197
Yamaguchi, Juan -pg 196
Yamaguchi, Manuel A -pg 196
Yamaguchi, Maria A -pg 197
Yamaguchi, Visitacion A -pg 197
Yamanaka, Alfonsina B -pg 385
Yamanaka, Carmelo U -pg 385
Yamanaka, Carmen B -pg 385
Yamanaka, Catalina M -pg 534
Yamanaka, Concepcion B -pg 385
Yamanaka, Diego -pg 534
Yamanaka, Iwakichi -pg 282
Yamanaka, Josefina M -pg 534
Yamanaka, Juan M -pg 534
Yamanaka, Maria B -pg 385
Yamanaka, Maria M -pg 534

Yamanaka, Paula B -pg 385
Yamasaki, Bonsuro O -pg 132
Yamasaki, Maria T -pg 132
Yamasaki, Pilar T -pg 132
Yamasaki, Vicente T -pg 132
Yamashita, Ana O -pg 516
Yamashita, Felicitas C -pg 516
Yamashita, Jesus C -pg 516
Yamashita, Kanzaboro -pg 443
Yamashita, Luis C -pg 516
Yamashita, Raymundo H -pg 516
Yaneyama, Hyojaro S -pg 386
Ynguillo, Carlos LG -pg 42
Ynguillo, Crispulo R -pg 42
Ynguillo, Martin LG -pg 42
Ynguillo, Trinidad LG -pg 42
Yokoi, Emilia Q -pg 166
Yokoi, Gertrudes Q -pg 166
Yokoi, Jose T -pg 166
Yokoi, Maria Q -pg 166
Yoshida, Ana C -pg 238
Yoshida, Concepcion A -pg 378
Yoshida, Dolores M -pg 378
Yoshida, Enrique A -pg 378
Yoshida, Guadalupe A -pg 378
Yoshida, Jose -pg 378
Yoshida, Juan A -pg 378
Young, Henry -pg 426
Zafra, Angusta E -pg 286
Zafra, Vicente E -pg 286
Zuniga, Alselmo -pg 502

www.ingramcontent.com/pod-product-compliance
Lightning Source LLC
Chambersburg PA
CBHW080254030426

42334CB00023BA/2816